How to Use

YOGA

Gen
phy ed

HOW TO USE YOGA

Edited & Compiled by

Prof. Dr. Amresh Kumar

M.P.E., Ph.D., LLB, MBA

KHEL SAHITYA KENDRA

7/26, Ansari Road, Darya Ganj,

New Delhi-110002

Published by:

KHEL SAHITYA KENDRA

7/26, Ansari Road, Darya Ganj, New Delhi-110002.

Ph.: (O) 011-65190343, 43551324, 42564726
(M) 9811088729 (Res.) 47091605

E-mail: *khelsahitya1@rediffmail.com*

Web: *www.khelsahitya.com*

Revised & Updated Edition

ISBN - 978-81-7524-477-1

PRINTED IN INDIA 2016

Laser Typeset by:
JAIN MEDIA GRAPHICS
Delhi

Printed by:
ASIAN OFFSET PRINTERS
Delhi

Price: Rs. 1100/-

CONTENTS

1

WHAT IS YOGA

What comes into your mind when you hear the word Yoga?

Well, if you think of women in seemingly impossible poses, then you may have an inkling of what Yoga is. But that's just it - an inkling. You've got a long way to go before fully understanding Yoga.

Yoga is an ancient Indian body of knowledge that dates back more than 5000 years ago. The word "Yoga" came from the Sanskrit word "yuj" which means "to unite or integrate." Yoga then is about the union of a person's own consciousness and the universal consciousness.

Ancient Yogis had a belief that in order for man to be in harmony with himself and his environment, he has to integrate the body, the mind, and the spirit. For these three to be integrated, emotion, action, and intelligence must be in balance. The Yogis formulated a way to achieve and maintain this balance and it is done through exercise, breathing, and Meditation - the three main Yoga structures.

In Yoga, the body is treated with care and respect for it is the primary instrument in man's work and growth. Yoga Exercises improve circulation, stimulate the abdominal organs, and put pressure on the glandular system of the body, which can generally result to better health.

Breathing techniques were developed based on the concept that breath is the source of life. In Yoga, students gain breathing control as they slowly increase their breathing. By focusing on their breathing, they prepare their minds for the next step - Meditation.

There is a general misconception that in Meditation, your mind has to go blank. It doesn't have to be so. In Meditation, students bring the activities of the mind into focus resulting in a 'quiet' mind. By designing physical poses and Breathing Techniques that develop awareness of our body, Yoga helps us focus and relieves us from our everyday stress.

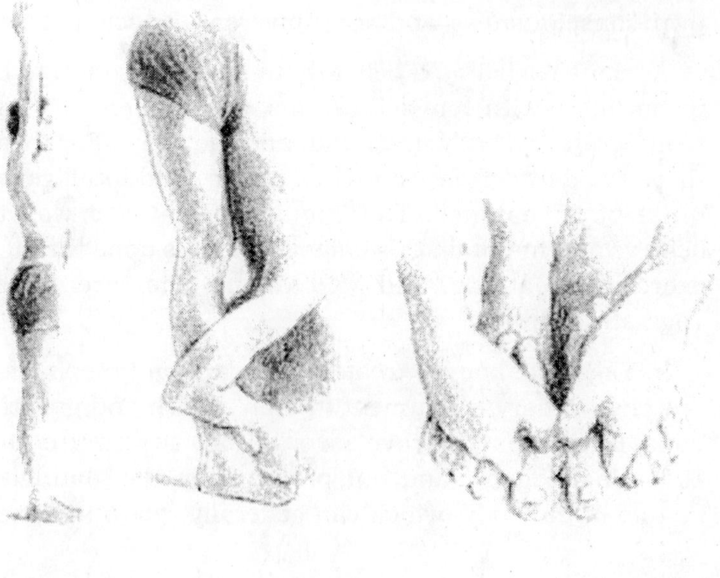

2

BRANCHES OF YOGA?

There are six branches of yoga which are as under:

1. Hatha Yoga or Yoga of Postures

Hatha Yoga is perhaps the path of Yoga you are most familiar with since this is the most popular branch of Yoga in the West. This branch of Yoga uses physical poses or Asana, Breathing Techniques or Pranayama, and Meditation to achieve better health, as well as spirituality. There are many styles within this path - Iyengar, Integral, Astanga, Kripalu, and Jiva Mukti to name a few.

If what you want is a peaceful mind and a healthy body to go along with it, Hatha Yoga may just be the path for you.

2. Bhakti Yoga or Yoga of Devotion

Bhakti Yoga is the path most followed in India. This is the path of the heart and devotion. Yogis who practice this branch sees the "One" or the Divine in everyone and everything. Bhakti Yoga teaches a person to have devotion to the "One" or to Brahma by developing a person's love and acceptance for all things.

3. Raja Yoga or Yoga of Self-Control

Raja means "royal". This path is considered to be the King of Yoga and this may be due to the fact that most of its practitioners are members of religious and spiritual orders. Raja Yoga is based on the teachings of the Eight Limbs of Yoga found in the Yoga sutras.

A Raja Yogi sees the self as central, and as such, respect to oneself and for all creation are vital to this path. They achieve self-respect by first learning to be masters of themselves.

If you wish to learn discipline, then Raja Yoga would perfectly suit that need.

4. Jnana Yoga or Yoga of the Mind

Jnana Yoga is the path of Yoga that basically deals with the mind, and as such, it focuses on man's intelligence. Jnana Yogis consider wisdom and intellect as important and they aim to unify the two to surpass limitations. Since they wish to gain knowledge, they are open to other philosophies and religion for they believe that an open and rational mind is crucial in knowing the spirit.

5. Karma Yoga or Yoga of Service

Karma Yoga is the path of service for in this path, it is believed that your present situation is based on your past actions. So by doing selfless service now, you are choosing a future that is free from negativity and selfishness. Karma Yogis change their attitude towards the good and in the process, change their souls, which leads to a change in their destiny.

6. Tantra Yoga or Yoga of Rituals

Perhaps the most misunderstood of all the paths, Tantra Yoga is about using rituals to experience what is sacred. Although sex is a part of it, sex is not the whole of it since this path aims to find what is sacred in everything we do. Tantra Yogis must possess certain qualities like purity, humility, devotion, dedication to his Guru, cosmic love, and truthfulness among other things.

There are still a lot of misconceptions about Yoga, for instance, Yoga being a religion. Yoga is not a religion. It is more of a set of techniques for us to find spirituality. In fact, Yoga is being practiced by a lot of people from different religions like Christians, Jewish, Buddhists, and Muslims.

Another misconception is that Yoga is an exercise, a way for us to keep fit. It is partly true, but if you think that Yoga is just that then you are greatly mistaken. Yoga develops the body since a weak one is a hindrance to spiritual growth. It does not simply focus on the physical but on the mental and spiritual aspects as well.

YOGA IN YOUR LIFE

You may ask, "Is Yoga for me?"

Definitely, yes! Yoga is for anyone who is willing to learn its ways and ideas. It does not actually require any special equipment or clothing. What it requires is your will to have a healthier, stress-free self.

You may first approach Yoga as a way to achieve a great body or to keep fit and that is perfectly alright. Yoga really does help in improving your health for stretching can tone your muscles and exercise your spine and your entire skeletal system.

Do not just take advantage of what Yoga can offer. Yoga encourages you to reflect on yourself and to find your inner peace. It exercises not just your body but your mind as well. With a healthy body and mind, you're on your way to a more fulfilling life.

3

THE PRINCIPLES OF YOGA

The Five Principles of Yoga are the basis of attaining a healthy body and mind through the Practice of Yoga. In this section, we give you detailed information on these Five Principles:

PRINCIPLE 1: PROPER RELAXATION

By releasing the tension in the muscles and putting the whole body at rest, you revitalize your Nervous System and achieve inner peace, making you feel relaxed and refreshed. This relaxed feeling is carried over into all your activities and helps you conserve your energy and let go of all worries and fears.

PRINCIPLE 2: PROPER EXERCISE

This principle revolves around the idea that our physical body is meant to move and exercise. Proper Exercise is achieved through the Yoga Postures or Asana which systematically works on all parts of the body - stretches and tones the Muscles and Ligaments, enhances the flexibility of the spine and the joints, and improves Blood Circulation. The asanas are designed to regulate the physical and physiological functions of the body. Practicing these Yoga Poses makes your body relaxed, gives you more strength and energy, and rejuvenates the various systems of the body. The Yoga Posture goes together with Proper Breathing. Each movement and stretch should be guided by your breath, making your movement and your breath coordinated and feel like one and the same. The execution of the Asana is beneficial to the body, and at the same time contributes to spiritual and Mental growth.

PRINCIPLE 3: PROPER BREATHING

This means breathing fully and rhythmically, making use of all the parts of your Lungs to increase your oxygen intake. Proper Breathing should be deep, slow and rhythmical. To achieve this, you need to be able to regulate the length and duration of your inhalation, exhalation, and the retention of air in your lungs or the pauses between breath. Yoga Breathing Exercises or Pranayama teaches you on how you can recharge your body and control your mental state by regulating the flow of Prana - the life force. This helps you achieve a calmer and more focused mind, and increases your energy level.

PRINCIPLE 4: PROPER DIET

What you eat extremely affects your mind. Improper diet results to mental inefficiency and blocks spiritual awareness. Proper Diet is one that nourishes both mind and body. It should be well balanced and based on natural foods. Proper Diet in Yoga also means eating in moderation and eating only when you are hungry. We sometimes tend to eat when we are upset, using food to fill the gap or the emptiness that we feel. Bad eating habits will cause our senses to be dull that we won't even notice how much we eat or how it tastes and may result to diet related ailments like Obesity and Diabetes. Food should sustain our body. It should keep the body light and supple, the mind calm, and it should also help in keeping a strong immune system.

PRINCIPLE 5: POSITIVE THINKING AND MEDITATION

The way we think highly affects our way of life. Practice keeping a positive outlook in life, this will facilitate in having a peaceful mind. Positive thinking and Meditation helps you remove negative thoughts and puts your mind under perfect control.

4

HISTORY OF YOGA

The saying, "What's in the past, should stay in the past" — doesn't work here.

We might already have an idea of what Yoga is but to understand it better, we have to know what it has become as well as its roots and beginnings. A quick look at the history of Yoga will help us appreciate its rich tradition and who knows, it might help us incorporate Yoga into our lives.

Although Yoga is said to be as old as civilization, there is no physical evidence to support this claim. Earliest archaeological evidence of Yoga's existence could be found in stone seals which depict figures of Yoga Poses. The stone seals place Yoga's existence around 3000 B.C.

Scholars, however, have a reason to believe that Yoga existed long before that and traced its beginnings in Stone Age Shamanism. Both Shamanism and Yoga have similar characteristics particularly in their efforts to improve the human condition at that time. Also, they aim to heal community members and the practitioners act as religious mediators. Though we know Yoga as focusing more on the self, it started out as community-oriented before it turned inward.

For a better discussion of the history of Yoga, we could

divide it into four periods: the Vedic Period, Pre-Classical Period, Classical Period, and Post-Classical Period.

VEDIC PERIOD

The existence of the Vedas marks this period. The Vedas is the sacred scripture of Brahmanism that is the basis of modern-day Hinduism. It is a collection of hymns which praise a divine power. The Vedas contains the oldest known Yogic teachings and as such, teachings found in the Vedas are called Vedic Yoga. This is characterized by rituals and ceremonies that strive to surpass the limitations of the mind.

During this time, the Vedic people relied on rishis or dedicated Vedic Yogis to teach them how to live in divine harmony. Rishis were also gifted with the ability to see the ultimate reality through their intensive spiritual practice. It was also during this time that Yogis living in seclusion (in forests) were recorded

PRE-CLASSICAL YOGA

The creation of the Upanishads marks the Pre-Classical Yoga. The 200 scriptures of the Upanishads (the conclusion of the revealed literature) describe the inner vision of reality resulting from devotion to Brahman. These explain three subjects: the ultimate reality (Brahman), the transcendental self (atman), and the relationship between the two. The Upanishads further explain the teachings of the Vedas.

Yoga shares some characteristics not only with Hinduism but also with Buddhism that we can trace in its history. During the sixth century B.C., Buddha started teaching Buddhism, which stresses the importance of

Meditation and the practice of physical postures. Siddharta Gautama, the first Buddhist to study Yoga, achieved enlightenment at the age of 35.

Later, around 500 B.C., the Bhagavad-Gita or Lord's Song was created and this is currently the oldest known Yoga scripture. It is devoted entirely to Yoga and has confirmed that it has been an old practice for some time. However, it doesn't point to a specific time wherein Yoga could have started. The central point to the Gita is that - to be alive means to be active and in order to avoid difficulties in our lives and in others, our actions have to benign and have to exceed our egos.

Just as the Upanishads further the Vedas, the Gita builds on and incorporates the doctrines found in the Upanishads. In the Gita, three facets must be brought together in our lifestyle: Bhakti or loving devotion, Jnana which is knowledge or contemplation, and Karma which is about selfless actions. The Gita then tried to unify Bhakti Yoga, Jnana Yoga, and Karma Yoga and it is because of this that it has gained importance. The Gita was a conversation between Prince Arjuna and God-man Krishna and it basically stresses the importance of opposing evil.

CLASSICAL PERIOD

The Classical Period is marked by another creation - the Yoga Sutra. Written by Patanjali around the second century, it was an attempt to define and standardize Classical Yoga. It is composed of 195 aphorisms or sutras (from the Sanskrit word which means thread) that expound upon the Raja Yoga and its underlying principle, Patanjali's Eightfold path of Yoga (also called Eight Limbs of Classical Yoga). These are:

1. Yama, which means social restraints or ethical values;

2. Niyama, which is personal observance of purity, tolerance, and study;

3. Asanas or physical exercises;

4. Pranayama, which means breath control or regulation;

5. Pratyahara or sense withdrawal in preparation for Meditation;

6. Dharana, which is about concentration;

7. Dhyana, which means Meditation; and

8. Samadhi, which means ecstasy.

Patanjali believed that each individual is a composite of matter (prakriti) and spirit (purusha). He further believed that the two must be separated in order to cleanse the spirit - a stark contrast to Vedic and Pre-Classical Yoga that signify the union of body and spirit.

Patanjali's concept was dominant for some centuries that some Yogis focused exclusively on Meditation and neglected their Asanas. It was only later that the belief of the body as a temple was rekindled and attention to the importance of the Asana was revived. This time, Yogis attempted to use Yoga techniques to change the body and make it immortal.

POST-CLASSICAL YOGA

At this point, we see a proliferation of literature as well as the practice of Yoga. Post-classical Yoga differs from the first three since its focus is more on the present.

It no longer strives to liberate a person from reality but rather teaches one to accept it and live at the moment.

Yoga was introduced in the West during the early 19th century. It was first studied as part of Eastern Philosophy and began as a movement for health and vegetarianism around the 1930's. By the 1960's, there was an influx of Indian teachers who expounded on Yoga. One of them was Maharishi Mahesh, the Yogi who popularized Transcendental Meditation. Another one is a prominent Yoga Guru Swami Sivananda. Sivananda was a doctor in Malaysia and he later opened schools in America and Europe. The most prominent of his works is his modified Five Principles of Yoga which are:

1. Savasana or proper relaxation;
2. Asanas or proper exercise;
3. Pranayama or proper breathing;
4. Proper diet; and
5. Dhyana or positive thinking and Meditation

Sivananda wrote more than 200 books on Yoga and Philosophy and had many disciples who furthered Yoga. Some of them were Swami Satchitananda who introduced chanting and Yoga to Woodstock; Swami Sivananada Radha who explored the connection between psychology and Yoga, and Yogi Bhajan who started teaching Kundalini Yoga in the 70's.

Up to this day, Yoga continues to proliferate and spread its teachings, crossing the boundaries of culture and language.

5

YOGA AND STRESS

While many people have always thought of Yoga as some mystic Hindu practice, that image is rapidly disappearing – almost as fast as the stresses of our modern lives are increasing. The American Academy of Family Physicians has noted that stress related symptoms prompt two-thirds of the office visits to family physicians. Exercise and alternative therapies are now commonly prescribed for stress-related complaints and illness. Even a recent issue of Consumer Reports suggests Yoga for stress relief.

As an effective method of stress management, yoga is spreading into the business world, the helping professions, nursing and old age homes. It is also being used in the treatment of alcoholics, hyperactive children and youngsters with learning disabilities. Yoga centers are getting stiff competition from adult education classes of community colleges, boards of education and parks and recreation departments.

There are many kinds of yoga to study, and there can be endless years of practice for the willing student. Many of the problems suffered in modern life can be erased by following a regular yoga routine.

REASONS TO PRACTICE YOGA

The following are some reasons to use yoga to cope with modern day stresses:

1. Yoga can release the tense muscles caused by hours of sitting at a desk.

Yoga differs from other forms of exercise in that it involves motions that don't cause strain on the body. It isn't an aerobic exercise, but it uses almost every muscle in your body. Over time, your limbs are strengthened – helping to combat the aches and pains caused by our sedentary lifestyles.

2. Mediation during Yoga can enhance concentration.

Breathing deeply can improve vitality by increasing the amount of oxygen that reaches the brain. All forms of yoga incorporate the practice of proper breathing techniques for relaxation, to rest the mind from its constant chatter, to experience an internal calm, and to energize and purify the body.

3. Yoga is fun an easy for children.

Yoga is great fun for children and teenagers and it's easy for them to do, as they are already flexible. Yoga can help them retain that flexibility. It can also help to develop their self-discipline. Practicing yoga is good for developing coordination and can help to improve concentration - which many children and teens find difficult.

4. Yoga is the ideal exercise during pregnancy.

Practicing yoga can improve backache and help to lift depression. Many women who practice yoga have said that it helped to make their labor easier and shorter. The meditation side of yoga is also calming and centering during pregnancy.

5. Yoga can combat feelings of anxiety and depression.

Practicing yoga can alter your brain chemistry. Some yoga positions in particular are effective in stimulating the pituitary gland to release endorphins and to reduce the level of cortisol (the stress hormone).

Many people beginning to practice yoga as stress management may feel unsure if they are doing it right. Trust yourself and trust the process and let it develop. Keep your focus on what is happening in each moment. As stress levels in our society reach new heights, yoga can provide you with the means for handling stress, diffusing tension and increasing the quality of your life!

YOGA : A MATTER OF COMMON SENSE

Through Hatha Yoga teachings, we learn that better health comes through purification of the body and caring for internal hygiene as well as external; that the body can only be built out of the nutritional ingredients which we eat; that occasional fasts help to eliminate toxins; that muscular strength is developed through both body building exercises as well as flexibility; and that full body movement should be encouraged to maintain youth and vitality.

We find that the practice of relaxation relieves stress both physical and psychological as the body and mind must work together to avoid inner conflicts; that breath is the primary nourishment for the body and links our body and soul; that breath provides the spiritual life link with universal life and energy outside; that quietude and meditation practices help to integrate our whole being and that self discipline is the only certain way to self improvement and happiness.

In Yoga classes we learn many physical techniques, postures and exercises for the purpose of improving physical health.

We hear of the importance of maintaining emotional equilibrium and the damage to our energy pattern when we give way to bad moods or violent behavior. We are taught more about our emotions in Bhakti Yoga.

Through Raja Yoga we are encouraged to understand our own personality and character make-up so that we can refresh our awareness and re-evaluate or re-create our own self-image, which potently determines so much of our life experiences.

Each layer of our nature is composed of energy of different grades and we begin to understand them all - firstly the physical energy layer, the emotional temperament, the two mental spheres related to rational thought and abstract thinking, in order to reach a more profound layer, the innermost harbor of our own soul.

It is the importance of the breath which convinces us that we are getting our energy from somewhere – it is the prime factor that makes our body, emotions, mind and soul function as they do. That the breath represents the spiritual or most subtle aspect of our selves is easy enough to comprehend. Although breath is invisible it is the most vital link with our Maker and the universal source of all life energy.

We practice stillness of the body. This is an

elementary technique to help still the mind and allow all our petty thoughts and sometimes quite destructive ones, to melt away. Then the mind is left as a clear slate, ready to deliberately use our thought faculty for positive outcomes. It is when our bodies, minds and emotions are all still that we find it easy to become aware of our real self, our soul. It is only in silence that we can expect to become aware of this quiet part of our inner nature which is 'heard' through a whisper rather than voice and has been called 'the still, small voice within', our intuition. So far so good!

We are reminded that health is natural, if we fulfill the natural physical and psychological needs, so happiness is natural when we have disciplined our thoughts, emotions and body and have determined our own life satisfactions and aims.

Peace of mind is natural, when we are living in accordance with all the rules, social, moral, ethical and obeying the kindness of the heart.

Spiritual awareness is natural, when we quietly sit in natural surroundings, or peaceful beautiful sanctuaries.

It really is a matter of what we wish to foster in ourselves and there is no one to do it for us. That's why it's necessary to find a well-qualified Yoga teacher who can give you a bit of encouragement and motivation.

The Yoga philosophy seems only to espouse the same old simple values of truth, beauty, love, kindness, care, self-effort, creative enterprise, generosity and others. The teaching reminds us of enduring values and the need for vigilance in maintaining them in our character and our habits. There seem to be no 'new' values to supplant the fundamental ones, which all religions and philosophies teach. We just need to keep polishing up our personality and keep practicing what we know is good... and keep persevering!

We have to keep strong to resist or avoid all the factors, which would tempt us away from our purpose of gradually developing human excellence of all kinds.

We need to apply ourselves now, though, if it is true that we have another life after this one and that we will have to face conditions, which will present us again with any problem we failed to resolve this time. Better to face the challenges presented by life to us now so we don't have to go through it all again!

Most of us hate to consider that we will have to repeat the painful lessons and experiences endured in this present life. This would seem to have been the main objection western people had to reincarnation. But the idea is becoming more popular now as we understand that once we are born human we are not reborn as an animal, or an ant!

Some of us may be dismayed to think of repeated experiences of the same frustrations and difficulties we presently endure. But what about a repeated opportunity to feel the sunshine, see the oceans, smell the roses, fall in love again and continue - or increase - our learning and our progress towards becoming a better human being? What a wonderful idea.

Yoga teachings seem to be just a matter of common sense.

HOW TO USE YOGA TO ALLEVIATE STRESS

It's a given, as technologically advanced as we may be we are still creatures with animal instincts. As we walk the fine line between modern life and our animalistic characteristics, we often times are left to find balance in our bodies, our minds, our environment, in our lives. That's where Yoga comes in.

As a result of being more inactive than ever and the over-stimulation of our minds, many of us suffer from the fatigue and imbalance that comes from chronic stress without sufficient recovery.

Well, the good news is yoga is an excellent way to soothe nerves that are in a constant state of overdrive. Yoga is indeed the oldest existing physical-culture system in the world. Besides being a systematic and scientifically proven path to attaining physical fitness, it delays ageing, rejuvenates and improves appearance, maintains suppleness and increases vitality and the creative part of life.

It's a fact that stress has become a chronic aspect of life for many of us; and it takes its toll. This often times wears out the body leaving us feeling depleted or overwhelmed.

The consequence of this is that the immune system weakens causing illness and fatigue, mood swings, lack of focus, and irritability

Since we are often engaged in many tasks at once, and feeling that we are constantly on the go, it should come as come as no surprise that it seems difficult to relax these days.

Thankfully, Yoga innately helps us to create balance;

to know our bodies, to recognize when we are not balanced both on and off of the mat. On a purely physical level hatha yoga creates strength, flexibility, grace.

Yoga helps to unlock and release tensions before they can accumulate over time and become chronic physical and psychological conditions. As we release physical blockages, toxins, and limitations from the body we also do so in mind, spirit, and emotions.

The Specific Poses Recommended will be the

-Sun Salutations

-The ShoulderStand

-The Corpse Pose

These three in particular are often recommended in several drug-free fraternities as being THE poses of stress relief.

So When next you feel overwhelmed with life's demands, stress, or just need a pick-me-up from lethargy, it won't hurt to do some Yoga. It won't hurt and will definitely help to rectify the situation.

YOGA AND EMOTIONAL HEALTH FOR LONGEVITY

How can Yoga have a positive impact on your emotional health? How does your emotional health affect your heart? What can Yoga do for the health of your heart? Let's look at taming our emotions for a more holistic and peaceful approach to a quality life.

How can Yoga have a real positive impact on your emotional health? Have you ever noticed that your heart, and the area around your solar plexus, feel terrible during times of severe anxiety? Medical and scientific experts often say, "Your heart cannot think," and we know this must be true. Yet, how do we explain that "gut wrenching" feeling, we have, when we feel stress, anguish, or remorse?

Let's look at the sequence of events, which create extreme anxiety, and learn how Yoga can help your emotional health. Firstly, you receive a thought, which creates images, within your mind. If they are good, your heart feels fine, but if they are not, you feel a "heart ache."

It is the mind's perception, which creates imagery, but how can we control that? Let's look at an extreme situation – instant grief. There is hardly anything worse than the death of a friend or family member. We have no control over death. We are helpless, and we mourn, because we will not see that person again in this life.

It has been said, "Time heals," but does it really? No, time goes by, filling your mind with chatter over weeks, months, and years. If you do manage to get over your grief, it was mind chatter that might have saved you.

There are cases where people carry loss around with them for the rest of their lives. Some people seek professional counseling for grief or loss because they cannot "get past it;" while some people may even die from a "broken heart."

How could Yoga help in this "worst case scenario?" When my mother passed away, at 50 years of age, it was a shock. She had one heart attack and she was gone. I was at the hospital, that night, and did not believe the doctor, who told me, "She has expired." I dashed into the room to see for myself, but he was right.

Did Yoga change my grief? Could I meditate the heart

ache away? No, but I did practice Pranayama, focused on positive memories, and quit smoking cigarettes, that day. Yes, once upon a time, I was a smoking Yogi.

Many of you have far worse stories to tell, but we have to take back control of our minds, or we will perish from the resulting damage to our hearts.

MEDITATION CUSHIONS: MAINTAIN CORRECT POSTURE DURING DAILY MEDITATION

Meditation was originally a Buddhist tradition, and has only spread to the western half of the world in recent decades, bringing peace and a sense of balance into the homes of thousands of Americans. Often complimented by Yoga and Pilates practices, meditation can be performed as often as you wish, and from the privacy of your own home. Some prefer to meditate on the floor, others in arm chairs, and sometimes on the bed, but meditation cushions are also growing in popularity.

Originally used as regular, everyday chairs in Asia, meditation cushions have become available in today's markets as the perfect way to meditate daily. They are extremely comfortable, and are designed to lend support for the lower back, knees, ankles, and buttocks. The traditional name for this cushions is zafu, which means "sewn seat." They are also accompanied by the zabuton, which is a large square cushion that is placed under the zafu for added support.

The zafu can be any size, but they are typically around 40cm in diameter and 20cm in hight. Some are shaped as balls or beans, while others can be square or crescent-shaped. Choosing the right size and shape depends on your body style, and which fits most comfortably. There are also different fillings for zafus, which include buckweat hulls, kapox (a natural fiber found in the east), cotton twil, or cotton drill. The substance that fills the zafu will also determine the price.

Meditation sessions vary in length, but it is absolutely essential that you are comfortable during this time. Your back should be complete straight, allowing for smooth and effortless breathing, and there should be no pressure on the lower back or tail bone. Sitting on the floor or even in a chair may not provide the type of support that you need; in this case, a zafu might completely fix the problem.

THE BENEFITS OF MEDITATION

The benefits of meditation are well documented. By using meditation, either alone, or with conventional treatments, you can reduce the negative effects of stress and strengthen your immune system. The effects of meditation are well documented. Various medical studies have shown the benefits of meditation to be numerous.

Cancer patients that are taught the benefits of meditation and how to meditate reduce their anxiety, anger, and confusion that are common with the disease. In cases of cancer and other chronic or terminal diseases, meditations benefits are a proven and documented way to strengthen a patient. By allowing the benefits of meditation to become part of a patients treatment plan, patients can gain some control over their illness.

Another interesting benefit of meditation has been documented in cases of patients suffering from atherosclerosis, or hardening of the arteries. When a sample group of patients were taught meditation, the benefits were amazing. The effects of meditation surprised everyone. The patients that practiced meditation actually showed a reduction of the thickening along their artery walls. The potential benefits of meditation are astounding, as many people do not realize that they may suffer from atherosclerosis until they are seriously ill.

Whether you are suffering from a long term or chronic illness, or just hoping to reduce the stress in your life, you can enjoy the benefits of meditation. Meditation effects the brain waves in such a way that, when practiced properly, you can decrease your heart rate, lower your blood pressure, and even lift mild depression.

Many people shy away from meditation because of the religious connection. The benefits of meditation can be enjoyed without practicing the more spiritual aspects of the process. Many studies have been conducted on the effects of meditation, and the results are pretty conclusive. You can enjoy the benefits of meditation without involving the religion.

The non-religious aspects of meditation involve focusing on a single object, clearing your mind, and relaxation. Although this sounds simple, unless done properly the benefits of meditation may be lost on you. The problem that many people have with meditation is the necessary quieting of the mind.

Particularly in times of stress, it can be difficult to quiet your mind. To enjoy the benefits of meditation, you must silence the inner voice that wants to worry about everything under the sun. To enjoy meditations effects, you must learn to truly clear your mind during your meditation time. If you spend this time allowing your mind to race about the worries and concerns that you face, the benefits of meditation will be lost to you.

Quieting your mind for meditation is not easy, and it is not something that you can turn on and off. The benefits of meditation outweigh the difficulties in establishing a meditation practice. When you first begin to mediate, you may only be able to clear you mind for a few seconds or minutes, and that is okay. As you stick with your practice, you will develop more control over your mind and be able to meditate for longer and longer periods of time.

The benefits of meditation are numerous. As you develop control over your mind you will find that your ability to concentrate is improved, you may be able to reduce or eliminate prescription drugs, you will sleep better, and your overall health will improve. Taking the time to establish a practice will allow you to enjoy the numerous benefits of meditation.

SOME USEFUL ASANAS FOR REDUCING STRESS

Asanas greatly influence the functioning of the endocrine system. We know the important role the endocrine glands play during stress adaptation, by secreting the stress hormones. There is such an intricate relationship between the glands that one malfunctioning gland can cause the disruption of the whole system.

Asanas bring about harmony in the functioning of the various other bodily systems, which are closely 'interwoven, such as the circulatory, nervous, respiratory, and digestive systems. Any disruption in the proper working relationship between these systems results in loss of health and body efficiency. Here again, all these systems play an active role during the body's adaptation to stress.

The subtle influence asanas bring about in the body is in the pranamaya kosha or the energy sheath. Pranamaya kosha is pervaded by what is known as bio-plasma or bioluminescence or prana, which the Kirlians had photographed for the first time. This energy travels in and around the body in specific pathways or the nadis, creating the aura around the bodies. These nadis or pathways become easily blocked, and prana gets congested in certain areas. When this happens, it leads to physical and mental disorders. Prana is also intimately connected to the mind. The free flow of prana brought about by asanas, leads to mental equilibrium and calmness.

Rapid and irregular breathing signifies tension in the mind and body, whereas slow, deep and rhythmical breathing indicates both calmness in the mind and good health. The practice of asana brings about mental and emotional equanimity, by slowing down the breathing, and by deepening the inhalation and exhalation.

Finally, the practice of asana with body and breath awareness, keeps the mind off tension and worry, at least during the practice. However, the temporary relaxation achieved during the practice, gradually builds up to bring permanent changes in one's mental and emotional makeup. As our mental attitude is reflected in our body, in the same way physical poise achieved during the practice of asanas has a corresponding effect on the mind.

1. Pawanmuktasana

The pawanmuktasana practices are taught preliminary to the practice of asanas, and are divided into

a) the anti-rheumatic group; and

b) the anti-gastric group.

'Pawan' means 'wind', 'mukta' means 'release' and the pawanmuktasana group of exercises releases excess of wind and acidity from the body.

Though in practice, these seem very simple, they exercise subtle effects on the different joints and organs of the body. That's why these are known as sukshma vyayama or subtle exercise in Sanskrit.

Along with the excess wind and acidity, the practice also removes or releases muscular tension from all over the body, from the head to the toes, and balances the pranas in the body. This in turn helps to keep the body balanced and stress-free throughout the day.

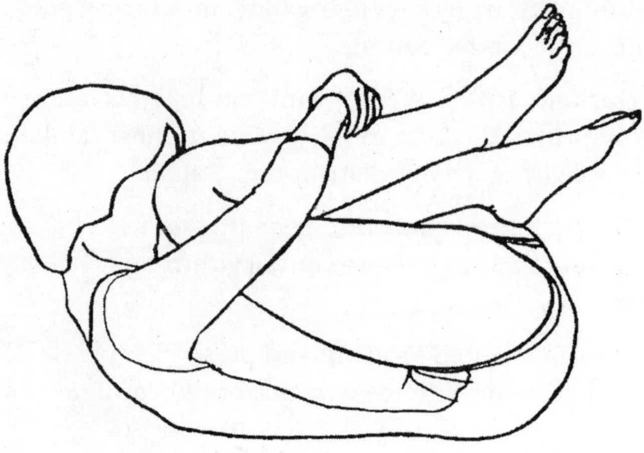

2. Surya Namaskara

The Sun Salutation or Surya Namaskar is a Yoga Pose which limbers up the whole body in preparation for the Yoga Asanas. It is a graceful sequence of twelve Yoga positions performed as one continuous exercise. Learn how to practice Sun Salutation in this section.

The Sun Salutation or Surya Namaskar limbers up the whole body in preparation for the yoga asanas. It is a graceful sequence of twelve yoga positions performed as one continuous exercise. Each position counteracts the one before, stretching the body in a different way and alternately expanding and contracting the chest to regulate the breathing. Practiced daily it will great flexibility to your spine and joints and trims your waist.

One round of Sun Salutation consists of two sequences, the first leading with the right foot in positions 4 and 9 (as illustrated), the second leading with the left. Keep your hands in one place from positions 3 to 10 and try to coordinate your movements with your breathing. Start by practicing four rounds and gradually build up to twelve rounds.

Method 1. Stand erect with feet together and palms in the prayer position in front of your chest. Make sure your weight is evenly distributed. Exhale.

2. Inhaling, stretch your arms up and arch back from the waist, pushing the hips out, legs straight. Relax your neck.

3. Exhaling, fold forward, and press your palms down, fingertips in line with toes - bend your knees if necessary.

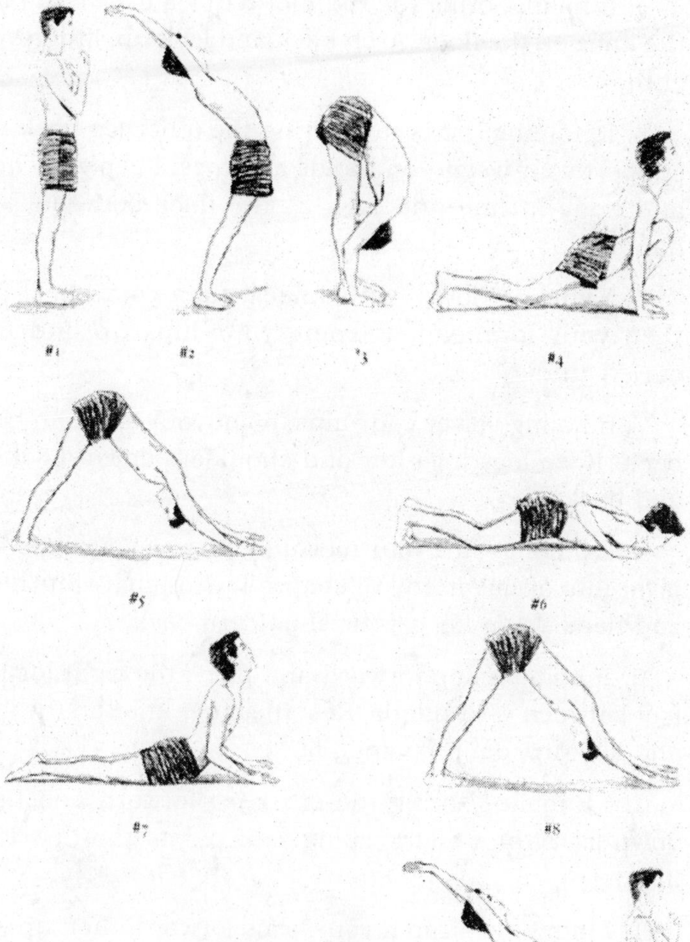
#1
#2
#3
#4
#5
#6
#7
#8
#9
#10
#11
#12

4. Inhaling, bring the right (or left) leg back and place the knee on the floor. Arch back and look up, lifting your chin.

5. Retaining the breath, bring the other leg back and support your weight on hands and toes. Keep your head and body in line and look at the floor between your hands.

6. Exhaling, lower your knees, then your chest and then your forehead, keeping your hips up and toes curled under.

7. Inhaling, lower your hips, point your toes and bend back. Keep legs together and shoulders down. Look up and back.

8. Exhaling, curl your toes under, raise your hips and pivot into an inverted "V" shape. Try to push your heels and head down keep your shoulders back.

9. Inhaling, step forward and place the right (or left) foot between your hands. Rest the other knee on the floor and look up, as in position 4.

10. Exhaling, bring the other leg forward and bend down from the waist keeping your palms as in position 3.

11. Inhaling, stretch your arms forward, then up and back over your head and bend back slowly from the waist, as in position 2.

12. Exhaling, gently come back to an upright position and bring your arms down by your side.

3. Siddhasana (Adept pose)

Technique

Sit on the folded rugged or folded blanket on the floor, bend the left leg and pull the foot in against the groin. Now bend the right leg and bring the foot across and insert its outer edge in the crevice between the calf and thigh of the left leg. The right heel should press against the pubic bone and both the knees should firmly touch the floor. Keep the palms of the right and left hands on the right and left knees. Sit upright keeping the head and the back in a straight line. For variation, change over the legs regularly. Place the heels near the groin carefully lest the pubic bone should be hurt.

4. Simhaasan (The Lion pose)

Technique

Sit on the folded blanket with legs stretched straight in front. Raise the seat, bend the right knee and place the right foot under the left buttock. Similarly bend the left knee and place it under the right buttock. The left ankle should be kept under the right one. Sit on the heels with toes towards backwards and put the weight of the body on the thighs and knees. Stretch the trunk forward and keep the back erect. Place the right and left palms on the right and left knees. Stretch the arms straight and keep them rigid. Then spread the fingers and press them against the knees. Open the mouth and eyes wide and protrude the tongue out and down as far as you can. Gaze at the centre of the eye brow or at the tip of the nose. Remain in this pose for a couple of seconds. Breathe through the mouth.

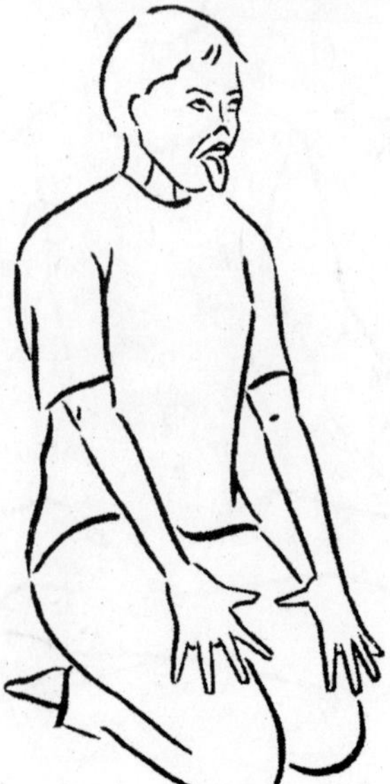

5. Padamasan (The Lotus pose)

Technique

Sit on the folded blanket with your legs outstretched. Bend each leg and place each foot on the opposite thigh, soles turned upwards. Pull the foot as high as you can. Keep the palms of the right and left hand on the right and left knees, touching the thumb with tips of index fingers and gaze at the tip of the nose. Keep the head, neck and spinal column straight and erect and breathe slowly.

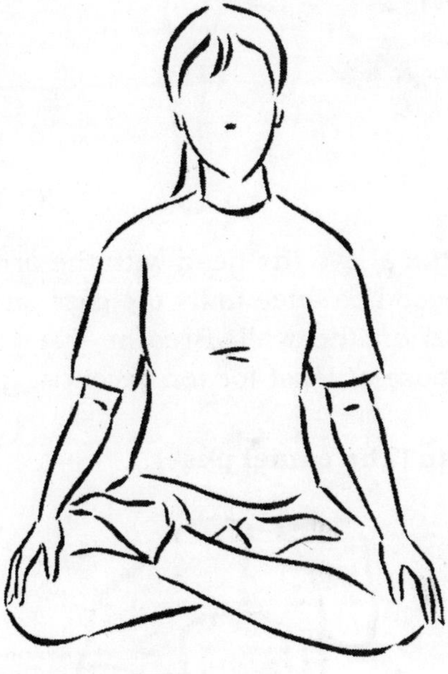

6. Vrikshasana (The Tree pose)

Technique

Stand up right. Fix the right leg on the ankle. Fix the right foot on the left thigh. Bring the palms of the hands

together a little above the head with the arms half bent. It will assist good balance to fix the gaze on a point level with the eyes on the wall. Breathe freely and deeply. Stay in this pose at least for ten seconds.

7. Ushtraasan (The camel pose)

Technique

Sit in Vajrasana pose with your feet and knees slightly apart. Stand on your keens and stretch the arms to the sides. Lean backward and put the hands on the keels. Stretch the neck backward and let the weight of the body rest on arms. Bend back as far as possible and push strongly. Remain in this pose for a couple of seconds and breathe slowly without any strain.

8. Gomukhasan (Face of a cow pose)

Technique

Sit on a folded blanket on the heels, knees together and head, and spine straight. Bend the right arms raise

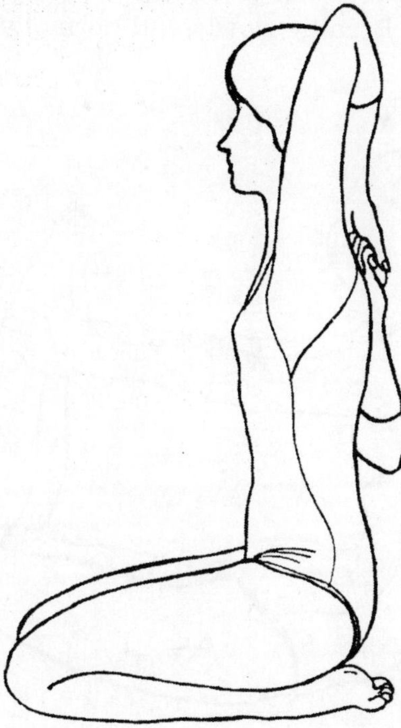

the elbow and lower the hand as far down the middle of the back without disturbing the upright posture. Bend the left arms and bring the left hand up the centre of the back until the finger of both hands interlock. Breathe deeply, remain in the pose for a couple of minutes. Unlock the hands and repeat the process in reverse manner. Return to the original position and relax.

9. Dhanurasan

Technique

Lie flat on the stomach and chest fix the legs bringing the feet back towards the head. Raise the legs, head and upper part of the body. While arching the back, take hold of your right ankle with your right hand and left ankle with left hand. Breathe slowly and normally. Remain in

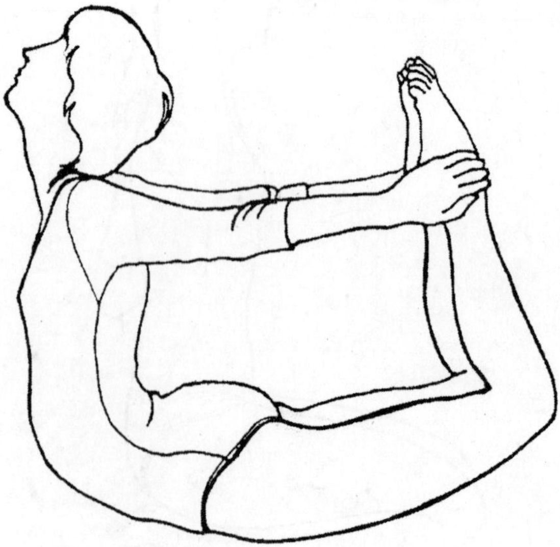

this pose for a couple of seconds. Return to the original position and relax.

10. Mayurasan

Technique

On a folded blanket kneel down. Join the two arms together and rest the hand on the floor, palms down with fingers pointing towards the toes. Keep the hands firm. Bring down the abdomen slowly against the joined elbows support your body on your elbows. Then stretch your legs. Inhale and raise the legs together from the floor. Remain in this pose for a couple of seconds. Exhale while raising the body of the floor and inhale while lowering the body.

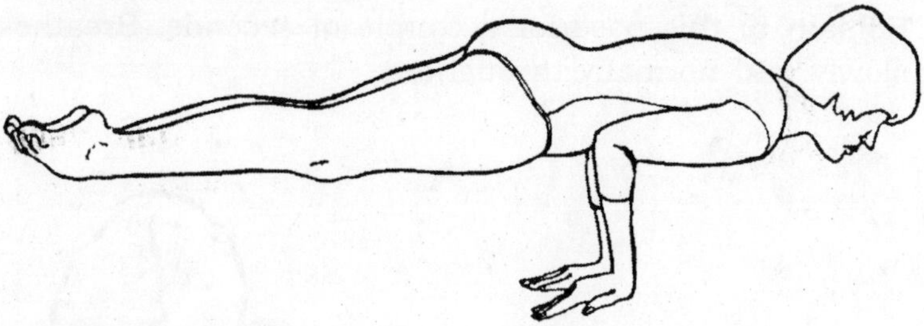

11. Shavasan

Technique

On a soft carpet or blanket or folded rug lie full length on back with arms away from the body with palms facing upward and feet slightly apart. Simply lying on the floor. The technique of this asana must be followed carefully. Rhythmic and deep breathing are absolutely necessary for concentration which gives complete relaxation. Savasan has been discussed in detail in "Yogic Relaxation".

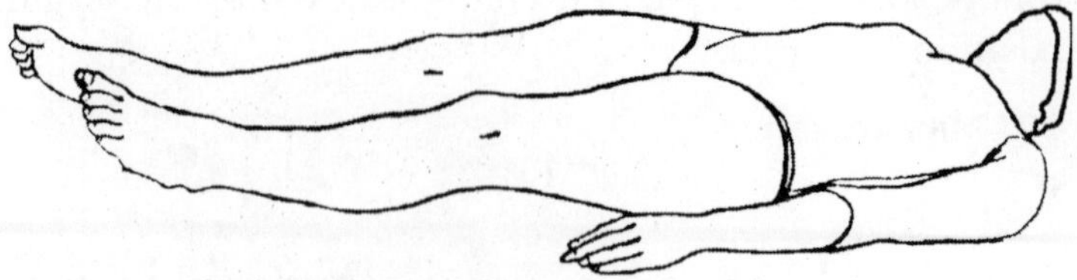

12. Bhujangasan

Technique

Lie flat on the stomach with legs straight and the feet extended. Place the hands, palms down under the shoulders. Slowly raise the body the navel until the arms are straight but the stomach and the legs must touch the floor. Bend the head back gazing diagonally upwards. Remain in this pose for a couple of seconds. Breathe slowly and normally throughout.

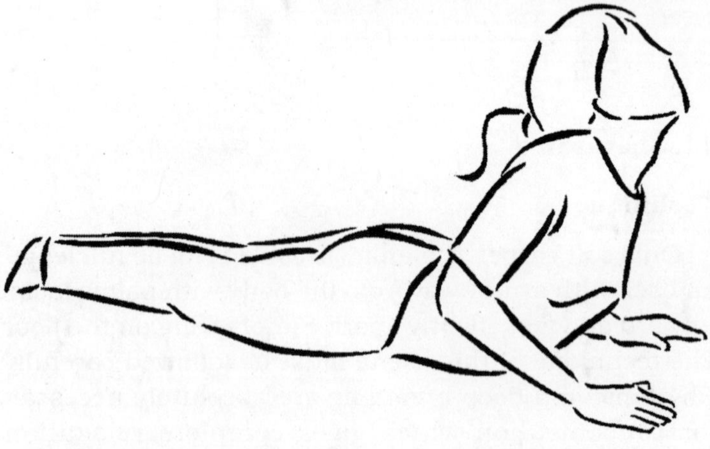

13. Paschimottanasana

Technique

Lie flat on the blanket and stretch the arms over the head and breathe in slowly and normally. Raise the arms, head and trunk, exhale and bend them over the legs

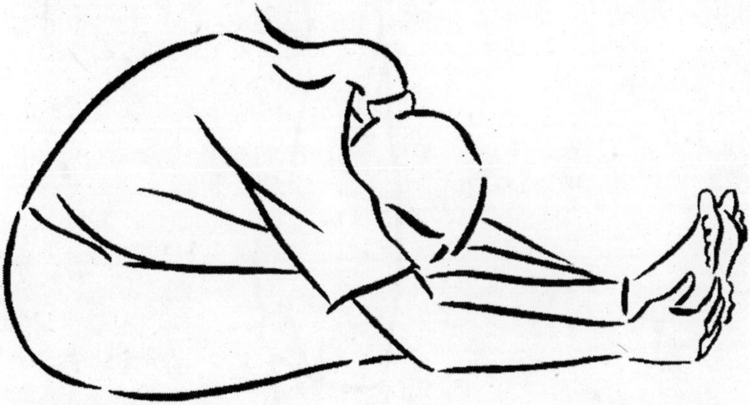

without raising the knees. Catch hold of the toes with fingers, contracting the abdomen and gently pressing the head against the knees. Pull the toe with the arms and lower the elbows. The bending should be done very slowly. Remain in this pose for a couple of seconds and increase the time gradually. Return to the original position and relax.

14. Sarvangasan

Technique

Spread a blanket on the floor and lie flat on your back. Then slowly raise the legs up lifting the trunk and hips vertically. The hips be supported by both hands. Let

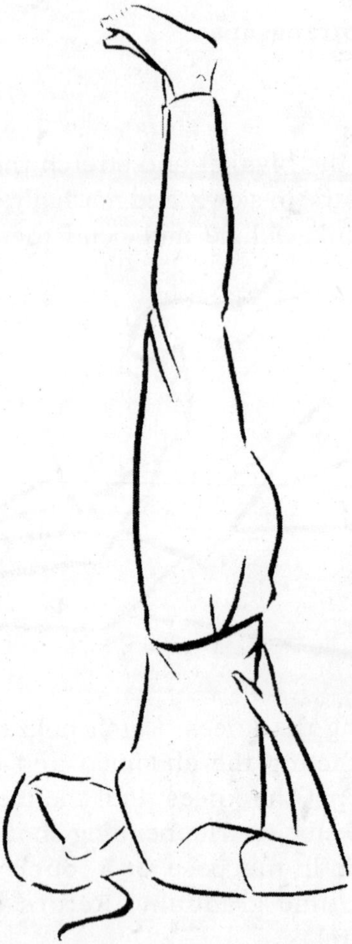

the elbows rest on the floor. The chin should be firmly pressed against the chest. In this pose the hinder part of the neck should touch the floor and trunk and legs should remain straight. Remain in this pose for a few minutes and breathe slowly and deeply and concentrate on the thyroid gland which is at the root of the neck. Return to the original position very slowly and relax.

15. Yog Mudra

Technique

Sit on folded blanket in Sidhasana pose. Relax the whole body and close the eyes. Place the hand behind the back catching hold of the left wrist in the right hand and keeping the spinal column erect, inhale and exhale slowly leaning forward touching the floor with forehead. Stay in this posture for as long as you can without any stress or strain. Focus your attention on the abdominal region. Then breathe in slowly and rhythmically. Sit upright and relax.

6

YOGA AND ANXIETY

WHAT IS ANXIETY?

Anxiety is a natural part of life, and most of us experience it from time to time. The word "anxiety" usually refers to worry, concern, stress, or nervousness. For most teens, anxiety is limited to particular situations such as tests, important dates (like the prom), or driving lessons.

Feeling anxious can sometimes be a good thing. Anxiety can actually help you by motivating you to

prepare for a big test or by keeping you on your toes in potentially dangerous situations. Occasional anxiety isn't something to be concerned about.

But for some teens, anxiety is a constant factor in their lives. When a person has an anxiety disorder, it interferes with their ability to function normally on a daily basis. Anxiety disorders can cause teens to suffer from intense, long-lasting fear or worry, in addition to other symptoms.

UNDERSTANDING ANXIETY DISORDERS

Anxiety disorders are conditions that involve unrealistic fear and worry. Anxiety disorders are very common - it is estimated that that they affect about 13% of the U.S. population. Anxiety disorders affect people of all ages, including kids and teens.

A teen who has an anxiety disorder isn't "crazy," and certainly isn't alone. Many teens have anxiety disorders, and have feelings of fear, worry, panic, or intense stress that can sometimes make it hard to get through the day. Anxiety can also interfere with things as basic as sleep, concentration, and appetite, not to mention the ability to enjoy life and relax. The good news is that anxiety disorders are very treatable.

There are several types of anxiety disorders that can affect teens. They include:

Generalized anxiety disorder, or GAD, for example, refers to constant, intense worry and stress about a variety of everyday things or situations. Teens with GAD may worry about school, health or safety of family members, the future, and whether they'll become ill or injured. They may always think of the worst that could happen. Along with the worry and dread, they may have physical symptoms, too, such as chest pain, headache, tiredness, tight muscles, stomachaches, or even vomiting. GAD can result in missed school days and avoidance of social activities.

Panic disorder is characterized by panic attacks, or episodes of intense fear that occur for no apparent reason. With a panic attack a person may have a sense that things are unreal, and may have physical symptoms like a pounding heart, shortness of breath, dizziness, numbness, or tingling feelings. Sometimes a person having a panic attack mistakenly feels he may be dying or having a heart attack. The panic symptoms are caused by overactivity of the body's normal fear response.

Agoraphobia is an intense fear of having a panic attack. People with agoraphobia have had a panic attack before, and worry so much about having another that they avoid going anywhere they think it could possibly occur. They are often left with very few places they feel comfortable going outside their own home.

Social anxiety disorder is an intense fear of social situations. Teens with social anxiety may feel too nervous to raise their hand or talk in class. They may fear making a mistake, saying the wrong answer, or looking foolish. They may feel extremely shy and anxious in situations where they have to interact with others, such as parties, the lunch table, or when they meet new people. They may be overly self-conscious about their clothes or hair, worrying that they might be criticized or teased, or that they might stand out or be noticed. With an extreme form of social anxiety called selective mutism, some kids and teens may be too anxious to talk at all in certain situations.

Obsessive-compulsive disorder (OCD) is characterized by obsessions - thoughts or impulses that occur again and again and that a person feels he can't control - and compulsions - behaviors or rituals that a person feels he must perform to control disturbing thoughts and relieve the anxiety the thoughts trigger. With OCD a teen may, for example, have constant worry and fear about illness or germs, and may become stuck in a pattern of washing and cleaning that becomes time-consuming, distressing, and feels impossible to control. The worries (obsessions) with OCD are unrealistic, but are frightening to the person who has them. For example, a teen with illness obsessions may worry that just by reading about an illness or driving past a hospital he could become ill.

Posttraumatic stress disorder (PTSD) refers to anxiety relating to a traumatic or terrifying past experience. With PTSD, a frightening, life-threatening event such as an accident, serious violence (such as rape, abuse, shooting, or gang violence), or a natural disaster (such as an earthquake, tornado, hurricane) causes such a severe fear response that the person may experience flashbacks, nightmares, or constant fear, worry, and stress after the fact. PTSD may occur within days or weeks after the life-threatening event, or it may be delayed and occur much later.

Phobias are intense unrealistic fears relating to specific situations or things (that are not actually dangerous), such as heights, dogs, or flying in an airplane. Phobias usually cause people to avoid what they are afraid of. Some people can work around a phobia if it involves something they do not have to encounter in their everyday life. Other phobias may involve more common situations or things, and may be harder to steer clear of even if people do their best to avoid them. Avoiding these things or situations tends to make the fear stronger each time the person encounters them.

If you have an anxiety disorder, you may feel that it's ruling your life. In addition to worrying much of the time, you may be easily distracted and have trouble concentrating. You may feel stressed and tense or unable to relax. You may experience physical symptoms such as headaches, sweaty hands, upset stomach, pounding heart, and muscle tension. Like Morgan, you may find it nearly impossible to fall asleep. Some people have extremely intense symptoms - for example, people who are experiencing panic attacks may fear that they are having a heart attack or might even die.

But whether you think you might have an anxiety disorder or you know someone who does, understanding the disorder and its treatment can help.

WHY DO PEOPLE GET ANXIETY DISORDERS?

There is no one cause for anxiety disorders. Several factors can play a role, including genetics, brain biochemistry, an overactive "fight or flight" response, life circumstances, and learned behavior.

Anxiety disorders tend to run in families, suggesting that there is a hereditary, or genetic, component to many of these conditions. A person who has a family member with an anxiety disorder has a greater chance of developing an anxiety disorder, though not necessarily the same type.

Genetics influence a person's brain biochemistry, and may make certain people more prone to problems with anxiety. The brain's biochemistry involves the brain's millions of nerve cells (called neurons) that constantly communicate with each other through chemicals called neurotransmitters.

Neurotransmitters are the brain's chemical messengers, and specific neurotransmitters help to regulate mood. Neurotransmitters are released from one neuron and attach to a receptor on another neuron. Sometimes there is interference with this process, such as if the receptor is blocked and unable to receive the neurotransmitter.

This interference can create an imbalance in the levels of the neurotransmitter in the brain, and can cause symptoms of anxiety. There are many kinds of neurotransmitters; two that are involved in anxiety are called serotonin and dopamine. When there's an imbalance of these chemicals, anxiety and other problems can occur.

Certain things that happen in a person's life can also set the stage for anxiety disorders. Frightening traumatic events that can lead to PTSD are a good example.

Early learning also plays a role. Growing up in a family where others are fearful or anxious can "teach" a child to view the world as a scary place. Likewise, if a child grows up in an environment that is actually scary or dangerous (if there is violence in the child's family or community, for example), the child may learn to be fearful or expect the worst.

The brain's automatic reaction to an anxiety-provoking situation also can fuel an anxiety disorder. Here's how this can happen: when a person senses danger (even if it doesn't turn out to be true danger), the brain quickly reacts by sending a signal to a small structure in the brain called the amygdala (pronounced: uh-mig-duh-luh). The amygdala immediately activates the body's automatic "fight or flight" response, and the body prepares itself for danger. This response is what triggers symptoms like sweating and a pounding heart.

Sometimes it turns out that as soon as the person processes the information in the thinking part of the brain (the cerebral cortex), which happens just moments later, the person realizes there's really no danger. The person then relaxes, and this fight or flight response stops.

But the amygdala is programmed to "remember" the trigger that set this process in motion in case it happens again. This is the brain's attempt to protect the person from future danger by keeping track of all cues that might signal danger. So, for example, if the person encounters the same thing that scared him once before (even if the person later realized it wasn't dangerous), the amygdala may activate the same anxiety reaction. It's possible for the amygdala to begin to overreact, and for the person to mistakenly interpret certain things as dangerous.

How Are Anxiety Disorders Diagnosed and Treated?

Some people go to their medical doctor because they're worried about the physical symptoms associated with anxiety. This is a good idea because symptoms like palpitations, chest pain, stomachaches, vomiting, shortness of breath, shakiness, numbness or tingling, or sleeping problems can be caused by certain medical illnesses.

A doctor can examine a person to determine whether he has any medical conditions that need treatment. But if the doctor doesn't find a medical cause for the symptoms, and sees that there's a certain pattern of physical symptoms, the doctor may diagnose anxiety and refer the person to a mental health specialist.

If you think you may have an anxiety disorder, you need to see a mental health specialist, such as a psychologist or psychiatrist, for an evaluation. Don't wait to ask for help - anxiety can be overwhelming, and it can prevent you from enjoying yourself, your friends, school, and social activities. There are treatments that can help teens with anxiety disorders feel much better, often fairly quickly.

Some people with anxiety try to medicate or relax themselves by using alcohol and drugs (even things like sleeping pills), which may seem to make the anxiety or stress go away temporarily. This is not a good solution for several reasons. Drugs and alcohol create only a false sense of relaxation, can be dangerous, and can lead to lots of other problems, which can make it that much harder to function.

You can expect the mental health specialist to ask about your medical history, your family situation, the symptoms you've been experiencing, and your general well-being. Don't be surprised if some of the questions are very personal - your responses will help the doctor to understand you more fully and create a treatment plan that's right for you.

Treatment for anxiety may include medication, cognitive-behavioral therapy or other types of talk therapy, and relaxation or biofeedback to control tense muscles. A combination of treatments may be prescribed.

When medications are part of the treatment for anxiety, often a certain class of medications called SSRIs is used. This is sometimes confusing to people with anxiety because the SSRI medications are commonly referred to as "antidepressants."

Here's the scoop to clear up the confusion: the SSRI medications were first developed as antidepressants, but it was recognized that they also have anti-anxiety effects. So, how could they work for both? Because depression and anxiety both involve, among other things, an imbalance of the neurotransmitter serotonin. SSRI medications help to restore the normal balance of serotonin, and therefore help with both depression and anxiety.

Though not every teen who has an anxiety disorder needs medication (in fact, most don't), the right medication can help to reduce symptoms of anxiety, and can be a great relief to someone whose anxiety symptoms are causing tremendous distress. Often when doctors prescribe medication, they begin with a very small dosage, and gradually increase to the dosage that works best. It may take some time to get the dosage that works best for you. And it may take several weeks before the full benefits of a certain medication are felt. As with any medication, it's very important to take it exactly as prescribed and to tell your doctor about any side effects.

In psychotherapy, or talk therapy, a teen talks with a mental health professional about the stresses and anxiety he's feeling. Getting support and sorting through problems by talking them through can be helpful to teens with anxiety.

In a particular type of talk therapy called cognitive-behavioral therapy (CBT), teens take an active role in "unlearning" some of their fear. CBT helps teens learn new ways to think and act when confronted with anxiety, and to manage and deal with stress so it doesn't get out of hand. In CBT, teens learn how to detect and measure their anxiety, recognize what triggers it, and practice ways to reduce it. They learn what makes their fear worse and what can ease it. Techniques vary, but may include relaxation and breathing exercises or exposure therapy, where a person is gradually exposed what triggers his fear. If it's done with proper support and new coping skills, exposure helps even intense fear fade away.

Don't hesitate to tell your doctor or therapist about what's working and what isn't - you're a member of your treatment team, and your ideas and feelings are important.

Dealing With an Anxiety Disorder

If you have an anxiety disorder, it may be difficult for your friends or family to understand just how you feel. Sometimes people give unrealistic advice - like telling you to just stop worrying. Though they may have the best intentions, they may not understand that it's not that simple. You may have to explain this to them.

Because others may not always understand, sometimes people are reluctant to let loved ones know what they are going through. Some people may be concerned that their fear or behavior may be seen as childish, silly, or weird. But communication is the key. Close friends and family can be part of the solution, and their care and support can be valuable. Let them know what they can do to help.

Yoga for Anxiety

Going as far back as 5,000 years ago Yoga is an ancient and timeless tradition enduring through the centuries as only a few things have done. Yoga is known primarily in the west for its healing and regenerative properties of the mind and body and started life in ancient India as a way for the dedicated follower to attain the highest form of enlightenment. In India this original practice of Yoga still continues much as it did 5,000 years ago with perhaps only a few changes.

The branches of Yoga that came over to the west were later modified to suit the western culture straying away from any overt religious teachings. Some of the ideas that are inherent in the original Yoga practices however are still to be found in the modern day western Yoga practices. This involves nothing more complicated than teaching a state of mindfulness and wellbeing to the student of Yoga to help them in understanding the underlying concept behind each posture or "asana" as it is called. You will also find that Hatha Yoga is the more predominant form of Yoga that is practiced here. Hatha Yoga leans more towards the physical aspect of Yoga and has more to do with poses and postural sequences than do any of the other branches of Yoga.

If you're interested in trying Yoga for yourself as a way to defeat your anxiety attacks don't be put off by what you might perceive as religious teachings. This is simply not the case especially if you're joining a class that's held at your local gym. Along with the stress releasing postures and mind relaxing techniques you'll also get an insight into the reason behind each posture and gradually be able to find the postures that suit you and that are able to relieve your anxiety.

As with all things these days, if you want to learn something it's as easy as picking up your phone or buying a how-to book, or even just walking into your gym and making enquiries. If you're able to cope with it I would suggest the gym method as it will get you on the right path from the get go. With the self teaching method you're prone to learn more of the wrong usage of techniques but if you're unable to leave the house or don't like crowds then this is a good way to start.

You also need to be aware that some more advanced postures should only be attempted when an experienced Yoga practitioner is present to help you. Some of the postures are also not recommended if you're suffering from certain ailments such as backache or even knee pain. These can be corrected through Yoga but only by doing the postures that are right for that condition as otherwise you might make it worse.

Yoga is a healthy and natural way to get rid of all your pent up stress and anxiety and will help to bring balance back into your world. As with any new thing however it will take time and practice before you get it right but if you persevere and continue I must say that the benefits to be had from practicing Yoga far outweigh any initial frustration you may have.

SOME USEFUL ASANAS FOR REDUCING ANXIETY

According to some experts, Yoga vies for pride of place alongside Tai Chi and meditation as the relaxation method of choice first thing in the morning. I found that where before I was always late to get up and just never had that zest for life to help get me through the day, when I took up Yoga I was filled with exuberance and the feeling that I could conquer the world if I wanted to.

Yoga was one of the very first things I took up in my quest to fight my frustrating anxiety attacks.

So just to start you off so that you know what your instructor is talking about when he/she starts you off on a Yoga jaunt I've named a few of the postures used commonly to treat anxiety disorders.

1. Savasana (Corpse Pose)

One of the simplest postures and one that is akin to meditation is the Savasana (Corpse Pose) - so named for the fact that you'll be lying flat and prone on whatever comfortable surface you have, ideally the floor, and practicing your breathing technique which I mentioned in both the "Breathing Properly" section and the "Meditation" section.

Method

On a soft carpet or blanket of folded rug lie full length on back with arms away from the body with palms facing upward and feet slightly apart. Close the eyes and mouth and withdraw the consciousness by stages beginning with the feet, the ankles the knees the adbomen the chest, the neck and the face. Finally keep the mind free. Simply lying on the floor, closing the eyes and breathing slowly does not mean Shavasan. The technique of this asana must be followed carefully. Deep, slow and long breathing and retaining breath for a couple of seconds is very essential in Shavasan—an excellent Asan for complete relaxation.

2. Padmasana (the Lotus Pose) -

Calms the brain; and is also one of those poses that I mentioned that needs an experienced Yoga practitioner to help you with. Although it looks simple enough it's really quite difficult to manage this one properly without some intensive practice. (I'm still working on it!)

Method

Sit on the folded blanket with your legs outstretched. Bend each leg and place each foot on the opposite thigh, soles turned upwards. Pull the foot as high as you can. Keep the palms of the right and left hand on the right and left knees, touching the thumb with tips of index fingers and gaze at the tip of the nose. Keep the head, neck and spinal column straight and erect and breathe slowly.

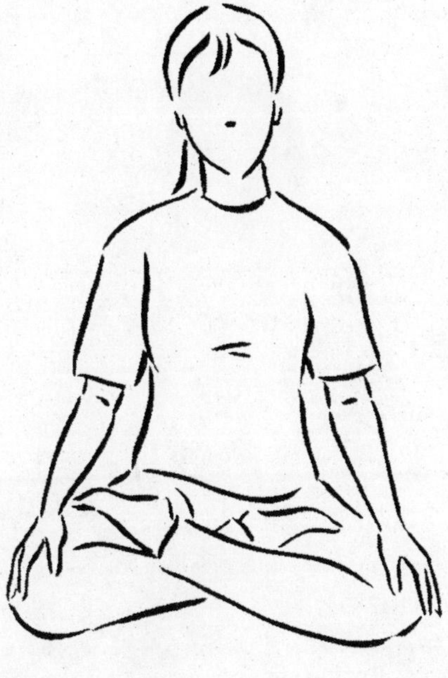

3. Anjali Mudra (Salutation Seal)

Mudras are hand gestures used in yoga and meditation in order to focus and direct energy. Anjali Mudra in Sanskrit means Reverence gesture. It is sometimes referred to as prayer position, and is used often in yoga asana practice. It can also be said to represent dualities, such as male and female.

Anjali Mudra is also called Pranamanjali. In India, people are greeted by this Mudra signifying grace and reverence. Its a gesture of respect and greeting, in which the two palms are held softly together and slightly cupped. Its often accompanied by the verbal salutation "Namaskar" which means "reverent salutation".

As you bring your hands together at your centre, you are literally connecting the right and left hemispheres of your brain.

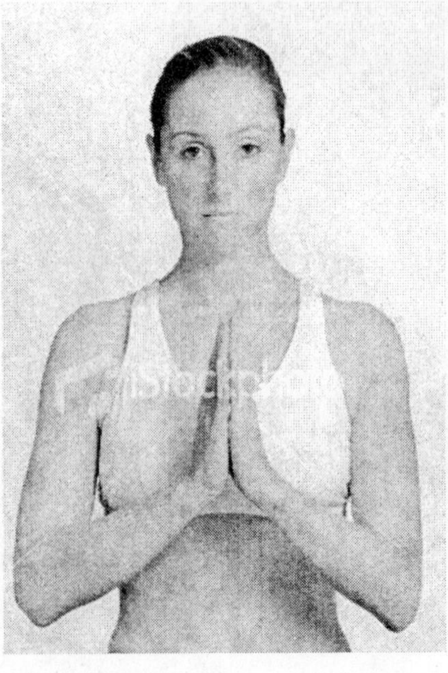

Anjali Mudra is used as a posture of composure, of returning to one's heart, whether you are greeting someone or saying goodbye, initiating or completing an action. This is the yogic process of unification, the yoking of our active and receptive natures.

In the yogic view of the body, the energitic or spiritual heart is visualized as a lotus of the centre of the chest. Anjali Mudra nourishes this lotus heart with awareness, gently encouraging it to open.

Method

1. Sit comfortably in Siddhasana or stand in Tadasana.

2. Inhale and bring your palms together. Rest the thumbs lightly on your sternum.

3. Press the hands firmly but evenly against each other. Make sure that one hand (usually your right hand if you are right-handed, your left if left-handed) doesn't dominate the other. If you find such imbalance, release the dominant hand slighly but don't increase the pressure of the non-dominant hand.

4. Bow your head slightly, drawing the crease of the neck toward the centre of your head.

5. Lift your sternum into your thumbs and lengthen down along the back of the armpits, making the back elbows heavy.

Practicing Anjali Mudra is an excellent way to induce a mediative state of awareness. Start your practice sitting in meditation in Anjali Mudra for 5 minutes. You can also use this hand position in Tadasana prior to beginning the Sun Salutation sequence, contemplating the "sun" or light of awareness the yogis say is resident in your heart.

Benefits

1. It reduces stress and anxiety.

2. Calms the brain.

3. Creates flexibility in the hands, fingers, wrists and arms.

4. Opens the heart.

4. Janu Sirsasana (Head-to-Knee pose)

It relieves mild depression, calms the brain, and also said to relieve anxiety.

Method

Janu-sirsasana: "Janu" means knee, "Sirsa" is the head.

This asana is effective for awakening the second chakra, Svadhisthana.

Chakra: The svadhisthana chakra is at the level of the sacrum, and at the front, between the navel and the pubic bone. This is the water centre; its qualities are expansion, expression and social response. It is the centre for desire, sex and pleasures in general, which are balanced and controlled from this chakra. The negative emotions associated with this centre are jealousy, fear, and anger.

The three water signs, Cancer, Scorpio, and Pisces are associated with this chakra. Identification with the svadhisthana chakra bestows a richly active and involved life with many ups and downs.

Method

1. Sit with legs outstretched and back straight. Place sole of right foot firmly against inside of left thigh.

2. Stretch arms overhead, straightening and opening the spine upwards, and leaning slightly back. Inhale while doing this.

3. Bending from hips, exhale and stretch forward keeping the back as straight as possible. Rest the hands on the legs where it is comfortable to hold the pose. Keep the foot pointing up. Relax the abdomen and neck as the head rests forward. Breathe while holding the position.

1

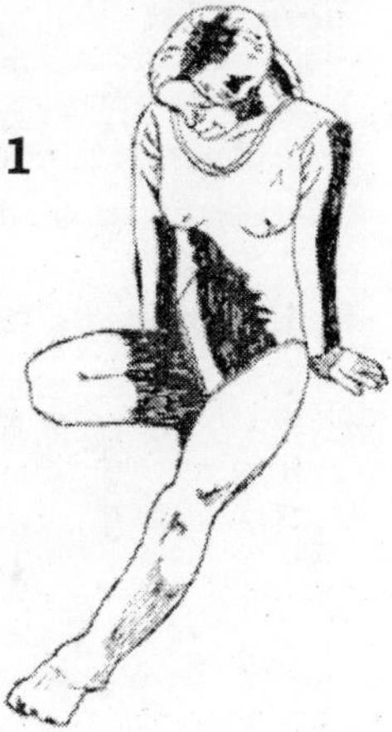

2

3

4. After holding the position for a count of 10, try to exhale and stretch a little farther down the leg, clasping the ankle or foot if possible. Hold for up to 1 minute if comfortable. Remember to breathe as you hold the pose.

5. When coming out of the pose, inhale and straighten the spine as you stretch the arms overhead. Exhale as you lower the arms to your sides. Repeat with the other leg.

NOTE: always hold the pose where it is comfortable, giving the muscles time to adapt and adjust to the stretch. Then continue to gradually move farther into the pose.

Benefits:

Janu-sirsasana is great for the lumbar/thoracic area, stretching the entire spine and back of the legs. It massages and stimulates the internal organs.

5. Uttanasana (Standing Forward Bend) -

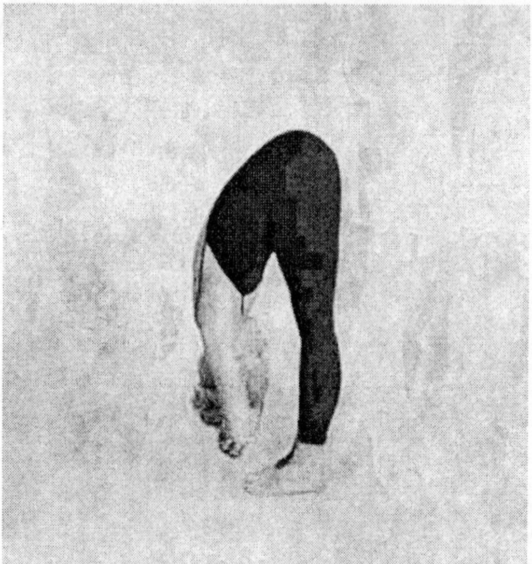

Uttanasana is the basic standing forward bend. It is a pose that brings about intense extension to your legs and spine. Your hamstrings will wake up and your mind will be soothed. Uttanasana is sometimes done between standing poses because of its recuperative benefits. It is a critical piece of Surya Namaskar, sun salutation sequences done in vinyasa and other styles of yoga. Vinyasa styles of yoga are sequences of poses performed one after another and linked in a dynamic flow by breath.

Method

1. Start in mountain pose (Tadasana) standing with the feet, ankles and toes as close together as possible. Place your hands at your hips with your fingers facing forward and the thumbs pointing back.

2. Inhale, then as you exhale bend forward. The goal is to place your fingers and then your palms on the floor.

3. As a basic forward bend, it is like all forward bends in that the work in the pose actually occurs in the muscles of the legs rather than in the spine. It is through lengthening the muscles in the back of the legs that one eventually can bend at the waist and fold the upper body flat against the legs in forward bending positions.

4. When performing Uttanasana lengthen the front of your body as you fold. Work towards placing the hands next to the feet and behind the heels. Do not bend your knees. When you have worked into the pose as deeply as you initially can with straight legs then stay there for some time attempting to breath into the stretching muscles in the legs and gradually easing a bit deeper into the pose.

5. It is important to extend continuously from the

base of the spine. Move the hips forward without pushing your buttocks back. Keep legs perpendicular with the floor. Soften as you hang from the hips. Let your own weight and gravity help you as you allow your spine to extend.

6. Keep breathing continuously and stay as long as it is easy to breathe normally in a continuous way without holding your breath.

7. Strive to extend the back leg muscles and thus bring the torso closer to the legs. The chin is moving towards the shin rather then the head to the knees.

8. Your knees should be lifted with active quadriceps muscles. Weight is equally divided between the left and the right leg and centered on each foot.

9. After some time, lift out of the pose on an inhalation. Raise your head from the knees, but, if possible, leave your palms or hands on the floor. If you are flexible, you can leave the palms there and lift up. Otherwise, your fingertips will be okay.

10. Complete two breaths and deeply inhale. Lift your hands from the floor and return to Tadasana (mountain pose). If this you experience any slight dizziness when finishing the pose it can often be alleviated by pressing the chin into the upper chest as you slowly return to an upright position.

Tips for Beginners:

1. Here is a variation. When you are in the pose, you can try bending elbows and holding each elbow. Hang like a rag doll and let the gravity help extend your spine. Play with bending your knees slightly during the pose,

which will lessen the intensity for the hamstrings.

2. Another variation is to do the pose against the wall. Stand a foot to a foot and half away from the wall, facing away from it. Bend forward and send your hips back to the wall. As you do the pose, your legs will be at an angle from the floor to the wall. Your sit bones should touch the wall, not your hips. Extend the spine and reach for the floor. Now try standing on your tiptoes. It should raise your sit bones on the wall. Leave your sit bones at the spot on the wall and come down onto your flat feet. As you do this, you will notice that your pelvis rotates and thus allows your spine to extend. The action of the raising of the sit bones and the pelvis is good to help your body understand when you do the pose in this variation or the other way.

3. Ardha Uttanasana, or half standing forward bend pose is an alternative to those who might have back problems. The Ardha Uttanasana pose is good for meditators and people who sit a lot. It helps stretch out the back. Instead of bending towards the floor, bend halfway to a ledge, like a windowsill or countertop. Arms are out in front of you resting on the ledge. Your torso is parallel with the floor. Your legs are still perpendicular to the floor. Don't lock your knees. If it feels good, bend them slightly in the pose which will make it less intense.

Tip for Intensifying the Pose:

Do the pose as described at the top under "Technique." Place a rolled mat under the balls of both feet bring your toes up with heels down. This makes the hamstrings and calves feel a more of a stretch.

More Variations

Do the pose and rest your head on a stool, chair, or block when your are tired and need restoration. Experiment in finding the right height for you. Add blankets to a surface to make it perfect. I like to use the yoga barrel standing on one end. I can grab the slats on the side of the barrel and pull yet the barrel provides a surface to rest the top of my head. Doing Uttanasana on a stool cools the head and relaxes the eyes. The fresh oxygenated blood going to the brain rejuvenates and refreshes the mind. Do the pose this way in the supported version when you are tired or exhausted. When you travel, try it and you will feel better.

Benefits

1. Uttanasana is said to soothe the mind and relieve stress. The pose may help alleviate mild depression. You will notice a stretch the hamstrings, calves, and hips and you want to be careful to not overstretch the hamstrings. Notice sensation and don't lock your knees in the pose.

2. The thighs and knees strengthen with lifting in the quadriceps. The supported version is useful during menopause. Uttanasana, especially supported, reduces fatigue and anxiety. For some headaches it may bring relief and it is a good pose to do to counteract fatigue. If you get excited and need calming, it will help. It may help digestion and menstrual pain in the abdomen. Your spine will appreciate the space between vertebrae created by the stretch. Those with asthma, high blood pressure, osteoporosis, and sinusitis may be assisted by this posture.

3. It calms the mind relieves stress and mild depression and also reduces anxiety and fatigue

Caution

If you have back pain when you do the pose, do Ardha Uttanasana described above in Beginner Tip #3. Bend your knees slightly and listen to your body as to not push it. A teacher is useful for guidance.

If you have high blood pressure or are prone to headaches, do the supported version shown above under "Variations."

7

SEXUAL HEALTH AND YOGA

YOUR CHANGING BODY

The Truth About Guys

Many people think of guys as being carefree when it comes to their appearance. But the reality is that a lot of guys spend plenty of time in front of the mirror. It's a fact — some guys care just as much as girls do about their appearance.

You may hear a lot about being a tough guy, but how often do you hear that being a guy is tough? Guys might think that they shouldn't worry about how they look, but body image can be a real problem for them. Unlike girls, guys are less likely to talk to friends and relatives about their bodies and how they're developing. Without support from friends and family, they may develop a negative self-image. The good news is that self-image and body image can be changed.

WHY IS BODY IMAGE IMPORTANT?

Body image is a person's opinions, thoughts, and feelings about his or her own body and physical appearance. Having a positive body image means feeling pretty satisfied with the way you look, appreciating your body for its capabilities and accepting its imperfections. Body image is part of someone's total self-image. So how a guy feels about his body can affect how he feels about himself. If he gets too focused on not liking the way he looks, a guy's self-esteem can take a hit and his confidence can slide. (The same thing can happen to girls, too.)

HOW PUBERTY AFFECTS BODY IMAGE

Although body image is just one part of our self-image, during the teen years, and especially during puberty, it can be easy for a guy's whole self-image to be based on how his body looks. That's because our bodies are changing so much during this time that they can become the main focus of our attention.

A change in your body can be tough to deal with emotionally — mainly because, well, your body is yours and you have become used to it.

Some guys don't feel comfortable in their changing bodies and can feel as if they don't know who they are anymore. Being the only guy whose voice is changing or who's growing body hair (or the only guy who isn't) can also make some guys feel self-conscious for a while.

Some guys go into puberty not feeling too satisfied with their body or appearance to begin with. They may have wrestled with body image even before puberty started (for example, battles with weight or dissatisfaction with height). For them, puberty may add to their insecurities.

It Could Be in Your Genes

It can be tough to balance what you expect to happen to your body with what actually does happen. Lots of guys can have high expectations for puberty, thinking they'll develop quickly or in a certain way.

The best way to approach your own growth and development is to not assume you'll be a certain way. Look at everyone in your family — uncles, grandfathers, and even female relatives — to get an idea of the kinds of options your genes may have in store for you.

WHEN EVERYONE ELSE SEEMS BIGGER

Not everyone's body changes at the same time or even at the same pace. It can be tough if all of your friends have already matured physically and are taller and more muscular. Most guys eventually catch up in terms of growth, although some will always be taller or more muscular than others — it's in their genes.

It's natural to observe friends and classmates and notice the different ways they're growing and developing. Guys often compare themselves with other guys in certain settings, and one of the most common is the locker room. Whether at a local gym or getting ready for a game at school, time in the locker room can be daunting for any guy.

Try to keep in mind in these situations that you aren't alone if you feel you don't "measure up." Many guys feel exactly the same way about their own bodies — even those whose physiques you envy. Just knowing that almost everyone else will go through the same thing can make all the difference.

You could try talking to a trusted male adult — maybe a coach, a doctor, a teacher, or your dad. Chances are they went through similar experiences and had some of the same feelings and apprehensions when their bodies were changing.

PICTURE PERFECT?

Guys put enough pressure on themselves, but what about the pressure society puts on them to be perfect?

It used to be that only girls felt the pressure of picture-perfect images, but these days the media emphasis on men's looks creates a sense of pressure for guys, too. And sometimes (actually many times) that "as advertised" body is just not attainable. The men you see in those pictures may not even be real. Magazines and ad agencies often alter photographs of models, either by airbrushing the facial and muscular features, or by putting a good-looking face on someone else's buff body.

BUILDING A BETTER BODY IMAGE

So in the face of all the pressure society places on guys — and guys place on themselves — what can you do to fuel a positive body image? Here are some ideas:

Recognize your strengths. Different physical attributes and body types are good for different things — and sometimes the things you did well as a kid can change during puberty. What does your body do well? Maybe your speed, flexibility, strength, or coordination leads you to excel at a certain sport. Or perhaps you have non-sports skills, like drawing, painting, singing, playing a musical instrument, writing, or acting. Just exploring talents that you feel good about can help your self-esteem and how you think of yourself.

A good body doesn't always translate into athletic success. Too often, the way guys see their body image is closely associated with their performance on a sports field or in the gym. The upside to this is that if you're good at a team sport, you might have a pretty good view of your body. But what if you don't like team sports or you got cut from a team you really wanted to make? In these cases, it helps to look at individual accomplishments.

If you don't like team sports, that's OK. Try finding another form of physical activity that really gets you going. Depending on your interests and where you live, that may be mountain biking, rock climbing, dancing, yoga, or even jogging. This will help you stay in shape and help you to appreciate skills may not have realized you had in a team environment.

If you like team sports but didn't make a particular team, don't let it get you down. Use this as an opportunity to discover what you're good at, not to lament what you aren't best at. Maybe try out for another team — so soccer wasn't for you, but maybe cross-country running will be.

If none of these appeal to you, continue to practice the sport you were cut from and try again next year. The people around you probably won't remember that you didn't make the team — not being picked was a much bigger deal to you than it was to them.

Look into starting a strength training program. Exercise can help you look good and feel good about yourself. Good physiques don't just happen — they take hard work, regular workouts, and a healthy diet. There's no need to work out obsessively. A healthy routine can be as simple as exercising 20 minutes to 1 hour three days a week. Another benefit to working out properly is that it can boost your mood — lifting weights can lift your spirits.

Don't trash your body, respect it! To help improve your view of your body, take care of it. Smoking and other things you know to be harmful will take a toll after a while. Treating yourself well over time results in a healthier, stronger body — and that contributes to a better body image. Practicing good grooming habits — regular showering; taking care of your teeth, hair, and skin; wearing clean clothes, etc. — also can help you build a positive body image.

Be yourself. Your body is just one part of who you are — along with your talent for comedy, a quick wit, or all the other things that make you unique. Your talents, skills, and beliefs are just as much a part of you as the casing they come in. So try not to let minor imperfections take over.

While it's important to have a positive body image, getting too focused on body image and appearance can cause a guy to overlook the other positive parts of himself. If you're like most guys who take care of their bodies and wear clothes that look good, you probably look great to others. You just might not be aware of that if you're too busy being self-critical.

DELAYED PUBERTY

Puberty is the time when your body grows from a child's to an adult's. You'll know that you are going through puberty by the way that your body changes. If you're a girl, you'll notice that your breasts develop and your pubic hair grows, that you have a growth spurt, and that you get your period (menstruation). The overall shape of your body will probably change, too — your hips will widen and your body will become curvier.

If you're a guy, you'll start growing pubic and facial hair, have a growth spurt, and your testicles and penis will get larger. Your body shape will also begin to change — your shoulders will widen and your body will become more muscular.

These changes are caused by the sex hormones (testosterone in guys and estrogen in girls) that your body begins producing in much larger amounts than before.

Puberty takes place over a number of years, and the age at which it starts and ends varies widely. It generally begins somewhere between the ages of 7 and 13 for girls, and somewhere between the ages of 9 and 15 for guys, although it can be earlier or later for some people. This wide range in age is normal, and it's why you may develop several years earlier (or later) than most of your friends.

Sometimes, though, people pass this normal age range for puberty without showing any signs of body changes. This is called delayed puberty.

WHAT CAUSES DELAYED PUBERTY?

There are several reasons why puberty may be delayed. Most often, it's simply a pattern of growth and development in a family. A guy or girl may find that his or her parent, uncle, aunt, brothers, sisters, or cousins developed later than usual, too. This is called constitutional delay (or being a late bloomer), and it usually doesn't require any kind of treatment. These teens will eventually develop normally, just later than most of their peers.

Medical problems also can cause delays in puberty. Some people with chronic illnesses like diabetes, cystic fibrosis, kidney disease, or even asthma may go through puberty at an older age because their illnesses can make it harder for their bodies to grow and develop. Proper treatment and better control of many of these conditions can help make delayed puberty less likely to occur.

A person who's malnourished — without enough food to eat or without the proper nutrients — may also develop later than peers who eat a healthy, balanced diet. For example, teens with the eating disorder anorexia nervosa often lose so much weight that their bodies can't develop properly. Girls who are extremely active in sports may be late developers because their level of exercise keeps them so lean. Girls' bodies require a certain amount of fat before they can go through puberty or get their periods.

Delayed puberty can also happen because of problems in the pituitary or thyroid glands. These glands produce hormones important for body growth and development.

Some people who don't go through puberty at the normal time have problems with their chromosomes (pronounced: kro-muh-soamz), which are made up of DNA that contain our body's construction plans. Problems with the chromosomes can interfere with normal growth processes.

Turner syndrome is an example of a chromosome disorder. It happens when one of a female's two X chromosomes is abnormal or missing. This causes problems with how a girl grows and with the development of her ovaries and production of sex hormones. Women who have untreated Turner syndrome are shorter than normal, are infertile, and may have other medical problems. Males with Klinefelter syndrome are born with an extra X chromosome (XXY instead of XY). This condition can slow sexual development.

WHAT DO DOCTORS DO?

The good news is that if there is a problem, doctors usually can help teens with delayed puberty to develop more normally. So if you are worried that you're not developing as you should, you should ask your parents to make an appointment with your doctor.

In addition to doing a physical examination, the doctor will take your medical history by asking you about any concerns and symptoms you have, your past health, your family's health, any medications you're taking, any allergies you may have, and other issues like growth patterns of your family members. He or she will chart your growth to see if your growth pattern points to a problem and also may order blood tests to check for thyroid, pituitary, chromosomal, or other problems. You may also have a "bone age" X-ray, which allows the doctor to see whether your bones are maturing normally.

In many cases, the doctor will be able to reassure you that there's no underlying physical problem; you're just a bit later than average in developing. If the doctor does find a problem, though, he or she might refer you to a pediatric endocrinologist (pronounced: en-doh-krih-nah-leh-jist), a doctor who specializes in treating kids and teens who have growth problems, or to another specialist for further tests or treatment.

Some teens who are late developers may have a difficult time waiting for the changes of puberty to finally get going - even after a doctor has reassured them that they are normal. In some cases, doctors may offer teens a short course (usually a few months) of treatment with hormone medications to get the changes of puberty started. Usually, when the treatment is stopped a few months later, the teen's own hormones will take over from there to complete the process of puberty.

DEALING WITH DELAYED PUBERTY

It can be really hard to watch your friends grow and develop when the same thing's not happening to you. You may feel like you're never going to catch up. People at school may joke about your small size or your flat chest. Even when the doctor or your parents reassure you that things will be OK eventually - and even when you believe they're right — it's difficult to wait for something that can affect how you feel about yourself.

If you're feeling depressed or having school or other problems related to delays in your growth and development, talk to your mom or dad, your doctor, or another trusted adult about finding a counselor or therapist you can talk to. This person can help you sort out your feelings and suggest ways to cope with them.

Delayed puberty can be difficult for anyone to accept and deal with — but it's a problem that usually gets solved. Ask for help if you have any concerns about your development. And remember that in most cases you will eventually catch up with your peers.

TIME TO CHANGE

When your body reaches a certain age, your brain releases a special hormone that starts the changes of puberty. It's called gonadotropin-releasing hormone, or

GnRH for short. When GnRH reaches the pituitary gland (a pea-shaped gland that sits just under the brain), this gland releases into the bloodstream two more puberty hormones: luteinizing hormone (LH for short) and follicle-stimulating hormone (FSH for short). Guys and girls have both of these hormones in their bodies. And depending on whether you're a guy or a girl, these hormones go to work on different parts of the body.

For guys, these hormones travel through the blood and give the testes the signal to begin the production of testosterone and sperm. Testosterone is the hormone that causes most of the changes in a guy's body during puberty. Sperm cells must be produced for men to reproduce.

In girls, FSH and LH target the ovaries, which contain eggs that have been there since birth. The hormones stimulate the ovaries to begin producing another hormone called estrogen. Estrogen, along with FSH and LH, causes a girl's body to mature and prepares her for pregnancy.

So that's what's really happening during puberty — it's all these new chemicals moving around inside your body, turning you from a teen into an adult with adult levels of hormones.

Puberty usually starts some time between age 8 and 13 in girls and 10 and 15 in guys. Some people start puberty a bit earlier or later, though. Each person is a little different, so everyone starts and goes through puberty on his or her body's own schedule. This is one of the reasons why some of your friends might still look like kids, whereas others look more like adults.

It Doesn't Hurt . . . It's Just a Growth Spurt

"Spurt" is the word used to describe a short burst of activity, something that happens in a hurry. And a growth spurt is just that: Your body is growing, and it's happening really fast! When you enter puberty, it might seem like your sleeves are always getting shorter and your pants always look like you're ready for a flood — that's because you're experiencing a major growth spurt. It lasts for about 2 to 3 years. When that growth spurt is at its peak, some people grow 4 or more inches in a year.

This growth during puberty will be the last time your body grows taller. After that, you will be at your adult height. But your height isn't the only thing that will be changing.

TAKING SHAPE

As your body grows taller, it will change in other ways, too. You will gain weight, and as your body becomes heavier, you'll start to notice changes in its overall shape. Guys' shoulders will grow wider, and their bodies will become more muscular. Their voices will become deeper. For some guys, the breasts may grow a bit, but for most of them this growth goes away by the end of puberty.

Guys will notice other changes, too, like the lengthening and widening of the penis and the enlargement of the testes. All of these changes mean that their bodies are developing as expected during puberty.

Girls' bodies usually become curvier. They gain weight on their hips, and their breasts develop, starting with just a little swelling under the nipple. Sometimes one breast might develop more quickly than the other, but most of the time they soon even out. With all this growing and developing going on, girls will notice an increase in body fat and occasional soreness under the nipples as the breasts start to enlarge — and that's normal.

Gaining some weight is part of developing into a woman, and it's unhealthy for girls to go on a diet to try to stop this normal weight gain. If you ever have questions or concerns about your weight, talk it over with your doctor.

Usually about 2 to 2 ½ years after girls' breasts start to develop, they get their first menstrual period. This is one more thing that lets a girl know puberty is progressing and the puberty hormones have been doing their job. Girls have two ovaries, and each ovary holds thousands of eggs. During the menstrual cycle, one of the eggs comes out of an ovary and begins a trip through the fallopian tube, ending up in the uterus (the uterus is also called the womb).

Before the egg is released from the ovary, the uterus has been building up its lining with extra blood and tissue. If the egg is fertilized by a sperm cell, it stays in the uterus and grows into a baby, using that extra blood and tissue to keep it healthy and protected as it's developing.

Most of the time, though, the egg is only passing through. When the egg doesn't get fertilized, the uterus no longer needs the extra blood and tissue, so it leaves the body through the vagina as a menstrual period. A period usually lasts from 5 to 7 days, and about 2 weeks after the start of the period a new egg is released, which

marks the middle of each cycle.

HAIR, HAIR, EVERYWHERE

Well, maybe not everywhere. But one of the first signs of puberty is hair growing where it didn't grow before. Guys and girls both begin to grow hair under their arms and in their pubic areas (on and around the genitals). It starts out looking light and sparse. Then as you go through puberty, it becomes longer, thicker, heavier, and darker. Eventually, guys also start to grow hair on their faces.

ABOUT FACE

Another thing that comes with puberty is acne, or pimples. Acne is triggered by puberty hormones. Pimples usually start around the beginning of puberty and can stick around during adolescence (the teen years). You may notice pimples on your face, your upper back, or your upper chest. It helps to keep your skin clean, and your doctor will be able to offer some suggestions for clearing up acne. The good news about acne is that it usually gets better or disappears by the end of adolescence.

PUTTING THE P.U. IN PUBERTY

A lot of teens notice that they have a new smell under their arms and elsewhere on their bodies when they enter puberty, and it's not a pretty one. That smell is body odor, and everyone gets it. As you enter puberty, the puberty hormones affect glands in your skin, and the glands make chemicals that smell bad. These chemicals put the scent in adolescent!

So what can you do to feel less stinky? Well, keeping clean is a good way to lessen the smell. You might want to take a shower every day, either in the morning before school, or the night before. Using deodorant (or deodorant with antiperspirant) every day can help keep body odor in check, too.

There's More?

Guys and girls will also notice other body changes as they enter puberty, and they're all normal changes. Girls might see and feel a white, mucous-like discharge from the vagina. This doesn't mean anything is wrong — it is just another sign of your changing body and hormones.

Guys will begin to get erections (this is when the penis fills with blood and becomes hard) sometimes. Erections happen when guys fantasize and think about sexual things or sometimes for no reason at all. They may experience something called nocturnal emissions (or wet dreams). This is when the penis becomes erect while a guy is sleeping, and he ejaculates. When a guy ejaculates, semen comes out of the penis — semen is a fluid that contains sperm. That's why they're called wet dreams — they happen when you're sleeping and your underwear or the bed might be a little wet when you wake up. Wet dreams become less frequent as guys progress through puberty, and they eventually stop. Guys will also notice that their voices may "crack" and eventually get deeper.

CHANGE CAN FEEL KIND OF STRANGE

Just as those hormones create changes in the way your body looks on the outside, they also create changes on the inside. While your body is adjusting to all the new hormones, so is your mind. During puberty, you might feel confused or have strong emotions that you've never experienced before. You may feel anxious about how your changing body looks.

You might feel overly sensitive or become easily upset. Some teens lose their tempers more than usual and get angry at their friends or families.

Sometimes it can be difficult to deal with all of these new emotions. Usually people aren't trying to hurt your feelings or upset you on purpose. It might not be your family or friends making you angry — it might be your new "puberty brain" trying to adjust. And while the adjustment can feel difficult in the beginning, it will gradually become easier. It can help to talk to someone and share the burden of how you're feeling — a friend or, even better, a parent, older sibling, or adult who's gone through it all before.

You might have new, confusing feelings about sex — and lot of questions. The adult hormones estrogen and testosterone are signals that your body is giving you new responsibilities, like the ability to create a child. That's why it's important to get all your questions answered.

It's easy to feel embarrassed or anxious when talking about sex, but you need to be sure you have all the right information. Some teens can talk to their parents about sex and get all their questions answered. But if you feel funny talking to your parents about sex, there are many other people to talk to, like your doctor, a school nurse, a teacher, a school counselor, or another adult you feel comfortable talking with.

DEVELOPING DIFFERENTLY

People are all a little different from one another, so it makes sense that they don't all develop in the same way. No two people are at exactly the same stage as they go through puberty, and everyone changes at his or her own pace. Some of your friends may be getting curves, whereas you don't have any yet. Maybe your best friend's voice has changed, and you think you still sound like a kid with a high, squeaky voice. Or maybe you're sick of being the tallest girl in your class or the only boy who has to shave.

But eventually everyone catches up, and the differences between you and your friends will even out. It's also good to keep in mind that there is no right or wrong way to look. That's what makes us human — we all have qualities that make us unique, on the inside and the outside.

FEMALE REPRODUCTIVE SYSTEM

All living things reproduce. Reproduction — the process by which organisms make more organisms like themselves — is one of the things that set living things apart from nonliving matter. But even though the reproductive system is essential to keeping a species alive, unlike other body systems, it's not essential to keeping an individual alive.

In the human reproductive process, two kinds of sex cells, or gametes (pronounced: gah-meetz), are involved. The male gamete, or sperm, and the female gamete, the egg or ovum, meet in the female's reproductive system to create a new individual. Both the male and female reproductive systems are essential for reproduction. The female needs a male to fertilize her egg, even though it is she who carries offspring through pregnancy and childbirth.

Humans, like other organisms, pass certain characteristics of themselves to the next generation through their genes, the special carriers of human traits. The genes that parents pass along to their children are what make children similar to others in their family, but they are also what make each child unique. These genes come from the father's sperm and the mother's egg, which are produced by the male and female reproductive systems.

WHAT IS THE FEMALE REPRODUCTIVE SYSTEM?

Most species have two sexes: male and female. Each sex has its own unique reproductive system. They are different in shape and structure, but both are specifically designed to produce, nourish, and transport either the egg or sperm.

Unlike the male, the human female has a reproductive system located entirely in the pelvis (that's the lowest part of the abdomen). The external part of the female reproductive organs is called the vulva, which means covering. Located between the legs, the vulva covers the opening to the vagina (pronounced: vuh-jigh-nuh) and other reproductive organs located inside the body.

The fleshy area located just above the top of the vaginal opening is called the mons pubis (pronounced: manz pyoo-bis). Two pairs of skin flaps called the labia (which means lips and is pronounced: lay-bee-uh) surround the vaginal opening. The clitoris (pronounced: klih-tuh-rus), a small sensory organ, is located toward the front of the vulva where the folds of the labia join. Between the labia are openings to the urethra (the canal that carries urine from the bladder to the outside of the body, which is pronounced: yoo-ree-thruh) and vagina. Once girls become sexually mature, the outer labia and the mons pubis are covered by pubic hair.

A female's internal reproductive organs are the vagina, uterus, fallopian tubes, and ovaries.

The vagina is a muscular, hollow tube that extends from the vaginal opening to the uterus. The vagina is about 3 to 5 inches (8 to 12 centimeters) long in a grown woman. Because it has muscular walls it can expand and contract. This ability to become wider or narrower allows the vagina to accommodate something as slim as a tampon and as wide as a baby. The vagina's muscular walls are lined with mucous membranes, which keep it protected and moist. The vagina has several functions: for sexual intercourse, as the pathway that a baby takes out of a woman's body during childbirth, and as the route for the menstrual blood (the period) to leave the body from the uterus.

A thin sheet of tissue with one or more holes in it called the hymen (pronounced: hi-mun) partially covers the opening of the vagina. Hymens are often different from person to person. Most women find their hymens have stretched or torn after their first sexual experience, and the hymen may bleed a little (this usually causes little, if any, pain). Some women who have had sex don't have much of a change in their hymens, though.

The vagina connects with the uterus (pronounced: yoo-tuh-rus), or womb, at the cervix. The cervix has strong, thick walls. The opening of the cervix is very small (no wider than a straw), which is why a tampon can never get lost inside a girl's body. During childbirth, the cervix can expand to allow a baby to pass.

The uterus is shaped like an upside-down pear, with a thick lining and muscular walls - in fact, the uterus contains some of the strongest muscles in the female body. These muscles are able to expand and contract to accommodate a growing fetus and then help push the baby out during labor. When a woman isn't pregnant, the uterus is only about 3 inches (7.5 centimeters) long and 2 inches (5 centimeters) wide.

At the upper corners of the uterus, the fallopian (pronounced: fuh-lo-pee-un) tubes connect the uterus to the ovaries (pronounced: o-vuh-reez). The ovaries are two oval-shaped organs that lie to the upper right and left of the uterus. They produce, store, and release eggs into the fallopian tubes in the process called ovulation (pronounced: av-yoo-lay-shun). Each ovary measures about 1 1/2 to 2 inches (4 to 5 centimeters) in a grown woman.

There are two fallopian tubes, each attached to a side of the uterus. The fallopian tubes are about 4 inches (10 centimeters) long and about as wide as a piece of spaghetti. Within each tube is a tiny passageway no wider than a sewing needle. At the other end of each fallopian tube is a fringed area that looks like a funnel. This fringed area wraps around the ovary but doesn't completely attach to it. When an egg pops out of an ovary, it enters the fallopian tube. Once the egg is in the fallopian tube, tiny hairs in the tube's lining help push it down the narrow passageway toward the uterus.

The ovaries are also part of the endocrine system

because they produce female sex hormones such as estrogen (pronounced: es-truh-jun) and progesterone (pronounced: pro-jes-tuh-rone).

What Does the Female Reproductive System Do?

The female reproductive system enables a woman to:

produce eggs (ova)

have sexual intercourse

protect and nourish the fertilized egg until it is fully developed

give birth

Sexual reproduction couldn't happen without the sexual organs called the gonads (pronounced: go-nadz). Although most people think of the gonads as the male testicles, both sexes actually have gonads: In females the gonads are the ovaries. The female gonads produce female gametes (eggs); the male gonads produce male gametes (sperm). After an egg is fertilized by the sperm, the fertilized egg is called the zygote (pronounced: zi-gote).

When a baby girl is born, her ovaries contain hundreds of thousands of eggs, which remain inactive until puberty begins. At puberty, the pituitary gland, located in the central part of the brain, starts making hormones that stimulate the ovaries to produce female sex hormones, including estrogen. The secretion of these hormones causes a girl to develop into a sexually mature woman.

Toward the end of puberty, girls begin to release eggs as part of a monthly period called the menstrual cycle. Approximately once a month, during ovulation, an ovary sends a tiny egg into one of the fallopian tubes. Unless the egg is fertilized by a sperm while in the fallopian tube, the egg dries up and leaves the body about 2 weeks later through the uterus. This process is called menstruation (pronounced: men-stray-shun). Blood and tissues from the inner lining of the uterus combine to form the menstrual flow, which in most girls lasts from 3 to 5 days. A girl's the first period is called menarche (pronounced: meh-nar-kee).

It's common for women and girls to experience some discomfort in the days leading to their periods. Premenstrual syndrome (PMS) includes both physical and emotional symptoms that many girls and women get right before their periods, such as acne, bloating, fatigue, backaches, sore breasts, headaches, constipation, diarrhea, food cravings, depression, irritability, or difficulty concentrating or handling stress. PMS is usually at its worst during the 7 days before a girl's period starts and disappears once it begins.

Many girls also experience abdominal cramps during the first few days of their periods. They are caused by prostaglandin, a chemical in the body that makes the smooth muscle in the uterus contract. These involuntary contractions can be either dull or sharp and intense.

It can take up to 2 years from menarche for a girl's body to develop a regular menstrual cycle. During that time, her body is adjusting to the hormones puberty brings. On average, the monthly cycle for an adult woman is 28 days, but the range is from 23 to 35 days.

If a female and male have sex within several days of the female's ovulation (egg release), fertilization can occur. When the male ejaculates (which is when semen leaves a man's penis), between 0.05 and 0.2 fluid ounces (1.5 to 6.0 milliliters) of semen is deposited into the vagina. Between 75 and 900 million sperm are in this small amount of semen, and they "swim" up from the vagina through the cervix and uterus to meet the egg in the fallopian tube. It takes only one sperm to fertilize the egg.

About a week after the sperm fertilizes the egg, the fertilized egg (zygote) has become a multi-celled blastocyst (pronounced: blas-tuh-sist). A blastocyst is about the size of a pinhead, and it's a hollow ball of cells with fluid inside. The blastocyst burrows itself into the lining of the uterus, called the endometrium (pronounced: en-doh-mee-tree-um). The hormone estrogen causes the endometrium to become thick and rich with blood. Progesterone, another hormone released by the ovaries, keeps the endometrium thick with blood so that the blastocyst can attach to the uterus and absorb nutrients from it. This process is called implantation (pronounced: im-plan-tay-shun).

As cells from the blastocyst take in nourishment, another stage of development, the embryonic stage, begins. The inner cells form a flattened circular shape called the embryonic disk, which will develop into a baby. The outer cells become thin membranes that form around the baby. The cells multiply thousands of times and move to new positions to eventually become the embryo (pronounced: em-bree-o). After approximately 8 weeks, the embryo is about the size of an adult's thumb, but almost all of its parts - the brain and nerves, the heart and blood, the stomach and intestines, and the muscles and skin - have formed.

During the fetal stage, which lasts from 9 weeks after

fertilization to birth, development continues as cells multiply, move, and change. The fetus (pronounced: fee-tus) floats in amniotic (pronounced: am-nee-ah-tik) fluid inside the amniotic sac. The fetus receives oxygen and nourishment from the mother's blood via the placenta (pronounced: pluh-sen-tuh), a disk-like structure that sticks to the inner lining of the uterus and connects to the fetus via the umbilical (proncunced: um-bih-lih-kul) cord. The amniotic fluid and membrane cushion the fetus against bumps and jolts to the mother's body.

Pregnancy lasts an average of 280 days — about 9 months. When the baby is ready for birth, its head presses on the cervix, which begins to relax and widen to get ready for the baby to pass into and through the vagina. The mucus that has formed a plug in the cervix loosens, and with amniotic fluid, comes out through the vagina when the mother's water breaks.

When the contractions of labor begin, the walls of the uterus contract as they are stimulated by the pituitary hormone oxytocin (pronounced: ahk-see-toh-sin). The contractions cause the cervix to widen and begin to open. After several hours of this widening, the cervix is dilated (opened) enough for the baby to come through. The baby is pushed out of the uterus, through the cervix, and along the birth canal. The baby's head usually comes first; the umbilical cord comes out with the baby and is cut after the baby is delivered. The last stage of the birth process involves the delivery of the placenta, which is now called the afterbirth. After it has separated from the inner lining of the uterus, contractions of the uterus push it out, along with its membranes and fluids.

Things That Can Go Wrong With the Female Reproductive System

Girls and women may sometimes experience reproductive system problems. Below are some examples of disorders that affect the female reproductive system.

Things That Can Go Wrong With the Vulva and Vagina

vulvovaginitis (pronounced: vul-vo-vah-juh-ni-tus), an inflammation of the vulva and vagina. It may be caused by irritating substances (such as laundry soaps or bubble baths). Poor personal hygiene (such as wiping from back to front after a bowel movement) may also cause this problem. Symptoms include redness and itching in the vaginal and vulvar areas and sometimes vaginal discharge. Vulvovaginitis can also be caused by an overgrowth of candida, a fungus normally present in the vagina.

nonmenstrual vaginal bleeding, most commonly due to the presence of a vaginal foreign body, often wadded-up toilet paper. It may also be due to urethral prolapse, a condition in which the mucous membranes of the urethra protrude into the vagina and form a tiny, donut-shaped mass of tissue that bleeds easily. It can also be due to a straddle injury (such as when falling onto a beam or bicycle frame) or vaginal trauma from sexual abuse.

Things That Can Go Wrong With the Ovaries and Fallopian Tubes

ectopic (pronounced: ek-tah-pik) pregnancy, when a fertilized egg, or zygote, doesn't travel into the uterus, but instead grows rapidly in the fallopian tube. Girls with this condition can develop severe abdominal pain and should see a doctor because surgery may be necessary.

endometriosis (pronounced: en-doh-mee-tree-o-sus),

when tissue normally found only in the uterus starts to grow outside the uterus — in the ovaries, fallopian tubes, or other parts of the pelvic cavity. It can cause abnormal bleeding, painful periods, and general pelvic pain.

ovarian tumors, although rare, can occur. Girls with ovarian tumors may have abdominal pain and masses that can be felt in the abdomen. Surgery may be needed to remove the tumor.

ovarian cysts, noncancerous sacs filled with fluid or semi-solid material. Although they are common and generally harmless, they can become a problem if they grow very large. Large cysts may push on surrounding organs, causing abdominal pain. In most cases, cysts will disappear on their own and treatment is unnecessary. If the cysts are painful, a doctor may prescribe birth control pills to alter their growth, or they may be removed by a surgeon.

polycystic (pronounced: pah-lee-sis-tik) ovary syndrome, a hormone disorder in which too many male hormones (androgens) are produced by the ovaries. This condition causes the ovaries to become enlarged and develop many fluid-filled sacs, or cysts. It often first appears during the teen years. Depending on the type and severity of the condition, it may be treated with drugs to regulate hormone balance and menstruation.

MENSTRUAL PROBLEMS

A variety of menstrual problems can affect girls. Some of the more common conditions are:

dysmenorrhea (pronounced: dis-meh-nuh-ree-uh), when a girl has painful periods.

menorrhagia (pronounced: meh-nuh-rah-zhuh), when a girl has a very heavy periods with excess bleeding.

oligomenorrhea (pronounced: o-lih-go-meh-nuh-ree-uh), when a girl misses or has infrequent periods, even though she's been menstruating for a while and isn't pregnant.

amenorrhea (pronounced: a-meh-nuh-ree-uh), when a girl hasn't started her period by the time she is 16 years old or 3 years after starting puberty, has not developed signs of puberty by age 14, or has had normal periods but has stopped menstruating for some reason other than pregnancy.

INFECTIONS OF THE FEMALE REPRODUCTIVE SYSTEM

Sexually transmitted diseases. These include infections and diseases such as pelvic inflammatory disease (PID), human immunodeficiency virus/ acquired immunodeficiency syndrome (HIV/AIDS), human papilloma virus (HPV, or genital warts), syphilis, chlamydia, gonorrhea, and genital herpes. Most are spread from one person to another by sexual intercourse.

Toxic shock syndrome. This uncommon illness is caused by toxins released into the body during a type of bacterial infection that is more likely to develop if a tampon is left in too long. It can produce high fever, diarrhea, vomiting, and shock.

If you think you have symptoms of a problem with your reproductive system or if you have questions about your growth and development, talk to your parent or doctor — many problems with the female reproductive system can be treated.

THE MALE REPRODUCTIVE SYSTEM

Ever wonder how the universe could allow the existence of someone as annoying as your bratty little brother or sister? The answer lies in reproduction. If people - like your parents (ew!) - didn't reproduce, families would die out and the human race would cease to exist.

All living things reproduce. Reproduction - the process by which organisms make more organisms like themselves - is one of the things that sets living things apart from nonliving matter. But even though the reproductive system is essential to keeping a species alive, unlike other body systems it's not essential to keeping an individual alive.

In the human reproductive process, two kinds of sex cells, or gametes (pronounced: gah-meetz), are involved. The male gamete, or sperm, and the female gamete, the egg or ovum, meet in the female's reproductive system to create a new individual. Both the male and female reproductive systems are essential for reproduction.

Humans, like other organisms, pass certain characteristics of themselves to the next generation through their genes, the special carriers of human traits. The genes parents pass along to their children are what make children similar to others in their family, but they are also what make each child unique. These genes come from the father's sperm and the mother's egg, which are produced by the male and female reproductive systems.

WHAT IS THE MALE REPRODUCTIVE SYSTEM?

Most species have two sexes: male and female. Each sex has its own unique reproductive system. They are different in shape and structure, but both are specifically designed to produce, nourish, and transport either the egg or sperm.

Unlike the female, whose sex organs are located entirely within the pelvis, the male has reproductive organs, or genitals (pronounced: jeh-nuh-tulz), that are both inside and outside the pelvis. The male genitals include:

the testicles

the duct system, which is made up of the epididymis and the vas deferens

the accessory glands, which include the seminal vesicles and prostate gland

the penis

In a guy who's reached sexual maturity, the two testicles (pronounced: tes-tih-kulz), or testes (pronounced: tes-teez), produce and store millions of tiny sperm cells. The testicles are oval-shaped and grow to be about 2 inches (5 centimeters) in length and 1 inch (3 centimeters) in diameter. The testicles are also part of the endocrine system because they produce hormones, including testosterone (pronounced: teh-stass-tuh-rone). Testosterone is a major part of puberty in guys, and as a guy makes his way through puberty, his testicles produce more and more of it. Testosterone is the hormone that causes guys to develop deeper voices, bigger muscles, and body and facial hair, and it also stimulates the production of sperm.

Alongside the testicles are the epididymis

(pronounced: eh-puh-dih-duh-mus) and the vas deferens (pronounced: vass de-fuh-runz), which make up the duct system of the male reproductive organs. The vas deferens is a muscular tube that passes upward alongside the testicles and transports the sperm-containing fluid called semen (pronounced: see-mun). The epididymis is a set of coiled tubes (one for each testicle) that connects to the vas deferens.

The epididymis and the testicles hang in a pouch-like structure outside the pelvis called the scrotum. This bag of skin helps to regulate the temperature of testicles, which need to be kept cooler than body temperature to produce sperm. The scrotum changes size to maintain the right temperature. When the body is cold, the scrotum shrinks and becomes tighter to hold in body heat. When it's warm, the scrotum becomes larger and more floppy to get rid of extra heat. This happens without a guy ever having to think about it. The brain and the nervous system give the scrotum the cue to change size.

The accessory glands, including the seminal vesicles and the prostate gland, provide fluids that lubricate the duct system and nourish the sperm. The seminal vesicles (pronounced: seh-muh-nul veh-sih-kulz) are sac-like structures attached to the vas deferens to the side of the bladder. The prostate gland, which produces some of the parts of semen, surrounds the ejaculatory ducts at the base of the urethra (pronounced: yoo-ree-thruh), just below the bladder. The urethra is the channel that carries the semen to the outside of the body through the penis. The urethra is also part of the urinary system because it is also the channel through which urine passes as it leaves the bladder and exits the body.

The penis is actually made up of two parts: the shaft and the glans (pronounced: glanz). The shaft is the main part of the penis and the glans is the tip (sometimes called the head). At the end of the glans is a small slit or opening, which is where semen and urine exit the body through the urethra. The inside of the penis is made of a spongy tissue that can expand and contract.

All boys are born with a foreskin, a fold of skin at the end of the penis covering the glans. Some boys have a circumcision (pronounced: sur-kum-sih-zhun), which means that a doctor or clergy member cuts away the foreskin. Circumcision is usually performed during a baby boy's first few days of life. Although circumcision is not medically necessary, parents who choose to have their children circumcised often do so based on religious beliefs, concerns about hygiene, or cultural or social reasons. Boys who have circumcised penises and those who don't are no different: All penises work and feel the same, regardless of whether the foreskin has been removed.

ALL ABOUR MENSTRUATION

Menstruation (a period) represents a major stage of puberty in girls; it's one of the many physical signs that a girl is turning into a woman. And like a lot of the other changes associated with puberty, menstruation can be confusing for girls (and guys). Some girls can't wait to start their periods, whereas others may feel afraid or anxious. Many girls and guys don't have a complete understanding of a woman's reproductive system or what actually happens during the menstrual cycle, making the process seem even more mysterious.

PUBERTY AND PERIODS

When girls begin to go through puberty (usually starting between the ages of 8 and 13), their bodies and minds change in many ways. The hormones in their bodies stimulate new physical development, such as growth and breast development. About 2 to 2 1/2 years after a girl's breasts begin to develop, she usually gets her first menstrual period.

About 6 months or so before getting her first period, a girl might notice an increased amount of clear vaginal discharge. This discharge is common. There's no need for a girl to worry about discharge unless it has a strong odor or causes itchiness.

The start of periods is known as menarche (pronounced: meh-nar-kee). Menarche doesn't happen until all the parts of a girl's reproductive system have matured and are working together.

Baby girls are born with ovaries, fallopian tubes, and a uterus. The two ovaries are oval-shaped and sit on either side of the uterus (womb) in the lowest part of the abdomen called the pelvis. They contain thousands of eggs, or ova. The two fallopian tubes are long and thin — like hollow strands of spaghetti (only a little bit thicker). Each fallopian tube stretches from an ovary to the uterus, a pear-shaped organ that sits in the middle of the pelvis. The muscles in a female's uterus are powerful and are able to expand to allow the uterus to accommodate a growing fetus and then help push the baby out during labor.

As a girl matures and enters puberty, the pituitary gland releases hormones that stimulate the ovaries to produce other hormones called estrogen and progesterone. These hormones have many effects on a girl's body, including physical maturation, growth, and emotions.

About once a month, a tiny egg leaves one of the ovaries — a process called ovulation — and travels down one of the fallopian tubes toward the uterus. In the days before ovulation, the hormone estrogen stimulates the uterus to build up its lining with extra blood and tissue, making the walls of the uterus thick and cushioned. This happens to prepare the uterus for pregnancy: If the egg reaches the uterus and is fertilized by a sperm cell, it attaches to the cushiony wall of the uterus, where it slowly develops into a baby.

If the egg isn't fertilized, though — which is the case during most of a girl's monthly cycles — it doesn't attach to the wall of the uterus. When this happens, the uterus sheds the extra tissue lining. The blood, tissue, and unfertilized egg leave the uterus, going through the vagina on the way out of the body. This is a menstrual period. This cycle happens almost every month for several more decades (except, of course, when a female is pregnant) until a woman reaches menopause and no longer releases eggs from her ovaries.

HOW OFTEN DOES A GIRL GET HER PERIOD?

Just as some girls begin puberty earlier or later than others, the same applies to periods. Some girls may start menstruating as early as age 9 or 10, but others may not get their first period until later in their teens. The amount of time between a girl's periods is called her menstrual cycle (the cycle is counted from the start of one period to the start of the next). Some girls will find that their menstrual cycle lasts 28 days, whereas others might have a 24-day cycle, a 30-day cycle, or even a 35-day cycle.

Irregular periods are common in girls who are just beginning to menstruate. It may take the body a while to sort out all the changes going on, so a girl may have a 28-day cycle for 2 months, then miss a month or have two periods with hardly any time in between them, for example. Usually, after a number of months, the menstrual cycle will become more regular. Many women continue to have irregular periods into adulthood, though.

As a girl gets older and her periods settle down — or she gets more used to her own unique cycle — she will probably find that she can predict when her period will come.

HOW LONG AND HOW MUCH?

The amount of time that a girl has her period also can vary. Some girls have periods that last just 2 or 3 days; other girls may have periods that last 7 days or longer. The menstrual flow — meaning how much blood comes out of the vagina — can vary widely from person to person, too. Some girls have such light blood flow that they wonder if they even have their period at all.

Other girls may be concerned that they're losing too much blood. It can be a shock to see all that blood, but it's highly unlikely that a girl will lose too much: For most girls an entire period consists of anywhere from a few spoonfuls to less than 1/2 cup (118 milliliters) of blood — it just looks like a lot! It is possible for a girl to lose an excessive amount of blood during her period, but it's not at all common. (In some cases, a girl can bleed too much because she has a medical condition — such as von Willebrand disease.) The amount of blood a girl loses and how long her period lasts can differ from month to month.

If you're worried about your blood flow or whether your period is normal in other ways, talk to a doctor or nurse. Some changes in menstrual periods can be normal — but only a doctor can help determine the cause of irregular, heavy, painful periods, or no periods at all.

CRAMPS, PMS, AND PIMPLES

Some girls may notice physical or emotional changes around the time of their periods. Menstrual cramps are pretty common — in fact, more than half of all women who menstruate say they have cramps during the first few days of their periods. Doctors think that cramps are caused by prostaglandin, a chemical that causes the muscles of the uterus to contract.

Depending on the girl, menstrual cramps can be dull and achy or sharp and intense, and they can sometimes be felt in the back or the thighs as well as the abdomen. These cramps often become less uncomfortable and sometimes even disappear completely as a girl gets older. In the meantime, many girls and women find that over-the-counter pain medications (like acetaminophen or ibuprofen) can relieve cramps, as can taking a warm bath or applying a warm heating pad to the lower abdomen. Exercising regularly throughout the monthly cycle may help lessen cramps, too. If these things don't help, ask your doctor for advice.

Some girls and women find that they feel depressed

or easily irritated during the few days or week before their periods. Others may get angry more quickly than normal or cry more than usual. Some girls crave certain foods. These types of emotional changes may be the result of premenstrual syndrome (PMS).

PMS is related to changes in the body's hormones. As hormone levels rise and fall during a woman's menstrual cycle, they can affect the way she feels, both emotionally and physically. Some girls, in addition to feeling more intense emotions than they usually do, notice physical changes along with their periods — some feel bloated or puffy because of water retention, others notice swollen and sore breasts, and some get headaches. PMS usually goes away soon after a period begins, but it can come back month after month. Doctors recommend that girls with PMS try to exercise to help feel better. And some girls notice that restricting caffeine intake may help relieve PMS.

It's not uncommon for girls to have an acne flare-up during certain times of their cycle; again, this is due to hormones. Fortunately, the pimples associated with periods tend to become less of a problem as girls get older.

PADS, TAMPONS, AND LINERS

Once you begin menstruating, you'll need to use something to absorb the blood — either a pad or a tampon. There are so many products out there that it may take some experimenting before you find the one that works best for you. Some girls use only pads (particularly when they first start menstruating), some use only tampons, and some girls switch around — tampons during the day and pads at night, for example. Girls who are very active, particularly girls who enjoy swimming, often find that tampons are the best option during sports.

Periods shouldn't get in the way of exercising, having fun, and enjoying life. If you have questions about pads, tampons, or coping with periods, ask a parent, health teacher, school nurse, or older sister.

Am I still a virgin if I use a tampon?

Some girls worry that if they use tampons, they will no longer be virgins. The truth is, a virgin is someone who has never had sexual intercourse. Inserting a tampon is definitely not the same as having sex!

So why do girls ask this question so often? Girls who are virgins usually have a hymen, a very thin piece of skin-like tissue that stretches partly across the opening of the vagina. A lot of people mistakenly think that a girl is still a virgin if her hymen has not been broken. Most of the time a girl's hymen breaks after having sex for the first time.

But a girl's hymen can tear in ways that have nothing to do with having sex. For example, it is possible that inserting a tampon might tear the hymen (although that usually doesn't happen). So even if a tampon does break a girl's hymen, she is still a virgin until she has had sexual intercourse.

Are Changes in My Vaginal Discharge OK?

Normal vaginal discharge has several purposes: cleaning and moistening the vagina and helping to prevent and fight infections. Although it's normal for the color, texture, and amount of vaginal fluids to vary throughout a girl's menstrual cycle, some changes in discharge may indicate a problem.

If you think you may have a problem, you should see a doctor as soon as possible. First, though, it helps to learn some of the differences between normal and abnormal vaginal discharge. This will help you to recognize changes that may occur.

Normal vaginal fluids can vary somewhat in texture and color. They can be somewhat thin, sticky, and elastic or thick and gooey. Vaginal fluids should be clear, white, or off-white in color.

It's important to keep an eye out for changes in vaginal fluids. The following changes may indicate a problem:

change in odor (especially an unpleasant odor)

change in color or texture (especially greenish, grayish, or anything looking like pus)

vaginal itching, burning, swelling, or redness

change in color that is caused by vaginal bleeding or spotting that is not a menstrual period

Vaginal infections, such as bacterial vaginosis, candidiasis (yeast infection), and trichomoniasis are common causes of abnormal vaginal discharge. Some infections are transmitted by having sex, such as gonorrhea. Other infections can occur with or without having sex, such as bacterial vaginosis or yeast infection.

Although the symptoms of these infections can be very similar, there are some differences to look for:

Yeast infections may cause your discharge to become very white and thick, resembling cottage cheese. A yeast infection usually does not cause a strong odor, but it may cause severe itching and burning.

Bacterial vaginosis (BV) may cause your discharge to be heavier than usual. The fluids may become foamy or frothy and grayish in color. BV often causes vaginal fluids to have an unpleasant, fishy odor.

Trichomoniasis, a common sexually transmitted disease (STD), may cause a musty, stale odor. Discharge may become grayish or yellow-green and may become thicker. Trichomoniasis also often causes vaginal itching and pain during urination.

It's very important to see a doctor or go to a teen clinic if you have any of the symptoms of abnormal vaginal discharge. This is really important for girls who have had sex, especially those who have had sex without using a condom. Many STDs cause changes in vaginal discharge or cause other infections that affect discharge as well.

BREAST AND PELVIC EXAMS

Your mom just made an appointment for your first gynecologic exam and you're feeling:

Totally panicked. You start praying for an avalanche, four flat tires on the car, anything to avoid that appointment.

Pretty calm. You don't really mind going to the doctor that much, and if your friends can handle it, so can you.

Confused. You don't feel sick at all, and you just had some vaccinations for school and a physical for sports. Why waste time going to a doctor when you're OK?

These are just some of the feelings that girls may have before their first gynecologic (or "gyn") exam, and it's not surprising. You might be asking yourself "Why me?

Why now?" The answer is that you're older and have gone through puberty, so you need to have a physical exam appropriate for a young woman. That's where breast and pelvic exams come in.

Why You Need These Exams

The American College of Obstetricians and Gynecologists recommends that a girl make her first visit to a gynecologist when she is between the ages of 13 and 15. Not all girls will need a pelvic exam during this initial visit, though. Many gynecologists will just do a regular health exam and talk to the girl about her development.

Yearly gyn visits are important for a number of reasons, including:

as a routine check. You'll want to be sure you're developing normally.

to prevent pregnancy or infection. If you have ever had sex, you are probably going to need a pelvic exam. Girls should have a pelvic exam before having sex to discuss methods of birth control and preventing sexually transmitted diseases (STDs).

to deal with a problem. There may be a number of concerns that lead to a pelvic exam. For example, if you have problems with your periods, missed periods, pain, signs of infection, and worries about development, it's a good idea to see a doctor.

Choosing the Right Doctor

If you're going to be involved in deciding who you'll see for your pelvic exam, you have a few choices. Many family doctors and pediatricians perform pelvic and breast exams and advise teens on birth control and STD prevention. So you may be able to see a doctor you already know and feel comfortable with for your first pelvic exam.

Also, a number of different kinds of doctors and nurses have special training in women's reproductive health:

Gynecologists are doctors who have been specially trained in women's health issues. Gynecologists are one of the doctors who can prescribe birth control and teach patients how to use it.

Adolescent medicine doctors have been trained in the health and management of teen issues. They are familiar with the concerns most young women have about their reproductive systems and can advise them on birth control and STD prevention.

Nurse practitioners have had advanced training that allows them to give gynecological exams and pay special attention to women's reproductive health.

Whether you want to see a male or female health care professional is up to you. Some women say that they prefer being examined by a female doctor or nurse because it puts them more at ease and they feel like they can talk more openly about women's health problems and sexuality issues. Other women feel comfortable being examined by a male doctor or nurse. If the doctor or nurse is male, he will usually have a female assistant in the room with him during all parts of the exam.

It's best to involve your parents in your health care. If you want to go to a doctor's office for your exam, you may need to involve an adult for insurance purposes (it may be expensive otherwise).

If for some reason you can't involve your parents, you can take advantage of health clinics like Planned Parenthood or your local teen clinic. These clinics have fully trained staff who often can care for you at a lower cost and respect your need for confidentiality. Each state has different guidelines on which medical issues teens can get confidential care for. Your doctor should be able to explain these issues to you.

The most important thing is that you feel comfortable with the person who is examining you. You want to be able to talk with him or her about important personal health and relationship issues, including birth control.

What Happens When You Go for Your Pelvic Exam

You don't need to do anything special before going for your exam. When you make the appointment, try to schedule the exam for a time when you won't have your period. For many young women, that can be hard to predict, though — lots of girls have irregular periods at first. Ask the doctor's office or clinic when you make the appointment what you should do if you get your period. Some doctors say it's OK to come for an exam if your period is just beginning or just ending and it's very light, but everyone has a different policy.

When you arrive for your appointment, you may be asked to fill out some forms while you wait. These forms ask questions about any illnesses or conditions you have, your health habits (like whether you drink or smoke), any family illnesses that you know of, and your history regarding sexual activity, pregnancy, and birth control. You might also be asked for the date of your last period (or a doctor or nurse will ask during your exam).

When you first go into the exam room, a nurse or medical assistant will do a few things that your doctor has probably done a million times before, such as recording your weight and taking your blood pressure. You'll then be left alone to change out of your clothes. It may feel weird taking off even your underwear because you may not have had to undress completely for a medical exam before. The nurse or medical assistant will leave you a paper sheet or gown — or maybe both — to cover you. If you're cold, most doctors and nurses won't mind if you keep your socks on.

After a few minutes, the doctor (or nurse practitioner, if that is who you choose to see) will knock on the door to make sure you're in your gown. If you're ready, he or she will come in and start the exam. The doctor may start by going over anything you wrote down on your forms, or you may talk about these things later.

If this is your first gynecologic exam, let the doctor know. That way, he or she will know to go slowly and explain everything that's going on. Now is also the time to ask about birth control or sexuality if you need to. Some doctors like to discuss these things before the exam, and some like to do it after. Your aim is to make sure you get your questions answered.

The Breast Exam

During the physical part of the gynecologic exam, you'll be asked to lie on your back on the table. You'll have the paper sheet or gown covering you, and the doctor will only uncover the parts of your body being examined.

The doctor will give you a breast exam by lightly pressing on different parts of your breasts. After finishing, he or she may show you how to examine your own breasts. This helps you become familiar with how your breasts feel so you know which lumps are normal and which may be the result of a change.

The Pelvic Exam

During the pelvic part of the exam, the doctor or nurse practitioner will ask you to move down so your behind is at the end of the table. You'll bend your knees and rest your feet in two stirrups, which are metal triangular loops that stick out from the end of the table. These might look a little scary, but they're just there to rest your feet in and keep you more comfortable. The doctor will ask you to relax your knees out to the sides as far as they will go. It might feel a little funny to be lying with your legs opened like this, but everyone feels that way at first.

The doctor will put on gloves and examine the outside of your vagina to make sure that there are no sores or swelling and that everything looks OK on the outside.

Next, the doctor will want to look at the inside of your vagina and will do so with the help of a speculum (pronounced: speh-kyuh-lum). A speculum is a thin piece of plastic or metal with a hinged piece on one end that allows it to open and close. The doctor or nurse will warm the speculum with water (some offices keep the speculum warmed in a drawer with a heating pad). The doctor or nurse will then slide the speculum into your vagina. Usually the doctor will tell you when he or she is about to place the speculum inside you so it doesn't come as a surprise.

Once the speculum is in the vagina, it can be opened to allow the doctor to see inside. Putting in and opening the speculum should not be painful, although some women say that it can cause a bit of pressure and discomfort. Naturally, if this is your first exam, you might feel a little tense. Because the vagina is surrounded by muscles that can contract or relax, the exam can be more comfortable if you try to stay calm and relax the muscles in that area.

If you feel like you're tensing up the muscles in your vagina, try breathing deeply or doing some breathing exercises to help you stay relaxed. Sometimes humming your favorite song or making small talk can distract you and allow you to feel more relaxed.

After the speculum is in place, the doctor will shine a light inside the vagina to look for anything unusual, like redness, swelling, discharge, or sores. He or she will then do a Pap smear, which involves touching the cervix to pick up cells from that area.

The cervix is the opening to the uterus, and it's located at the very top of the vagina. The Pap smear should not hurt, but it might be uncomfortable, especially if this is your first pelvic exam. The good news is this part of the exam is over quickly.

The cells that have been collected are sent to a laboratory where they are studied for any abnormal cells, which might indicate infection or warning signs of cervical cancer. (Like breast cancer, cervical cancer is very unusual in teen girls.)

If you have had sex, the doctor or nurse practitioner may test for STDs. He or she will swab the inside of the cervix with what looks like a cotton swab. The speculum is then slid out of the vagina. As with the Pap smear, the sample is sent out to a laboratory where it is tested for various STDs.

Talk to your doctor or a nurse about how you want to be contacted with results, and what they should do if they are unable to reach you. Again, doctors and nurses will do their best to maintain confidentiality, but they need to be able to reach you.

Because the ovaries and uterus are so far inside a girl's body that they can't be seen at all, even with the speculum, the doctor will need to feel them to be sure they're healthy. While your feet are still in the stirrups, and after the speculum is removed from the vagina, the doctor will put lubricant on two fingers (while still wearing the gloves) and slide them inside your vagina. Using the other hand, he or she will press on the outside of your lower abdomen (the area between your vagina and your stomach). With two hands, one on the outside and one on the inside, the doctor can make sure that the ovaries and uterus are the right size and free of cysts or other growths.

During this part of the exam, you may feel a little pressure or discomfort. Again, it's important to relax your muscles and take slow, deep breaths if you feel nervous.

At this point, the physical part of the exam is usually over. Your own doctor may do the exam in a different order, but it will probably include all these steps.

After the Exam

Although reading this article may make it seem long, the entire pelvic exam (the parts involving your vagina, cervix, uterus, and ovaries) really only takes about 3 to

5 minutes. Afterward, you'll be left alone to get dressed. Some women say that they bleed a tiny bit from the Pap smear after the exam, so they like to put a pantiliner in their underwear as they get dressed. If you bleed a tiny bit, it's no big deal — it's nothing like a period and it won't last.

If you haven't discussed your questions before the exam, now's the time. Don't be afraid of questions that sound stupid or silly — no question about your body is stupid, and this is the best time to get answers.

The Pap smear is almost always normal in teen girls. But if for any reason the doctor or nurse practitioner needs to see you again, the office or clinic will let you know. Unless you notice any health problems, you won't need to go for an exam for another 6 months to a year.

It's very important to go for pelvic exams on a yearly basis — even when you're feeling good — because they help detect any problems early on. If you don't want to return for another exam because you didn't like the doctor or nurse practitioner, look into finding a new doctor or clinic.

Why Bother with Bras?

Bras not only minimize jiggling and shape the appearance of a girl's breasts, they're also helpful from a health standpoint. Wearing the right bra keeps a girl's breasts supported while she's playing a sport and can help prevent injury to breast tissue. A well-fitting bra is also important for a woman's posture, particularly if she has large breasts. A bra that doesn't fit can cause back problems, muscle tension, and even headaches.

Yet 8 out of 10 women wear bras that don't fit.

All About Straps, Snaps, Bands, and Cups

Finding the right bra doesn't have to be an ordeal if you know the basics of bra sizing. There are two parts to a bra's size: the chest size (also called the band size) and the cup size.

The chest, or band, size is the part of the bra that runs across a girl's chest and around her back. The cups are the parts of the bra that hold the breasts. Bras come in many sizes, which are different combinations of the chest sizes (shown as numbers — in the United States, these are 32, 34, 36, etc.) and cup sizes (shown as letters — AA, A, B, C, etc.)

It's important to get both the chest and cup sizes right to ensure a proper fit. Some bra manufacturers are now starting to offer cup options in half sizes in addition to regular cups to help girls get a better fit.

If a girl wears a bra that's the wrong chest size, the bra's band will either feel tight and uncomfortable around her rib cage or it will be too loose and ride up her breasts. Bras that are too small in the cup will compress a girl's boobs and force them to bulge out the sides (think armpit boobs). And cups that are too big can wrinkle and pucker, which won't look good under clothes.

So how do you calculate your chest and cup measurements? It's easy, and it's something you can do in the privacy of your own room at home. All that you need is a tape measure.

Chest measurement. Bra fitting experts offer two methods of calculating the chest measurement. The most common method involves running a tape measure just under your breasts, all the way around your back and rib cage. The tape measure should rest flat on your skin and lie straight across your back — not so tight that it digs in, but not so loose that it sags down in back. Make a note of your measurement and add 5 inches. That's your chest size.

You can also estimate your chest size by running a tape measure across your chest above your breasts, under your armpits, and around your back (measure from the same back position as in the first chest measurement option). This method is easier because you don't have to do any addition or other calculation, but some people feel it's less accurate than using the first method.

If your chest measurement comes out as an odd number (such as 31 inches or 33 inches), it's usually a good rule to round up to the next number. Most bras have a few sets of adjustable hooks and eyes, so you can adjust the tightness. It's a good idea to round up, rather than round down, because when you buy a new bra that hooks on the first or middle hooks — rather than on the last — you can leave room for growth.

Cup measurement. As with the chest measurement, when you're measuring for cup size, make sure the tape is not too loose or too tight. If you already own an unpadded bra that fits well, wear it when measuring for cup size. Be careful about the type of bra you wear to take your measurements, though. Sports bras can flatten breasts and give a cup reading that's too small, and padded or lined bras have the opposite effect.

This time, when you run the tape measure around your body, you're going to take the measurement across the fullest part of your breasts. Write down this number. Now subtract your chest measurement. If the difference between the two numbers is less than 1 inch, your cup size is AA. If it's 1 inch, your cup size is A; 2 inches, you're a B; 3 inches you're a C, and so on.

So you've taken your measurements and you're in the fitting room trying a bra in what's supposed to be your size — but it doesn't seem to fit. Now what?

Before you pile on all your clothes just to go out and look for a different size, experiment by making some adjustments to the bra. Extend or shorten the band around your chest slightly by moving the hooks to a different eye on the hook and eye closure (or adjust the velcro if the bra has a velcro closing). The bottom band of a properly fitting bra should ride across the middle of your back and pass under your shoulder blades to provide the right support.

A bra's straps allow you to modify how the cups fit and support your breasts. When the straps are the right length, a bra lifts the breasts comfortably and the back of the bra will run straight across your back (if a bra is pulling upward in the back, it may be a sign that the straps are too tight). You should be able to get one finger under the straps to prevent them from digging into your shoulders. In general, girls who are petite will need to wear their bra straps shorter than girls who are tall.

Bra Booby Traps

In addition to fit, there are some other things you might want to take into account when choosing a bra.

Breast growth. A girl's breasts can grow and change rapidly during the teen years, which means that until you stop developing, you might have to change your bra size several times. If your breasts are still growing, consider buying fewer bras and measure yourself frequently to double-check your size.

Because growth can make a girl's breasts sensitive, you might find certain styles or fabrics work better for you. For example, some girls like seamless cups because they don't irritate the nipples; others choose styles that minimize jiggle to ease the occasional aches of breast development.

Menstrual changes. Some girls' breasts change size or shape at different times in their menstrual cycles. Many girls find they like to wear different styles of bras at different times in their cycle.

Different-sized breasts. Most girls' breasts grow at different rates — and many girls find themselves with one boob that's bigger than its partner. This is so common that bra manufacturers design their products so they can be adjusted to accommodate asymmetrical breasts. Start by moving the strap adjusters on a bra to different lengths to see if this helps.

Some girls also use the trick of buying a bra that has removable padding and then taking the extra padding out of the cup for the larger breast. Push-up bras can work well for this because they often come with an easily removable padded section (called a "cookie") that sits under the breast.

Hooks, wires, and other hazards. Take a look at the bra you're about to buy and imagine how it might survive a full day of wear. If the front closure pops open too easily, could this bra let you down in front of your entire drama class? The bra's straps may feel fine in the fitting room, but if the adjusters are sitting right on your shoulder or collarbone, how will that feel under your backpack?

Test to see if the bra band is too loose by lifting your arms in the air and putting them back down by your sides a couple of times. If the bra rides up across your breasts, the band is too loose. If you're looking for a sports bra, jump up and down in the fitting room a couple of times to evaluate the bra's bounce control.

You may also want to try on a T-shirt or sweater over a bra you're thinking of buying to get the finished effect. That pink rose on the front may look cute on the bra itself, but does it make you look as if you've sprouted a third breast once your T-shirt's on?

No matter what the size or shape of a girl's breasts, the most important thing to remember in choosing a bra is comfort. Try on a variety of bras to find the one that's right for you. Some girls prefer the comfort of cotton, others like the support of synthetics or underwires. There are minimizer bras for girls who'd like their breasts to look smaller, or padded bras for girls who'd like a little extra shape. No one bra is better than another — it all depends on which style works best for you.

SEXUAL ATTRACTION AND ORIENTATION

It's a natural part of life to have sexual feelings. As people pass from childhood, through adolescence, to adulthood, their sexual feelings develop and change.

Adolescence is a Time of Change

During the teen years, sexual feelings are awakened in new ways because of the hormonal and physical changes of puberty. These changes involve both the body and the mind, and teens may wonder about new — and often intense — sexual feelings.

It takes time for many people to understand who they are and who they're becoming. Part of that understanding includes a person's sexual feelings and attractions.

The term sexual orientation refers to the gender (that is, male or female) to which a person is attracted. There are several types of sexual orientation that are commonly described:

Heterosexual. People who are heterosexual are romantically and physically attracted to members of the opposite sex: Heterosexual males are attracted to females, and heterosexual females are attracted to males. Heterosexuals are sometimes called "straight."

Homosexual. People who are homosexual are romantically and physically attracted to people of the same sex: Females who are attracted to other females are lesbian; males who are attracted to other males are often known as gay. (The term gay is sometimes also used to describe homosexual individuals of either gender.)

Bisexual. People who are bisexual are romantically and physically attracted to members of both sexes.

Teens — both guys and girls — often find themselves having sexual thoughts and attractions. For some, these feelings and thoughts can be intense — and even confusing or disturbing. That may be especially true for people who are having romantic or sexual thoughts about someone who is the same sex they are. "What does that mean," they might think. "Am I gay?"

Thinking sexually about both the same sex and the opposite sex is quite common as people sort through their emerging sexual feelings. This type of imagining about people of the same or opposite sex doesn't necessarily mean that a person fits into a particular type of sexual orientation.

Some teens may also experiment with sexual experiences, including those with members of the same sex, during the years they are exploring their own sexuality. These experiences, by themselves, do not necessarily mean that a person is gay or straight.

Do People Choose Their Sexual Orientation?

Most medical professionals, including organizations such as the American Academy of Pediatrics and the American Psychological Association, believe that sexual orientation involves a complex mixture of biology, psychology, and environmental factors. A person's genes and inborn hormonal factors may play a role as well. These medical professionals believe that — in most cases — sexual orientation, whatever its causes, is not simply chosen.

Not everyone agrees. Some believe that individuals can choose who they are attracted to — and that people who are gay have chosen to be attracted to people of the same gender. No matter what someone's sexual orientation is, in some cases it may be affected by the life experiences that person has had.

There are lots of opinions and stereotypes about sexual orientation, though, and some of these can be hurtful to people of all orientations. For example, having a more "feminine" appearance or interest does not mean that a guy is gay. And having a more "masculine" appearance doesn't mean a girl is lesbian. As with most things, making assumptions just based on looks can lead to the wrong conclusion.

What's It Like for Gay Teens?

For many people who are gay or lesbian, it can feel like everyone is expected to be straight. Because of this, some gay and lesbian teens may feel different from their friends when the heterosexual people around them start talking about romantic feelings, dating, and sex. They may feel like they have to pretend to feel things that they don't in order to fit. They might feel they need to deny who they are or that they have to hide an important part of themselves.

These feelings, plus fears of prejudice, can lead people who aren't straight to keep their sexual orientation secret, even from friends and family who might be supportive.

Some gay or lesbian teens tell a few accepting, supportive friends and family members about their sexual orientation. This is often called coming out.

Many lesbian, gay, and bisexual teens who come out to their friends and families are fully accepted by them and their communities. They feel comfortable about being attracted to someone of the same gender and don't feel anxious about it.

But not everyone has the same feelings or good support systems. People who feel they need to hide who they are or who fear rejection, discrimination, or violence can be at greater risk for emotional problems like anxiety and depression.

Some gay teens without support systems can be at higher risk than heterosexual teens for dropping out of school, living on the streets, using alcohol and drugs, and even in some cases for attempting to harm themselves.

These difficulties are thought to happen more frequently not directly because they are gay, but because gay and lesbian people are more likely to be misunderstood, socially isolated, or mistreated because of their sexual orientation.

This doesn't happen to all gay teens, of course. Many gay and lesbian teens and their families have no more difficulties during the teen years than anyone else.

The Importance of Talking

No matter what someone's sexual orientation is, learning about sexuality and relationships can be difficult. It can help to talk to someone about the confusing feelings that go with growing up, perhaps a parent or other family member, a close friend or sibling, or a school counselor. It's not always easy to find somebody to talk to, but many people find that confiding in someone they trust and feel close to, even if they're not completely sure how that person will react, turns out to be a positive experience.

In many communities, resources such as youth groups composed of teens who are facing similar issues can provide opportunities for people to talk to others who understand. Psychologists, psychiatrists, family doctors, and trained counselors can help teens cope — confidentially and privately — with the difficult feelings that go with their developing sexuality. These experts can also help teens to find ways to deal with any peer pressure, harassment, and bullying they may face.

Whether gay, straight, bisexual, or just not sure, almost all teens have questions about physically maturing and about sexual health (for example, avoiding STDs). It's important to find a doctor or health professional to discuss these issues with — someone who can provide reliable health advice.

Although sexual feelings and behavior are important parts of human development, there are still many unanswered questions about human sexuality. Researchers are constantly learning new information, and undoubtedly people will know more about sexual orientation in the coming years.

ABOUT SEXUALLY TRANSMITTED DISEASES (STDs)

Sexually transmitted diseases — also known as STDs and once called venereal diseases or VD — are infectious diseases that spread from person to person through intimate contact. STDs affect guys and girls of all ages and backgrounds who are having sex — it doesn't matter if they're rich or poor.

STDs are becoming more and more common: By the age of 21, almost 1 in 5 Americans requires treatment for an STD. Because teens are more at risk for getting some STDs, it's important to learn what you can do to protect yourself. STDs are more than just an embarrassment. They're a serious health problem. If untreated, some STDs can cause permanent damage, such as infertility (the inability to have a baby) and even death (HIV/AIDS is one of the STDs that are on the rise in teens).

How STDs Spread

One reason STDs spread is because people think they need to have sexual intercourse to become infected. That's wrong. A person can get some STDs, like herpes or genital warts, through skin-to-skin contact with an infected area or sore. Another myth about STDs is that you can't get them if you have oral or anal sex. That's also wrong because the viruses or bacteria that cause STDs can enter the body through tiny cuts or tears in the mouth and anus, as well as the genitals.

STDs also spread easily because you can't tell whether someone has an infection. In fact, some people with STDs don't even know that they have them. These people are in danger of passing an infection on to their sex partners without even realizing it.

Some of the things that increase a person's chances of getting an STD are:

Sexual activity at a young age. The younger a person starts having sex, the greater his or her chances of becoming infected with an STD.

Lots of sex partners. People who have sexual contact — not just intercourse, but any form of intimate activity — with many different partners are more at risk than those who stay with the same partner.

Unprotected sex. Latex condoms are the only form of birth control that lessen your risk of contracting an STD. Spermicides, diaphragms, and other birth control methods may help prevent pregnancy, but they don't protect a person against STDs.

Preventing and Treating STDs

As with many other diseases, prevention is key. It's much easier to prevent STDs than to treat them. The only way to completely prevent STDs is to abstain from all types of sexual contact. People who are considering becoming sexually active should get regular gynecological or male genital examinations. There are two reasons for this. First, these exams give doctors a chance to teach people about STDs and protecting themselves. And second, regular exams give doctors more opportunities to check for STDs while they're still in their earliest, most treatable, stage.

Don't let embarrassment at the thought of having an STD keep you from seeking medical attention. Waiting to see a doctor may allow a disease to progress and cause more damage. If you think you may have an STD, or if you have had a partner who may have an STD, you should see a doctor right away.

If you don't have a doctor or prefer not to see your family doctor, you may be able to find a local clinic in your area where you can get an exam confidentially. Some national and local organizations operate STD hotlines staffed by trained specialists who can answer your questions and provide referrals. Calls to these hotlines are confidential. One hotline you can call for information is the CDC (Centers for Disease Control and Prevention) National STD Hotline at 1-800-227-8922.

Not all infections in the genitals are caused by STDs. Sometimes people can get symptoms that seem very like those of STDs, even though they've never had sex. For girls, the vaginal infection bacterial vaginosis can easily be confused with both STDs and yeast infections. Guys may worry about bumps on the penis that turn out to be pimples or hair follicles. That's why it's important to see a doctor if you ever have questions about your sexual health.

SOME USEFUL YOGASANAS FOR SEXUAL HEALTH

1. Padmasana (the Lotus Pose) -

Calms the brain; and is also one of those poses that I mentioned that needs an experienced Yoga practitioner to help you with. Although it looks simple enough it's really quite difficult to manage this one properly without some intensive practice. (I'm still working on it!)

Method

Sit on the folded blanket with your legs outstretched. Bend each leg and place each foot on the opposite thigh, soles turned upwards. Pull the foot as high as you can. Keep the palms of the right and left hand on the right and left knees, touching the thumb with tips of index fingers and gaze at the tip of the nose. Keep the head,

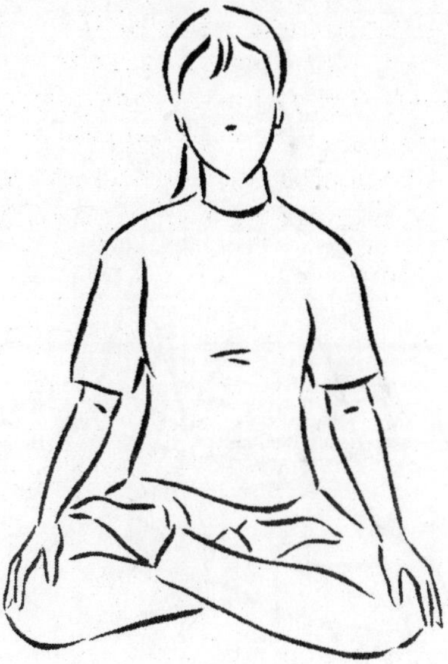

neck and spinal column straight and erect and breathe slowly.

2. Siddhasana (Perfect Pose, Accomplished Pose)

"Siddha" in Sanskrit means adept. Yogis and rishis have spoken high of this Asana. Great saints and sages like Nityamatta, Niranjana, Kapali, Sabar used to meditate in this Asana for hours together. The knees of the beginners may find it difficult to stay flat on the ground but by practice they can overcome this difficulty.

One of the most popular meditation postures is Siddhasana. The Sanskrit name means "Perfect Pose," because one attains perfection in Yoga by meditating in this position. Siddhasana is useful to learn, since it is used as the practice seat for some of the pranayamas and the mudras. The positions of the legs and the hands also contain the body energies by closing the circuits and allowing awakened vital forces to remain in the system during meditation practice.

Technique

1. Sit down with both legs outstretched.

2. Bend the left knee and place the sole of the left foot against the right thigh so that the heel touches the perineum.

3. Bend the right knee and put the right heel against the public bone.

4. Keep hands with palms open if done between sunrise and sunset; otherwise reverse the palms.

5. The spine should always be held erect.

3. Uthata Padangusthasana

Technique

Start from the sitting on floor position. Bending the knees draw back the feet and catch the right big toe with the right hand the left big toe with the left hand. Straighten the legs and arms so that you balance on the buttocks, the trunk and the legs forming a V shape. Hold the pose for at least fifteen seconds, breathing normally.

The balancing big toe posture stretches and firms the legs and improves abdominal fitness.

4. Baddha Padamasana

Fixing the right foot on the left thigh and the left (foot) on the right thigh, the big toes are to be held by both hands, arms crossing behind the back, the chin to be fixed on the chest, and the tip of the nose to be gazed at. This is known as Padmasana (Baddha) which destroys (all) the diseases of Yogis and helps in maintaining the sexual health.

Note:- Generally this Asana is called Baddha-Padmassi.

Technique :-

1. Sit erect, stretch both the legs together, hands by the side, palms resting on the ground, fingers together pointing forward.

2. Slowly place one leg (right) on the left thigh by holding toes of the leg by left hand and ankle by the right.

3. Similarly hold the toes of the other leg by right hand and ankle by left.

4. Now place it well on the right thigh.

5. Cross both the hands at back like a scissor, hold the big toe of the right leg with right hand and that of left leg with left hand.

6. Place the chin on the chest making Jugular knotch. Gaze should be nasal, This is baddha-padmasana.

7. While retrurning back to the original position, straighten your head, release the big toes, keep the hands

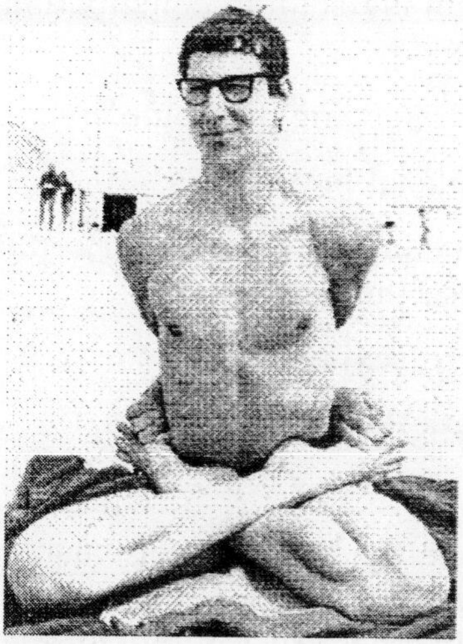

by the side.

8. Holding the left leg by ankle remove it from the right thigh and stretch it in front.

9. Similarly remove the right leg from the left thigh, stretch it and come back to the original position.

Remember

1. It is a further development of simple Padmasana.

2. Before practising Baddha-Padmasana practise simple Padmasana well.

3. In the beginning one knee might not remain placed on the ground but by practise it can be achieved.

4. Keep waist and chest erect.

5. Gaze at the tip of nose.

Benefits and Limitations :-

1. This Asana is useful in constipation and improves digestive power.

2. It helps in keeping the spine erect.

3. It is beneficial in Arthritis.

4. Those, feeling trouble in performing this Asana should not force themselves.

5. It improves sexual health.

5. Utthita Hasta Padangusthasana

Technique

1. Experience the challenge of balancing on one foot with this pose which calls for strength and flexibility, building steadfastness in the practitioner.

2. Stand in Tadasana. Shift weight onto the left foot. Extend the foot and press it firmly onto the floor. Press down with all corners of the foot and your toes.

3. Square the hips facing forward and continue to be this way throughout the pose even when you raise your leg.

4. Raise your right leg towards your chest by bending it at the knee. Hold your right big toe with two fingers curled around it. Rest your left hand on your left hip. On an exhalation extend the right leg so that it becomes straight while pulling the foot inwards so the extended leg moves to come in line with your torso.

5. Gaze at a single spot on the floor about a body's length in front of you to help with balance. Flex your foot so the toes curl back toward you. Take a couple of breaths and settle into the posture.

6. Extend your torso, keeping as much space between

sternum and pubic bone as possible. Continue to keep this "Tadasana" alignment even after one leg is in the air. That means that you should be careful to avoid collapsing on your lifted leg side. There is a tendency for the raised leg's hip to move up towards the lower ribs. Correct this collapse by lowering the raised leg's side hip down as you move its sit-bone towards the upper inner thigh of the standing leg.

7. Keep the hips at the same level, parallel with the floor.

8. If you want, you can deepen the pose by taking your foot in two hands and bringing the leg up and toward you. Really flexible yogis can bring the

straight up with the knee to the face and the hips and sit-bones parallel.

9. As you exhale, release the hands, and lower the leg to the floor to stand in Tadasana pose again. Repeat the pose on the other side.

Additional variation: The pose can be done with the leg extended to the side of the body. This variation has several names. It is called Parsva Utthita Hasta Padangusthasana, Utthita Parsvasahita and even Utthita Hasta Padangushthasana II by other practitioners.

The pose involves bringing your foot to the the side with an extended leg while balancing on the other foot. Open your right hip by bringing your leg out to the right. Extend the left arm out to the side so it is parallel to the ground. If you are flexible, draw the right foot towards your head by using your arm muscles as your hips stay level. In this variation it is also important to keep the side hips and sitbones aligned. As in the main pose this alignment is facilitated by bringing the sit-bone of the raised leg down towards the inner upper thigh of the straight leg. The head may face to the side in the opposite direction or straight forward.

Beginners Tips:

1. Try using a yoga strap looped around the foot and held with one hand. The strap will extend the reach of your arm which will make this pose accessible to everyone.

2. If balance is difficult, try the following:

3. Make sure your practice space is firm, level surface.

4. Do the pose as one of the first ones in your practice

session when you are feeling more energized.

5. Focus your eyes on one point.

6. Use a wall for support for your left hand. Reach and touch it or press your back against it during the pose. A window ledge for your left hand is also useful.

7. Use a prop of an elevated surface to support the lifted foot during the pose. Possible props include a dancer's bar, a "pune pony", a stair banister or a window ledge. Position yourself so that the standing leg is perpendicular to the floor and the hips aligned facing the prop as the heel of the extended raised leg is supported by the prop.

8. As you acquire better balance you won't need these props.

Benefits:

1. This is one of a short list of standing poses which are recommended by the eminent yogis and that are said to be good to do during menstruation.

2. This posture is suggested by some for pregnancy especially for the second and third trimesters. It is suggested that one does a supported version against the wall or on a ledge. Some yogis recommend this pose in pregnancy only if it was being practiced unsupported before pregnancy. When the belly gets big and in the way, do the variation with the leg extended to the side.

3. The pose strengthens and stretches the inner and back legs and the spine. It also improves balance and coordination.

Contraindications and Caution:

1. Do not do the pose if you have a recent or chronic injury to the legs, arms or shoulders.

2. Be cautious of your hamstrings to not overstretch them in this pose.

3. Consult with your yoga teacher and health care provider if you are pregnant and want to do the pose. Work with a teacher who is experienced with pregnant students.

4. Always listen to your body and notice messages that it gives you as you do yoga.

6. Hero Pose (Virasana)

The Hero Yoga Pose is one of the basic sitting postures, also excellent for Meditation. The internal rotation of the upper legs and knees is opposite to the movement involved in Lotus Yoga Pose; as such, it both loosens the hips, knees and ankles in preparation for the Lotus and acts as a mild counterpose. The Hero is also the starting

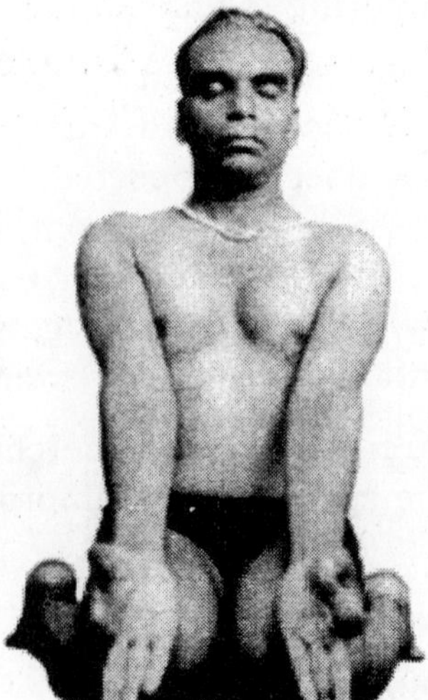

Yoga Position for several forward bends, backward bends, and twists.

Start on your hands and knees as in Cat Pose. Have your knees hip-width apart so the thighs are parallel with one another, and separate your feet until they are slightly wider than your hips. Check that your feet are pointing directly backward, not turning in or out.

Sit between your feet by first supporting yourself with your hands and then slowly lowering your hips to the floor (photo 1). If you are unable to sit comfortably, or if you feel any pain in your knees, elevate your hips by placing a folded Yoga Blanket or Zafu (Zen pillow) beneath you. Use this support until you experience a feeling of ease (this may take several months). Eventually you will be able to sit between your feet with no discomfort with your buttocks firmly on the ground.

Sit tall. Counteract the tendency to slump by adjusting the buttock muscles sideways and back with your hands, and tilting the pelvis slightly forward so you are positioned on the frontal edge of each sitting bone. Then draw the abdomen backward toward the spine and delicately adjust your hips toward cat tilt to establish neutral alignment of your center, your pelvis making a ninety-degree angle with the thighs. You are now on the tips of the sitting bones.

Rest your hands in your lap, on your thighs, or on your ankles, then close your eyes. Elevate and free your chest, relax the shoulders back and down away from your ears, then lift or lower your chin until your head feels perfectly balanced, weightless on top of the spine. Sit quietly for at least a minute.

7. Dhanur Asana

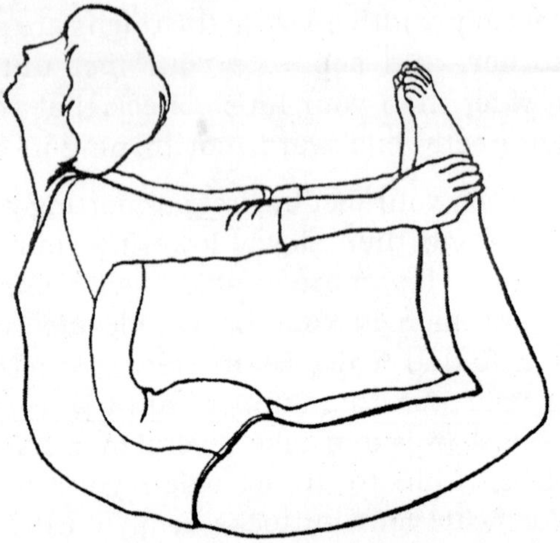

Technique

Lie flat on the stomach and chest, fix the legs bringing the feet back towards the head. Raise the legs head and upper part of the body. While arching the back, take hold of your ankle with your right hand and left ankle with left hand. Breathe slowly and normally. Remain in this pose for a couple of seconds. Return to the original position and relax.

8. Uthita Padmasana

Technique

On a folded blanket, adopt Padamasana pose. Lie on the back and place the palms of the hands under buttocks and raise the trunk so that it is supported by the elbows. Then raise the head, legs and trunk further

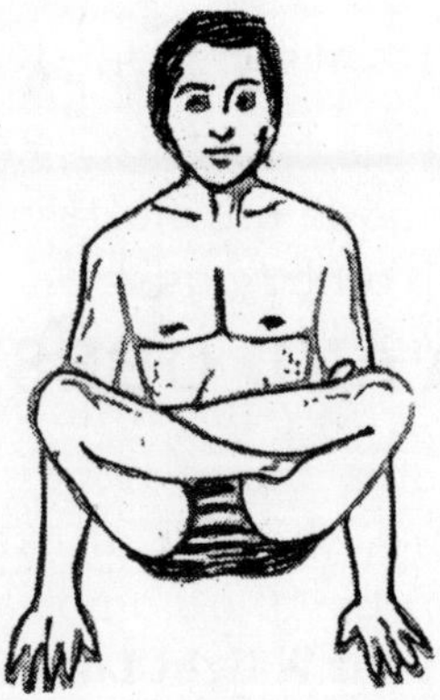

off the floor so that the whole body rests on the buttocks and forearms. Remain in this pose for as much time as you feel convenient. Breathe in and out slowly. Come to the original position and relax.

8

YOGA AND OBESITY

How To Use Yoga In Your Weight Loss For Great Results

Yoga can be put to good use for taking off excess pounds through the power of creating a state of mental and physical well being. Promoting a healthy lifestyle and when combined with a calorie reduction can help to speed up your weight loss is the basic tenets of Yoga. It also increases your metabolism by increasing the caloric burning process. Using more calories than you take in is all the basis of weight loss. It will allow you to increase your ability to concentrate and focus.

What regulates your metabolism is your thyroid. Thyroid is responsible for the chemical processes that transform food into energy. A series of twisting poses are used in Yoga to help you to stimulate the work flow of the internal organs. This will cause your metabolism to increase. This can also burn more calories which will eventually cause you to have a lower body weight. Another side effect is that it will help to improve your circulation and increase your energy level.

Helping to stimulate the metabolism is combining the various back bends with the forward bends. The poses that affect the neck region can be helpful in stimulating the thyroid if the weight problem is caused by a hormonal imbalance. Camel, rabbit, plow, bridge and head stand are the poses that will help the most. Going quickly between the various poses can help to accelerate the weight loss. You should beware though that those seriously overweight may find some of these poses extremely difficult and should start slowly with the easier poses and add others as they become more confident in the easier ones.

To increase muscle strengthening, you can use standing poses such as the warrior. These will help to create higher endurance. These can also increase your caloric usage.

What is best with all Yoga practices is a gradual approach. The long term effects on your weight loss regime will become evident and even more so the inner peace and general well feeling that Yoga will promote within you.

WEIGHT LOSS FACTS

Low Fat Foods Don'T WORK

You cannot lose weight using Low Fat Diets. Low fat foods have been popular for more than 15 years, but yet our society is getting more overweight as each year passes. This fact alone should tell you that eating a purely low fat menu is not the answer to losing weight.

Low Calorie Diets Don't Work.

You won't lose weight using a Low Calorie Dieting Plan either. In fact, eating low calories is the worst thing that you can do to your body, since that will only slow down your body's fat burning engine and ruin all chances of losing weight (low calorie diets may allow a few pounds of weight loss for the first few days, but then after that all weight loss comes to a halt --- known as a dieting plateau). You can never get slim by starving yourself.

Low Carb Plans Don't Work

You'll probably find it extremely difficult to get slim using a Low Carb Dieting Plan. Low carb diets have recently become popular over the last couple years, but the problem with low carb menus is that they are too strict and TOO HARD TO FOLLOW for average people. Low carb menus tend to rob your body of too much energy (carbohydrates) and make it nearly impossible to remain on the program for very long. This is why so many dieters find it difficult to follow a strict low carbohydrate menu.

Two Basic Laws of Weight Loss

Effective, lifelong weight loss is simple...not easy, just simple.

Everyone is seeking the ultimate weight loss secret. However, the "weight loss secret" has been known for years. Simply stated, if you take in more calories than you use, you gain weight. If you use more calories than you take in, you lose weight.

In their attempts to wiggle around those two simple facts, people have discovered that some foods, and some diet products, are effective in "helping" you cut down on the calories; and they have found lifestyles, and diet products, that "help" you burn more calories, but two simple laws have remained for healthy, effective, lifelong weight loss and weight management.

1. Get regular, moderate exercise

2. Regularly eat tasteful, nutritionally satisfying foods in reasonable quantities.

Do those two things, and your body will automatically adjust itself to a healthier, leaner, more fit state of existence.

Are there other things you can do to help the process along?

Of course there are. Drink more water, get more sleep, serve meals on smaller plates, eat more slowly...and so on. All these things and many other tips help the weight loss process, but, in the final analysis, it all comes down to those two rules up there.

Now, it is advisable that if you do those two things, your body will automatically adjust itself to a healthier, leaner level. Unfortunately, since we are all different...in upbringing, in ethnicity, in learned habits, in likes and dislikes, in daily lifestyle, in metabolism, and in so many other ways, a perfect weight loss program for one person may seem to be not very effective for another. Also, since we may attack our weight loss problem with a different intensity or attitude or expectation, what we perceive as "being effective" may not satisfy our neighbor...or may seem miraculous to him or her.

In the absence of individual coaching from a personal fitness trainer, and a trained dietician to prepare our meals, some of our actions in the areas of nutrition and exercise are going to be a little hit and miss. Add into that mix the process by which most of us go about our daily lives...staying up too late, rushing around to get all our obligations (real and imaginary) properly discharged, eating unhealthy food in a state of stress and on the go...and from a point of ignorance...and there is no surprise at that statement which is made about weight loss being simple, but not necessarily easy.

All that being said, however, most of us can easily make regular attempts to meet the requirements of the two laws already outlined above. We can easily find ways to insert more activity, both planned and opportunistic, into our lives, and we can exercise more control over the food we put in our mouths. A great knowledge of physiology and the science of exercise is not necessary, nor is it a requirement that we be extremely knowledgeable in the science of nutrition either.

Most of us are perfectly aware that a five, ten, or fifteen minute walk is probably better for us than sitting in front of a TV watching a completely mindless show. Okay, I confess, I watch "WWF" regularly. Hmmm! Why does my wife keep calling me Manoj? Anyway, we all understand that a few minutes of yard work is better for us than raiding the fridge for another beer or that other piece of pie.

We also know that if we have to slip into the kitchen for something to munch, a handful of nuts or an apple is probably going to be better for us than that piece of pie. Doing the healthy things from day to day is what will help us live up to the two laws already mentioned.

Would we be able to more effectively exercise with a little more knowledge and training on the subject? Of course.

Would we be able to more effectively take control of our dietary and nutritional lifestyle with a bit more information? Of course we would.

If we have more knowledge about exercise and

nutrition, will we be better able to make that weight loss plan of ours more effective? Without a doubt.

There is nothing stopping anyone from learning and applying knowledge about exercise and nutrition. No one needs to learn all the knowledge of the fitness trainer or the dietician. A simple, basic understanding of the two fields will suffice in most cases.

I would like to make one last point. In both of the two laws it is mentioned above, the words "regular" and "regularly" appear. In terms of weight loss, fitness, and health, what you do today is not worth a hill of beans unless it is tied to events either before or after it. To go out and walk a mile today is a good thing, of course, but in terms of weight loss, health, and fitness, it will be a habit of walking a mile a day several days a week, over many weeks which will eventually result in the change you and I are seeking.

A good side to this is the empowering knowledge that a slip in our program today is not going to matter that much as long as we get back into the swing of things as soon as possible. If you are exercising regularly and eating properly, a piece of pie at a friend's house, a dish of ice cream at a birthday party, just one more piece of that delicious pot roast will not destroy all that you are attempting to accomplish...just don't let it happen too often.

Hoodia Helps Weight Loss by Suppressing Appetite

The Hoodia cactus plant extract has recently gained quite a lot of publicity in the media. The BBC and CBS 60 Minutes both sent reporters to investigate Hoodia, and interest in it is growing as a result.

Although there are several kinds of Hoodia plants, the one known for its remarkable ability to suppress the appetite is Hoodia Gordonii. For hundreds of years, this plant has been used by the San Bushmen of Africa's Kalahari Desert. In this most inhospitable region, where food and water can be extremely scarce, the San people learned that they can go for long periods of time without craving food or water if they first eat a particular plant.

In the 1990s, the Council for Scientific and Industrial Research (CSIR) was doing research on the plants the San Bushmen eat, and they discovered that Hoodia Gordonii not only was non-toxic, but it reduced the desire for food of the animals that tested it.

After more study, researchers discovered that a molecule in Hoodia Gordonii works on the part of the brain that responds to high levels of glucose in the blood that come from having eaten a satisfying meal. Nerve centers in the hypothalamus located in the mid-brain, sense the glucose and tell the body it has had enough food. What Hoodia is believed to contain is a molecule that is thousands of times more active than glucose, so when Hoodia is ingested, the brain is tricked into believing the stomach is full, and the appetite is lowered.

How well does Hoodia work in stopping people from craving to eat? This was demonstrated dramatically in an experiment conducted in the United Kingdom. A group of people diagnosed as morbidly obese were chosen for the test. Half the group was given Hoodia and the other half a placebo (sugar pill). All were allowed to eat as much food as they wanted. In about two weeks, the group using Hoodia were eating an average of 1,000 fewer calories per day than the control group.

People who desire to lose weight are often concerned about whether there are any harmful side effects caused by diet products they may be considering to use. Weight loss products such as Hoodia Gordonii Plus have been found to have no harmful side effects. Of course, people using Hoodia who consume less food should be concerned about getting enough nutrition in their systems. That is why Hoodia Gordonii Plus was formulated to include magnesium, mangosteen oil extract and green tea extract. Magnesium is an essential nutrient the body requires to function in a healthy manner. Mangosteen oil extract, Garcinia Cambogia, contains significant amounts of Vitamin C and may help prevent excess calories from being converted to body fat. Green tea has been associated with not only weight control but also help in treating arthritis, high cholesterol levels and heart disease. It contains the powerful anti-oxidant EGCG.

Hoodia Gordonii Plus users should be cautioned, however, that it should not be used during pregnancy, by children, lactating mothers or anyone who is underweight.

Losing Weight Through a Healthy Eating Program

Like many people today there are many who have tried every food fad, weight loss program and diet that is out there. Yet although they lose the weight initially after some time they find that they have regained it. Unfortunately many people are beginning to realize that using healthy eating weight loss programs do not work on their own and you need to actually do some form of exercise as well.

However if you do decide to look for a healthy eating

weight loss program the best thing you can do before making a final decision on which one to use is to talk to your doctor first. Even if you do find it difficult to discuss your weight problem with your doctor it is important to remember that they are there to help you and to ensure that you live the happiest, longest and healthiest life possible.

Also what is important to remember is that these types of programs are not a quick fix solution to your weight problem and will need to stick with it in order that you can lose the weight and then keep it off. However the most successful types of healthy eating weight loss programs should combine the following: -

1. Healthy Eating - They should ensure that you are get sufficient amounts of protein, carbohydrates, vitamins, minerals and other essential products in order that your body remains in top condition even whilst you are trying to lose the weight.

2. Nutrition should be balanced - These programs should ensure that the nutritional value of any healthy eating weight loss program will not cause any problems to your body and yet still allows you to lose the excess weight.

3. Regular Exercise - This is an extremely vital part of any healthy eating weight loss program as without exercise you will find that you lose some weight but after a while you may find that you regain it. In many cases combining a healthy eating weight loss program with exercise will help you not only to lose the weight but also help to keep it off, plus you will find that you are much better to cope with the stresses and strains of everyday life.

A great way of ensuring that you are sticking to any healthy eating weight loss programs that you decide to use is by changing your favorite dishes to low calorie versions. This is pretty simple to do and if you were to carry out a search of the Internet there are plenty of sites that are offering low calorie version recipes of some if not all of your favorite dishes.

What is the Difference Between Male and Female Fat Metabolism?

So what is fat metabolism? Fat metabolism is a process that will break down the facts that we ingest into the body into glycerol and fatty acids. Fat metabolism with glyceral and fatty acids are broken down into very simple substances so that the body can be utilized by the cells of the body. So what does all of this really means?The fat in your body can be broken down converted into the energy. So how does this really affect you? If you are a person who is trying to lose some weight, fat metabolism will have a lot to do if it! What happens is the fact that gets broken down and uses energy this is what causes you to eventually lose weightDid you ever wonder why it is bad man and women will lose weight at different rates? Well you have to understand that this also has to do with fat strength metabolism. There are a few differences in the fat metabolism between men and women.

The metabolic variationsThere are a few differences when it comes to fat storage and fat metabolism in men and women. The first thing that you need to know is that a woman's body fat percentage is tend to be higher than those of men.What you usually see is that while women will store more of their fat in the gluteal-femoral region (the hips and thighs), while the men would tend a store more of their fat in the abdominal region. These differences between men and women and fat metabolism are supported by scientific studies.Scientists say that the abdominal zone and the fat located there is easier to metabolize them the fat that is located in the hips and thighs or the gluteal-femoral region. Another factor that makes the difference between men and women and losing weight and storing fat is there are a greater number of Alpha receptors, which promote the storage of fat, are generally some in the hips and thighs of women. These two factors alone show that men usually have a faster metabolism than women and are more successful at shedding those unwanted pounds.

When is low fat metabolism dangerous? One of the side effects of a person being overweight or obese is that they you can develop high blood pressure which is extremely harmful to your health. We also know and talked about it earlier, that low fat metabolism is a factor to being overweight. Could there be a connection? Of course there is! So now we know that low fat metabolism is bad for your health and according to studies, maybe affected too high blood pressure. More importantly, is that high blood pressure could cause low fat metabolism in your heart.There are some people that are over weight and have been blaming this excess weight on their metabolism. Well come to find out, they are not that far from the truth. But you must know that this is no excuse to try to lose some weight. When you start to look at the health concerns that are associated with being overweight, you should focus your effort on a healthy diet and plenty of exercise. What you don't want do is allow the fat metabolism from stopping you from living your life to the fullest!

FIVE WAYS TO LOSE WEIGHT FASTER

If one has to think back to about twenty years ago the biggest thing that he would remember is that people used to be skinny! The waistlines of society are expanding at a rapid pace and he, for one, don't like it.

Then again, he might be of a different breed. He've thought about this a lot, you see, and this is what he came up with: he must be an alien. He go for walks, he ride his bike, and he even work out- all things that a "normal" person in our society today simply just does not do.

He often get asked how he is able to stay as thin he is. He never had an answer simply because he thought it all made sense to him. But, the more he got to thinking about it, the more he decided to offer his top five ways of losing weight (and keeping it off once it's gone). These are the exact same methods usually follow to keep one's shape.

1. Phentramin. The one word that's made a world of difference for so many people. Phentramin is like a diet pill (though it isn't has harsh on your system). Phentramin effectively controls your appetite, while at the same time increasing your metabolism and helping suppress the hormones that exasperate stress.

Phentramin works fast and, compared to many "diet" pills, is pretty inexpensive. It's been called the "lazy mans way out" simply because it works and doesn't require frequent trips to the gym to make it happen.

2. Early morning cardio. Yes, you read that right. The next time you feel a bit chubby you might want to get up nice and early and go for a morning jog (or walk). Do this before you eat as you will burn the calories that your body consumed the day before. A calorie surplus is, as you probably know, why you gained the weight in the first place.

3. Weight machines. It is not considered to be the most pleasant activity, but lifting weights will do wonders for your body. It's like supercharging your workout- any cardio that you've been doing will become more effective and your body will literally begin to shed pounds! Don't believe anybody else? I don't blame you- it's not like getting up and actually trying it actually did anyone any good anyway.

4. Salads. Meat and potatoes are one's favourite meal. Unfortunately, too much clogs your system and expands your waistline. People enjoy a good steak and mashed potato meal twice a week. The other five days they eat smart and enjoy a lot of salads.

Why salad, you ask? Easy- a good salad is healthy, filling, and helps with the digestion of your meal. Eating salad never killed anyone, but too much red meat sure has. Think about it.

And lastly...

5. Discipline. The one thing that nearly everybody is missing. You need to be disciplined and motivated to stay on your diet and to keep your workout routine going. As soon as you stop your results stop with it, and there is nothing more frustrating than losing 10 pounds only to gain it all back again.

Some of those might sound difficult, I know, but remember that there's always an easy way out. If working out and eating right just aren't for you, taking Phentramin might just do the trick.

How to Lose 10 Pounds Every Month

There's no "secret" to losing weight. The problem is that every person that gives advice does so from a very biased perspective: a nutritionist will always recommend that you completely rearrange your diet (and plug their service at the same time), a personal trainer will always recommend going to the gym (and they will probably offer their services), and a wellness advisor will always recommend a complete routine change.

Losing weight, however, is unique to each person. Not everyone, unfortunately, will respond to each different type of method- some people have slow metabolisms, others simply can't work out. This leads to a lot of frustrations as people trying to lose weight lose their motivation. There's no clear-cut guide to losing weight, but there is a standard idea on making it happen.

Weight gain (and loss) is all about calories. You gain weight when you consume more than you burn, and you lose weight when you burn more than you consume. I can't tell you exactly how to lose a few pounds, but I can tell you how to get started (and lose ten pounds your first month).

1. Regulate your metabolism. For many people this can be as simple as going for walks every night or cutting the junk out of their diet. Others, however, might benefit significantly from taking a supplement to help regulate their metabolism. There are numerous products on the market that can do this. Of all of the options, I recommend Phentramin because of its quality and price. Phentramin contains ingredients that have been proven to help regulate your metabolism and promote weight loss.

2. Eat healthy foods. I know that everyone and their mother is always telling you to eat healthy- and for good reason. You are what you eat. If you dine exclusively on

McDonald's and deep-fried foods you should expect it to be impossible for you to lose weight. As a matter of fact, you should expect to gain weight (and plenty of it).

3. Go for a walk every now and then. Physical activity elevates your heart rate, releases crucial hormones, and reduces stress. If you are taking a supplement (such as Phentramin) it will compound the effects and promote rapid weight loss.

Now, when I say rapid, I don't mean that you're literally going to lose inches every day. What I mean is that as your body adjusts to its new routine you will begin to lose weight. You will be lighter, healthier, and almost certainly happier.

4. Drink lots of water. Water cleanses the system of toxins and junk that's not supposed to be there. Water also suppresses your bodies hunger pains and, as a result, helps you lose weight.

By following the above mentioned advice anyone may get useful tips which will helps him/her in losing the bodily weight.

Get Rid of Obesity

The most fret point is that more than half of the population of the world either in developed or developing nations is effected by overweight or obesity. And one day it will seriously affect the general health of the nation and considering the health cost of the countries, think of the consequence when majority of the population will be suffering from one disease or other due to their overweight.

There are lots of weight reducing medicines, pills etc., are available in the market which usually has the fatal side effects on the human body after consuming them. Out of several medicines, drugs and pills recommended for weight reducing, Alli which is the over the counter version of Xenical for weight loss is now on the market so that people can use this as a aid to their weight. . Food and Drug Administration (FDA) approved the weight-loss product orlistat 60 mg capsules for over-the-counter (OTC) use in the United States. Alli helps people lose 50 percent more weight than with diet alone. Alli is the only FDA-approved weight loss product available to consumers without a prescription, and it is the first support program.

GSK Consumer Healthcare selected Alli as the brand name as it conveys the concept of cooperation with consumer in their weight- loss efforts. Peoples spend billions of dollars each year on fad diets and weight loss pills that may not works. Alli is the clinically proven option to these overvalued and quick fix products that mislead overweight adults away from weight-loss strategies that are backed by medical science.

Unlike other diet pills Alli is a proven medicine with a comprehensive support program. The optional dose of alli is one 60 mg capsule three times a day with meals containing fat. Alli works by blocking about 25 percent of the fat in the food a person eats because alli must be used in combination with a reduced calorie, low fat diet containing about 15 grams of fat per meal. The person who is taking Alli should take a multivitamin once a day, at bedtime, because alli can reduce the inclusion of some vitamins.

Alli diet pill is safe and effective when used as directed but as other prescription drugs Alli having also some side effects. So it is advisable that first consult with your doctor before start the course.

But Alli diet pill is safe compare to other diet pills as

has no effect on the heart or brain. Alli Diat Pill should not taken by individuals below the age of 18 years.

Alli should keep in a cool and dry place as moisture has the conditions to break down the ingredients in the medicine which can increase its side effects.

Avoid These Dieting And Weight Loss Mistakes

Dieting can be tough work. Even for ongoing successful dieters, it can be difficult to keep it up. Here are a few things to avoid that can otherwise lead you away from your dieting goals and progress. Avoid them at all costs if you plan on successfully losing weight.

1. Rushing into the toughest diet you can find

This happens to many beginning dieters. Deciding to improve your health with a new diet is great, but don't just rush into the strictest diet you can find. Make sure you pick a diet you can stick with, and work it into your natural lifestyle so it becomes second nature to you.

2. Stick to reality.

Losing weight takes time. Don't expect to lose 10 pounds overnight. When deciding how much weight you want to lose, spread it over a longer period of time, like a few months. Stay motivated about your goals if you hear someone saying they lost a lot of weight quickly. Remember, everyone is different so don't try to match exactly what they did. Instead try to find things to work into your lifestyle

3. Going to the gym way too often

Another often overlooked mistake when getting started in your diet is going to the gym every day. This is not good because muscles need time to heal and expand after your workouts. Going to the gym can cause problems for this process and besides, a few days hitting the gym won't offset 10 to 20 years of couch potato lifestyle.

4. *Worrying too much about calories*

Cutting down calories seems like a good way to lose weight and is a big part of any popular diet. Be careful and don't just try to cut out all calories or your body will be trying to store anything it can. Again moderation is the key.

5. *Skipping or avoiding meals*

Having only one or two meals a day won't help you lose weight any faster. It's all about eating the right foods at the right amounts, never starve yourself, or overeat.

6. *Checking the bathroom scale every day*

Everyone who tried to lose weight wants to see fast results. Let your diet plan take its course and and try not to check the scale every day. The natural, small daily changes in your weight will only make you depressed and want to quit dieting. Some people avoid the scale altogether and judge their results by the way they feel

7. *Letting emotions get the best of you*

Other emotions affect your dieting habits besides wanting to check the scale. If you tend to grab an ice cream or other fatty snacks while you are bored, frustrated or angry, think of your ideal body image when this happens and you will soon find your emotions won't get in the way of your goals and progress.

8. *Not asking for help when you need it*

There is no need to go at it alone. If you need any help or advice, ask friends and family or even professionals for it. You should be able to find others supportive of you and your goals

9. Totally denying yoursel your favorite foods as a treat

Dieting helps you control your eating habits, but go ahead and enjoy a treat sometimes. It's good for your overall willpower and motivation. Totally cancelling out your favorite foods will only make dieting more difficult over time.

10. Relying on willpower and memory alone

Be smart about your efforts. Keep a journal and write down what you eat so you will know if you ate something you shouldn't. Learn about yourself and make dieting easier with a clear mind.

Mark Daily lost 55 pounds by following sound weight loss advice and testing the most popular herbal weight loss pills. He is also a nutritionist who recommends effective weight loss supplements to his several clients.

YOGA & WEIGHT MANAGEMENT (OBESITY)

What is Obesity or Overweight?

It may be defined as excess weight or deposition of excess fats on body, which leads to various diseases like diabetes, heart diseases, hypertension, lowered pulmonary functions, lowers life expectancy.

Medical words, it may be defined as an abnormal growth of the adipose tissue due to enlargement of fat cell size (Hypertrophic) or an increase in fat cell number (Hyperplastic).

It can be of 2 types, first is Abdominal obesity and second is Gluteal obesity. Generally 20 % excess weight is considered as health risk.

Obesity Reasons-

- Physical inactivity (lack of proper exercise)
- Eating Habits –

o Eating in between meals

o Preference to sweets, refined food, fats, preserved food

o Composition & periodicity of meals

- Psychological Factors

o Emotional disturbances

o Depression and anxiety

o Frustration and loneliness

- Endocrine glands problems
- Familial tendency
- Males are at high risk during age 29 to 35 and females are at risk during the age 45 to 49
- The risk increases with age.

Assessment of Obesity –

1. Body Mass Index = Weight in kg./ (Height in meter)* (Height in meter)

If the BMI is in between 19 to 23, it is considered as normal, but if it is more then 23 then it can be called as obesity.

2. Waist to Hip ratio = if it is more than 1 in male is Obesity and 0.85 in females.

There are other methods to assess the obesity.

The obesity results in various diseases like diabetes mellitus, hypertension, coronary heart diseases, reduced pulmonary functions and resulting in lower life expectancy.

Yoga

Yoga has an important role to play in the treatment of Obesity. Yoga techniques affect body, internal organs, endocrine glands, brain, mind and other factors concerning Body – Mind complex. Various Yoga techniques can be practiced effectively to reduce the weight and achieve normal healthy condition of Body and Mind.

Asanas – Yoga positions or postures are especially useful to reduce the fats in various parts, especially forward bending, twisting and backward bending asanas help reduce the fats near abdomen, hips and other areas. Also the practice of asanas improves functioning of internal organs, strengthening heart, lungs, kidneys, excretory & reproductive organs. Regular practice builds strength in muscles.

Asanas can be practiced with fast speed like exercise with good effects, the practitioner may increase repetitions instead of maintaining the asana for long.

Sun salutations are very beneficial in Obesity management, every day 24 sun salutations with a speed of 4 rounds in 1 minute gives great benefits of Yoga Asanas and exercise as well. The practice of Sun salutation is a sequence of 7 asanas practiced in order which tones almost all of the muscles and also internal organs are stretched increasing blood & oxygen supply to these parts. Regular practice of sun salutation with breathing gives good exercise to the lungs. Mantras have relaxing effect on mind.

The following are some useful yogic postures which helps in reducing bodily fatness and stay free your body from obesity:

1. Easy Pose (Sukhasana)

This is one of the classic Meditative Poses and is usually performed after doing the Corpse Pose. The Easy Pose helps in straightening the spine, slowing down metabolism, promoting inner tranquility, and keeping your mind still.

After relaxing in the Corpse Pose for a few minutes, come up and sit in the Easy Yoga Pose or Sukhasana for Pranayama and the neck, shoulder and eye exercises. This Yoga Asana is one of the classic Meditative Poses, which help to straighten the spine, slow down metabolism and still the mind. If you find that holding the Yoga Pose is uncomfortable, place a folded Yoga Blanket under the back of your buttocks.

In order to stretch the leg muscles evenly, be sure put each leg alternately on top in this Yoga Posture. When

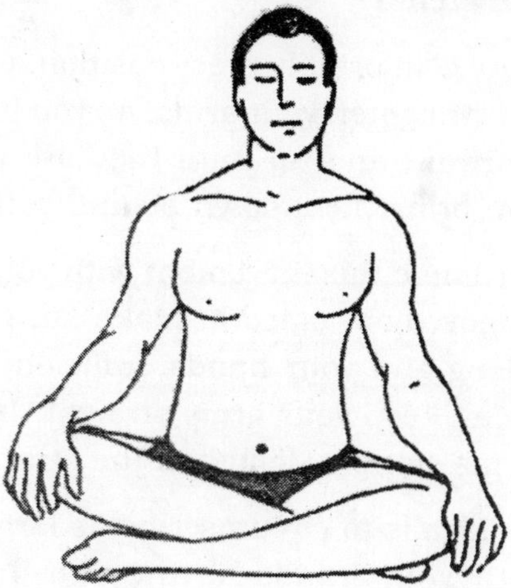

you are ready, substitute the Half Lotus or Lotus at this point.

Method: Sitting on the floor and bend your knees. Clasp your arms around them and press them to your chest to make the spine erect. Now, release your arms and cross your legs, letting your knees drop down toward the floor. Keep your head and body straight.

2. Shoulder Stretches

Shoulder Stretches are great in relieving stress and tension on your shoulders, as well as your entire upper back. Practice them daily for several weeks and notice the changes.

The following Shoulder Stretches are great in relieving stress and tension on your shoulders, as well as your entire upper back. Practice them daily for several weeks and notice the changes. You will need a long strap for the first three.

Shoulder Stretch 1:

1. Sit in any comfortably erect position. Clasp hold of the strap and straighten your arms. As you inhale, sweep your arms forward and up until they are vertical, and exhale as you bring them down behind you.

2. Coordinate this movement with your breathing, making the movement smooth. Make sure the strap is sufficiently long and your hands sufficiently far apart, so that you call keep your arms straight. If you cannot keep your arms straight, lengthen the strap.

3. The idea is to circumscribe as large a circle as possible with your hands as they go up and over.

Therefore, at every given moment you are stretching outward through your arms in the direction they are pointing.

Shoulder Stretch 2 :

1. Shorten the strap so your hands are approximately twenty-four to thirty inches apart. Adjust the distance to suit your need. Raise both arms up, bringing the right arm alongside the ear, and swivel the left arm around and down behind you.

2 . Inhale as you energize upward through the right arm, and exhale as you reach outward through the left arm and pull down with the hand. This is a fantastic stretch. Breathe smoothly and create the degree of intensity you find pleasurable. Be here several breaths, then change sides.

Shoulder Stretch 3 :

1. Shorten the strap until your arms are parallel with one another and your hands are shoulder-width apart. Pull outward with your hands until the strap is taut.

2 . Take your arms up. Get as long as you can from your navel to your hands. Be here a few moments.

3. Slowly bend your arms. Pull hard on the belt as you slowly bring it down behind your head until it touches the back of your neck. Keep the abdominals in, your chest lifted, and firmly squeeze the elbows backward - and continue pulling the strap taut. Then slowly take the strap back up again, straightening the arms. Try to feel every subtle change of sensation. Do not be surprised if the strap starts jiggling. It's a long way up. This is more difficult than you'd think. Do this

several times, then release the strap.

Shoulder Stretch 4 :

1. Clasp your hands behind you, straighten your arms, then lift your hands as high as you can. Roll the shoulders backward, gently squeezing the shoulder blades together, and expand your chest by lifting it up and pressing it forward. Pull straight backward through your arms in the direction they are pointing. Be here several breaths.

2. Bring your interlaced hands to the left side of your waist. Pull the abdominals in and lift the chest, then roll both shoulders backward as you squeeze the elbows inward toward one another and press forward with your hands. Breathe deeply and expand your chest, deliberately pressing it forward through the shoulders. Be here several breaths, then change sides.

Shoulder Stretch 5 :

1. Stretch the left arm straight up, then bend your elbow and bring your hand down behind your back. Clasp the left elbow with your right hand. Find the groove of your spine with your left fingertips.

2. Keeping your abdomen in, backward toward the spine, and your chest lifting and expanded, use your right hand to pull the left elbow behind your head. Maneuver your fingertips down the groove of the spine, gently squeeze the right elbow comfortably far backward, and allow the stretch to penetrate for half a minute. Breathe smoothly. Change sides.

Shoulder Stretch 6 :

1. Place the back of your right hand on your lower back, then wriggle it up your back as far as it will comfortably go. Pause here, acclimatize for a moment, then wriggle it farther up.

2. Stretch the left arm straight up, bend your elbow so your hand comes down behind your back, and clasp your hands. Move the left elbow away from your head and elevate your chin slightly. Stretch straight up, into the left elbow, straight down into the right elbow, and attempt to move both elbows baackward - chest up, shoulder blades down, navel backward toward the spine. Be here half a minute, breathing smoothly, then switch sides.

Shoulder Stretch 7 :

1. Entwine your arms and bring your palms together. Turn your palms until they are straight. Be here half a minute, then entwine them with the other arm on top.

2. Bring your hands into prayer position behind your back. Start with your fingertips together, pointing down, then turn your hands inward and bring them up into prayer position.

3. Bring the abdominals in, lift and expand the chest, then roll the shoulders backward. Move the elbows backward so the shoulder blades flatten into your back, and gently press your palms together. Wriggle your hands higher when you can. The higher you get them, the more comfortable this will be. Be here several breaths.

3. Sun Salutation (Surya Namaskar)

The Sun Salutation or Surya Namaskar is a Yoga Pose which limbers up the whole body in preparation for the Yoga Asanas. It is a graceful sequence of twelve Yoga positions performed as one continuous exercise. Learn how to practice Sun Salutation in this section.

The Sun Salutation or Surya Namaskar limbers up the whole body in preparation for the yoga asanas. It is a graceful sequence of twelve yoga positions performed as one continuous exercise. Each position counteracts the one before, stretching the body in a different way and alternately expanding and contracting the chest to regulate the breathing. Practiced daily it will great flexibility to your spine and joints and trims your waist.

One round of Sun Salutation consists of two sequences, the first leading with the right foot in positions 4 and 9 (as illustrated), the second leading with the left. Keep your hands in one place from positions 3 to 10 and try to coordinate your movements with your breathing. Start by practicing four rounds and gradually build up to twelve rounds.

Method 1. Stand erect with feet together and palms in the prayer position in front of your chest. Make sure your weight is evenly distributed. Exhale.

2. Inhaling, stretch your arms up and arch back from the waist, pushing the hips out, legs straight. Relax your neck.

3. Exhaling, fold forward, and press your palms down, fingertips in line with toes - bend your knees if necessary.

4. Inhaling, bring the right (or left) leg back and place

#1
#2
#3
#4
#5
#6
#7
#8
#9
#10
#11
#12

the knee on the floor. Arch back and look up, lifting your chin.

5. Retaining the breath, bring the other leg back and support your weight on hands and toes. Keep your head and body in line and look at the floor between your hands.

6. Exhaling, lower your knees, then your chest and then your forehead, keeping your hips up and toes curled under.

7. Inhaling, lower your hips, point your toes and bend back. Keep legs together and shoulders down. Look up and back.

8. Exhaling, curl your toes under, raise your hips and pivot into an inverted "V" shape. Try to push your heels and head down keep your shoulders back.

9. Inhaling, step forward and place the right (or left) foot between your hands. Rest the other knee on the floor and look up, as in position 4.

10. Exhaling, bring the other leg forward and bend down from the waist keeping your palms as in position 3.

11. Inhaling, stretch your arms forward, then up and back over your head and bend back slowly from the waist, as in position 2.

12. Exhaling, gently come back to an upright position and bring your arms down by your side.

4. Half Spinal Twist (Ardha Matsyendrasana)

If done properly, the Half Spinal Twist lengthens and

strengthens the spine. It is also beneficial for your liver, kidneys, as well as adrenal glands. Practice this Yoga Pose under the supervision of a Yoga instructor.

The Spinal Twist Yoga Pose, which takes its Sanskrit name from the great Yogic Sage Matsyendra, is one of the few Yoga Poses in the Basic Session that rotates the spine. Most bend the Spinal Column either backward or forward, but to become truly flexible it must be twisted laterally as well. The movement also tones the spinal nerves and ligaments, and improves digestion. Keep your spine erect and your shoulders leveled in the position. Breathe steadily. Twist a little more each time you exhale. Twist first to the left, as below, then repeat the sequence twisting to the right.

Method

1. 1. Kneel down with your legs together, resting on your heels.

2. Then sit to the right of your feet, as illustrated.

3. Lift your left leg over your right, placing the foot against the outside of the right knee. Bring your right heel in close to your buttocks. Keep the spine erect.

4. Stretch your arms out to the sides at shoulder level, and twist around to the left.

5. Now bring the right arm down on the outside of the left knee and hold the left foot in the right hand, placing your left hand on the floor behind you. As you exhale, twist as far as possible to the left. Look over the left shoulder.

The Half-Spinal Twist or *Ardha Matsyendrasana*, taught here, has similar benefits and prepares the body for the full Yoga Posture.

5. Stand Spread Leg Forward Fold

Practicing the Standing Spread Leg Forward Fold can strengthen and stretch your inner and back legs and your spine. It is also good for toning the abdominal organs and calming the Brain Doing this pose can relieve mild Headaches.

Start in the Mountain Posture. Step out to the right with your right foot in a wide stance, approximately 3 feet for taller people, less if you are shorter. As you inhale, raise your arms out from the sides forming a T with your torso.

As you exhale, bend forward from the hips and hand down, holding each of your bent elbows with the opposite side hand. Soften your knees to where you are comfortable.

Stay in the folded position for 6-8 breaths. Roll your body up and return to the Mountain posture.

People with Lower-Back problems should avoid doing the full forward bend. For beginners, you may use props like a folding chair to support your forearms.

6. Tree Pose (Tadasana)

The Tree Pose helps strengthen your thighs, calves, ankles and back. It can also increase the flexibility of your hips and groin. Your balance and concentration can also be improved with constant practice. This Yoga Pose is recommended for people who has Sciatica and flat feet.

Start with the Mountain Posture.

As you exhale, place the sole of your left foot on the inside of your right leg above your knee, toes, pointing toward the ground.

As you inhale, bring your arms out from your sides to form a T, and then, as you exhale, bring your hands together in prayer position with your thumbs touching your breast bone and fingers toward the ceiling. As a variation, bring your arms overhead and join your palms together. Look at a spot on the floor 6-8 feet in front of you.

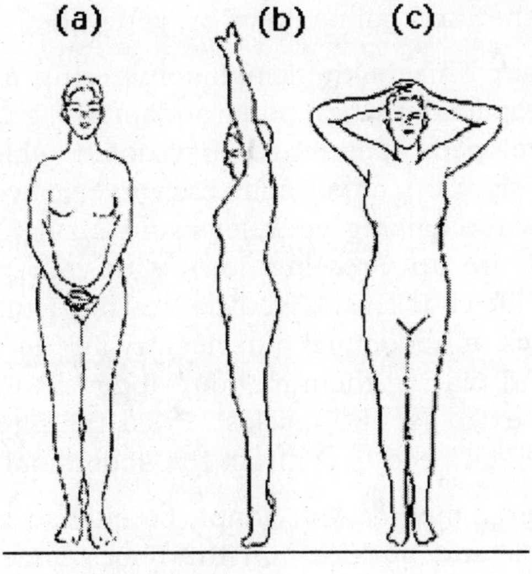

Stay for 6-8 breaths and then repeat on the other side.

People who are suffering from Headache, insomnia, low blood and High Blood Pressure should take extra caution in doing this pose. People with high blood pressure should not raise their arms overhead.

In the beginning, you may use a back brace against a wall to help you keep yourself steady.

7. Double Leg Raises

This simple Yoga Exercise prepares your body for the other Yoga Asanas. It strengthens the abdominal and Lower Back muscles and is often used to come up into the Headstand. Performing the Double Leg Raise trims the waist and the thighs. If your muscles are weak, you may find yourself arching your lower back or using your shoulders to help lift your legs. To get the most benefit from this Yoga Postures, make sure that the full length of your back is resting on the floor and your shoulders and neck are relaxed. These Yoga Exercise begins with legs together and palms down on your side.

Method: This is the most demanding of the Leg Raises, especially when your abdominal muscles are underdeveloped. At first you may not be able to raise your legs right up, or you may have to bend your knees slightly while raising your legs and straighten them once they are up. Pressing down with your palms will help you lift your legs. If you have a particularly weak Lower Back or abdominal muscles, try interlocking your fingers and placing them on your abdomen in order to create an extra set of "muscles". Press the fingers down each time you need to contract the abdominal muscles.

Whichever method you adapt, be sure to keep your lower back and buttocks on the floor. Once you can

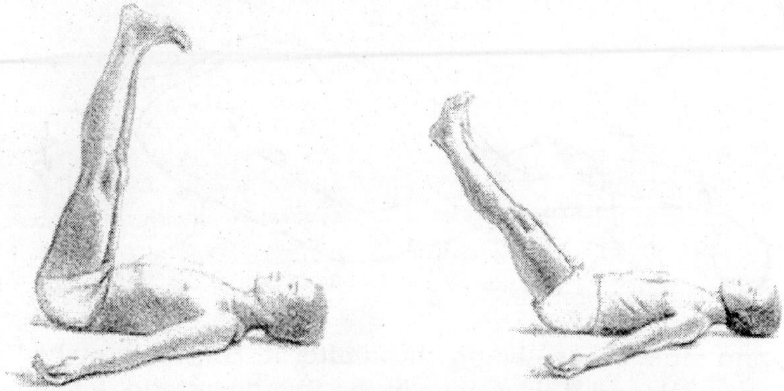

perform the Double Leg Raise without strain, lower your legs slowly as possible and keep your feet an inch or so off the floor between raises to make your muscles work harder.

1. Lie flat on the floor. Inhaling, raise both legs, keeping your knees straight and your buttocks on the floor.

2. Exhale and lower your legs. Repeat ten times. Make sure that your lower back remains flat on the floor while you bring the legs down, to avoid injuring your spine.

8. Fish Pose (Matsyasana)

Doing the Fish Pose relieves stiffness of the neck and shoulder muscles and improves flexibility of your spine. It is the counter-pose of the Shoulderstand. Hold the Fish Pose for at least half the amount of time you spent in the Shoulderstand in order to balance the stretch.

Matsya, the Fish, was one of the incarnations of the Hindu God Vishnu Vishnu assumed this form to save the world from the Flood. The Fish Yoga Pose or in Hindi Matsyasana, is the counter-pose to the Shoulderstand

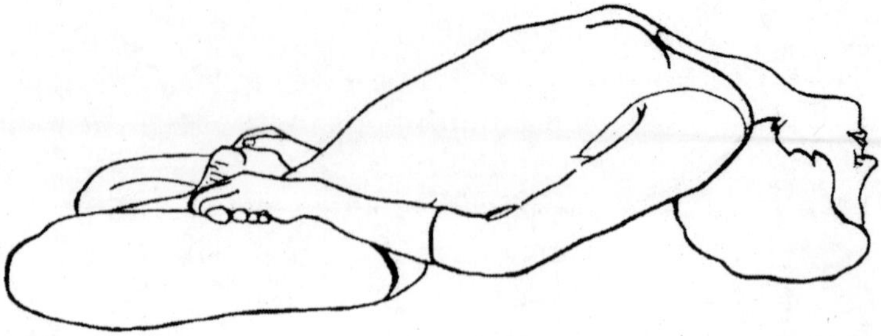

and must always be practiced after it. Having stretched the neck and upper spine in the Shoulderstand, Plough or Bridge, you now compress them as you arch your back. Doing the Fish Pose also relieves the stiffness of your neck and shoulder muscles and corrects any tendency of having rounded shoulders. Holding this Yoga Pose exercises the chest, tones the nerves of the Neck and Back, and ensures that the Thyroid and Parathyroid Glands obtain the maximum benefits from the Shoulderstand. Performing the Fish Pose also expands the ribcage fully, increasing your lung capacity and aids in deep breathing. You should remain in this Yoga Posture for at least half the amount of time you spent in the Shoulderstand in order to balance the stretch.

Method

1. Lie down on your back with your legs straight and your feet together. Place your hands, palms down, underneath your thighs.

2. Note: Your hands should rest palms down, side by side, and your elbows should be as close together as possible under your back.

3. Pressing down on your elbows, inhale and arch your back. Drop your head back so that the top of your

head is on the floor, but your weight should rest on yuor elbows. Exhale. Breathe deeply while in the position, keeping your legs and lower torso relaxed. To come out of the pose, first lift your head and place it gently back down, then release the arms.

9. Corpse Pose (Savasana)

Even relaxation can bring out the best in you — but make sure you do it properly. The Corpse Yoga Pose or Savasana may look like a simple relaxing pose that is done in between or after an Asana, but this exercise requires a lot of concentration and will develop through continued practice. This exercise, if done correctly, will stimulate blood circulation and will lessen or relieve fatigue, nervousness, asthma, constipation, diabetes, indigestion, and insomnia. It will also improve one's mental concentration.

These are the steps in doing the Corpse Pose:

1. Rotate your legs in and out, and then let them fall gently out to the sides.

2. Let your arms fall alongside your body, slightly separated from the body, palms facing upwards.

3. Rotate the spine by turning your head from side to side to center it.

4. Then start stretching yourself out, as though someone is pulling your head away from your feet, your shoulders down and away from your neck, your legs down and away from your pelvis.

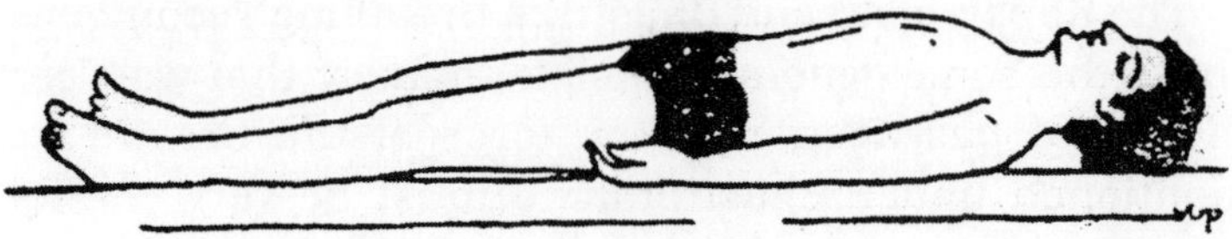

5. Breathe deeply and slowly from your abdomen.

6. Hold the pose for several minutes. Make your mind still and concentrate on your breath or the body.

7. After doing the pose, bend your knees. Using your legs, push yourself onto one side.

8. Push yourself in a sitting position.

Note: No Yoga Session is complete without the Corpse Yoga Pose. It is the body's time to process information after a Yoga exercise, and it is a must that you stay awake during the five to ten minute-duration of this pose.

10. Breathing Exercise (Pranayama) - Kapalabhati (Cleaning Breath)

Kapalabhati is a Breathing Technique used specifically for cleansing. If we have a lot of mucus in the air passages or feel tension and blockages in the chest it is often helpful to breathe quickly. In this practice, we deliberately breathe faster and at the same time use only Abdominal Breathing, that is, diaphragmatic, not Chest Breathing. In Kapalabhati, the Breath is short, rapid, and strong. We use the lungs as a pump, creating so much pressure as they expel the air that all the waste is removed from the air passages, from the lungs up through the nostrils. Kapala means "skull," and bhati means "that which brings lightness." Kapalabhati is a good thing to do when we feel heavy or foggy in the head. If we have problems with the sinuses or feel numb around the eyes, Kapalabhati can help to clear this area as well.

The Kapalabhati and Bhastrika Breathing Techniques share the same general principle, namely that we clear the nasal passages with the force of the breath. As mentioned under Bhastrika, we must be very careful with these techniques because there is a danger of creating tension in the breath. We may also become dizzy when we breathe rapidly; for this reason we always conclude the practice of Kapalabhati with some slow breaths. It is important not to breathe rapidly too many times, but after a few rapid breaths take several slow ones in which we emphasize the long Exhalation.

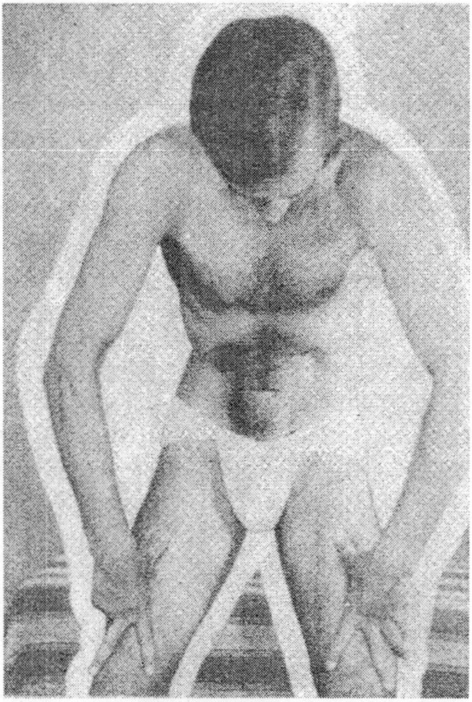

One Round of Kapalabhati (Cleaning Breath)

Take two normal breaths. Inhale. Now exhale, pulling in your abdomen. Repeat twenty times, keeping a steady rhythm and emphasizing the exhalation each time. Then inhale, exhale completely, inhale fully and hold your breath for as long as you comfortably can. Slowly exhale.

11. Simple Meditation

Meditation is a principle of yoga often portrayed by the mass media as an activity of sitting in silence while listening to your inner self and tuning out of the physical, material world. It is indeed an act of contemplation and reflection, but meditation has various ways and techniques.

Meditation's roots can be traced way back ancient times. There are speculations that it even started during the primitive years. Meditation then developed into a structured practice, and was even noted 5000 years ago in the Indian scripture called the "tantras". Around 500 B.C., the major icon of meditation, Buddha, made his mark in history through His practice and teachings.

There is not just one way to meditate. It is up to you to experience and decide which meditation practice is best for you. But for starters, here's a simple Meditation you could apply in your daily routine. Set aside 10 to 20 minutes same time each day, if possible. Before

breakfast is a good time. Then follow these steps to a moment of prayer and internal dialogue:

1. Choose a quiet spot where you will not be disturbed by other people.

2. Sit quietly in a comfortable position. Refer to the section on postures for recommendations on sitting positions.

3. Eliminate distractions and interruptions during the period you'll be meditating.

4. Commit yourself to a specific length of time and try to stick to it.

5. Pick a focus word or short phrase that's firmly rooted in your personal belief system. A non-religious person might choose a neutral word like one, peace, or love. Others might use the opening words of a favorite prayer from their religion such as 'Hail Mary full of Grace', "I surrender all to you", "Hallelujah", "Om", etc.

6. Close your eyes. This will make it easy to concentrate.

7. Relax your muscles sequentially from head to feet. This helps to break the connection between stressful thoughts and a tense body. Starting with your forehead, become aware of tension as you breathe in. Let go of any obvious tension as you breathe out. Go through the rest of your body in this way, proceeding down through your eyes, jaws, neck, shoulders, arms, hands, chest, upper back, middle back and midriff, lower back, belly, pelvis, buttocks, thighs, calves, and feet.

8. Breathe slowly and naturally, repeating your focus word or phrase silently as you exhale.

9. Assume a passive attitude. Don't worry about how well you're doing. When other thoughts come to mind, simply say, "Oh, well," and gently return to the repetition.

10. Continue for 10 to 20 minutes. You may open your eyes to check the time, but do not use an alarm. After you finish: Sit quietly for a minute or so, at first with your eyes closed and later with your eyes open. Do not stand for one or two minutes.

Meditation has been scientifically proven to have health benefits. First of all, it lowers blood pressure and aides the asthmatics in their breathing. Meditation also balances the person's physical, emotional and mental states. Moreover, it relaxes the mind and body, and reduces stress and tensions in our body. This practice is like recharging our mind, body and spirit to be energized again to live a life connected with God. By having simple Meditation a part of your life, you can achieve true happiness and peace of mind through spiritual growth and detachment from the physical world.

12. Anuloma Viloma

Anuloma Viloma is also called the Alternate Nostril Breathing Technique. In this Breathing Technique, you inhale through one nostril, retain the breath, and exhale through the other nostril.

Anuloma Viloma is also called the Alternate Nostril Breathing Technique. In this Breathing Technique, you inhale through one nostril, retain the breath, and exhale through the other nostril in a ratio of 2:8:4. The left nostril is the path of the Nadi called Ida and the right nostril is the path of the Nadi called Pingala. If you are really healthy, you will breathe predominantly through

the Ida nostril about one hour and fifty minutes, then through the Pingala nostril. But in many people, this natural rhythm is disturbed. Anuloma Viloma restores, equalizes and balances the flow of Prana in the body.

One round of Anuloma Viloma is made up of six steps, as shown below. Start by practicing three rounds and build up slowly to twenty rounds, extending the count within the given ratio.

The Vishnu Mudra

In Anuloma Viloma, you adopt the Vishnu Mudra with your right hand to close your nostrils. Tuck your index and middle finger into your nose. Place the thumb by your right nostril and your ring and little fingers by your left.

One Round of Anuloma Viloma (Alternate Nostril Breathing)

1. Inhale through the left nostril, closing the right with the thumb, to the count of four.
2. Hold the breath, closing both nostrils, to the count of sixteen.
3. Exhale through the right nostril, closing the left with the ring and little fingers, to the count of eight.
4. Inhale through the right nostril, keeping the left nostril closed with the ring and little fingers, to the count of four.
5. Hold the breath, closing both nostrils, to the count of sixteen.
6. Exhale through the left nostril, keeping the right

closed with the thumb, to the count of eight.

Benefits of Anuloma Viloma

The exercise of the Anuloma Viloma produces optimum function to both sides of the brain: that is optimum creativity and optimum logical verbal activity. This will make both sides of the brain, the left side which is responsible for logical thinking and the right side which is responsible for creative thinking to function properly. This will lead to a balance between a person's creative and logical thinking. The Yogis consider this to be the best technique to calm the mind and the Nervous System.

Anuloma Viloma: The Scientific Confirmation

Medical science has recently discovered the nasal cycle, something that was already discovered by the Yogis thousands of years ago. Modern scientists found out that we do not breathe equally on both nostrils, that is one nostril is much easier to breathe through than the other at any particular time. Each nostril alternates about every three hours. The Yogis claim that the natural period is every two hours, but we must remember these studies were done on people who do not have an optimum Health level.

Scientists also discovered that the nasal cycle corresponds with brain function. The electrical activity of the brain was found to be greater on the side opposite the less congested nostril. The right side of the brain controls creative activity, while the left side controls logical verbal activity. The research showed that when the left nostril was less obstructed, the right side of the brain was predominant. Test subjects were indeed found to do better on creative tests. Similarly when the right nostril was less obstructed the left side of the brain was predominant. Test subjects did better on verbal skills.

Medical science has not quite caught up with the ancient Yogis yet. The Ancient Yogis even went one step further. They observed that a lot of diseases were due to disturbances of the nasal cycle or if a person breathe for too long through one nostril. To prevent and correct this condition, they developed the Alternate Nostril Breathing Technique. This clears any blockage the airflow in the nostrils and reestablishes the natural nasal cycle. For example, the Yogis have known for a long time that prolonged breathing through the left nostril only (over a period of years) will cause Asthma. They also know that this so-called incurable disease can be easily treated by teaching the patient to breathe through the right nostril until the Asthma is cured and prevent it from recurring by doing the Alternate Nostril Breathing Technique. The Yogis also believe that Diabetes is caused, to a large extent, by breathing mainly through the right nostril.

13. Relaxation Pose

In this section, we present the technique of relaxation, that is an essential part of your yoga practice. There are three parts to proper relaxation - physical, mental and spiritual relaxation. To relax the body, you lie down in the Corpse Pose and first tense then relax each part of the body in turn, working from up your feet to your head. This alternate tensing then relaxing is necessary because it is only by knowing how tension feels that you can be sure that you have achieved relaxation. Then just as in normal life your mind instructs the muscles to tense and contract, you now

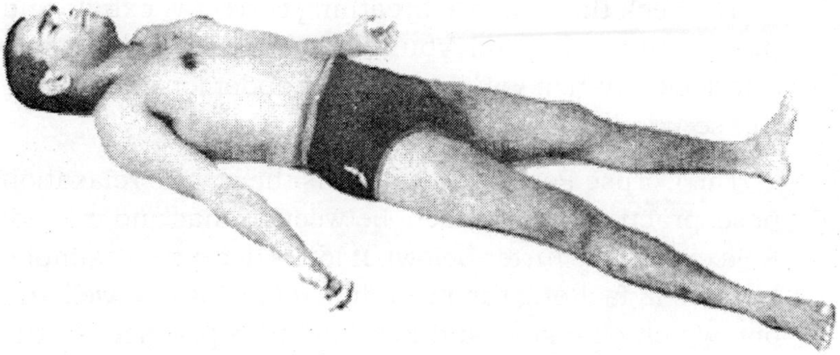

use autosuggestion to send the muscles a message to relax. With practice you will gradually learn to use your subconscious mind to extend this control to the involuntary muscles of the heart, the digestive systems and other organs too.

The Corpse Pose

The Front Corpse Pose

Lie down on your front, legs slightly apart, toes touching, and allow your heels to fall out to the sides. Make a pillow with your hands. Lengthen the body, tense and relax the muscles. Feel your body sinking into the floor as you exhale. Use this pose after any asana performed on the abdomen (such as the Cobra or Bow), alternating on which side you place your head.

The Corpse Pose

Lie on your back, feel spread about 18 inches apart, and hands about 6 inches from your sides, palms up. Ease yourself into the pose, making sure the body is symmetrical. Let your thighs, knees and toes turn outward. Close your eyes and breathe deeply.

Abdominal Breathing

To check that you are breathing correctly, exhale and place your hands on your abdomen, fingers loosely interlocked.When you inhale, your abdomen should rise up, separating your hands.

The Corpse Pose or Savasana is the classic relaxation pose, practised before each, between asanas and in Final Relaxation (see furter below). It looks deceptively simple, but it is in fact one the most difficult asanas do well and one which changess and develops with practice. At the end of an asana session your Corpse Pose will be more complete than at the beginning because the other asanas will have progressively stretched and relaxed your muscles. When you first lie down, look to see that you are lying symetrically as symmetry provides proper space for all parts to relax. Now start to work in the pose. Rotate your legs in and out, then let them fall gently out to the sides. Do the same with your arms. Rotate the spine by turning your head from side to side to centre it. Then start stretching yourself out, as through someone were pulling your head away from your feet, your shoulders down and away from your neck, your legs down and away from your pelvis. Let gravity embrace you. Feel your weight pulling you deeper into relaxation, melting your body into the floor. Breathe deeply and slowly from the abdomen, riding up and down on the breath, sinking deeper with each exhalation. Feel how your abdomen swells and falls. Many physiological changes are taking places, reducing the body's energy loss, removing stress, lowering your respiration and pulse rate, and resting the whole system. As you enter deep relaxation, you will feel your mind grow clear and detached.

Final Relaxation (Savasana)

Your yoga practice will help to be more in touch with your body, able to recognize tension and relaxation and thus to bring them under your conscious control. At the end of session of asanas, you should spend at least ten minutes in Final Relaxation. During this time, you relax each part of the body in turn. But in order to experience relaxation, you must first experience tension. Working up from the feet, as shown below, you first tense and lift each part, then drop (but don't place) it down. Now let your mind travel throughout the body, commanding each part to relax. Let yourself go. Sink deep into the quiet pool of the mind. To bring your consciousness back to your body, gently move your fingers and toes, take a deep breath and as your exhale, sit up.

Feet and Legs

Lift your right foot just an inch off the floor. Tense the leg, hold, then let it drop. Repeat on the other side.

Hands and Arms

Raise your right hand an inch off the floor. Make a fist, tense the arm, then let it drop. Repeat on the other side. Relax.

Buttocks

Clench your buttocks tightly together, lift the hips a little way off the floor and hold. Relax and drop them down

Chest

Tense and lift up the back and chest, keeping your hips and head on the floor. Relax and drop them down.

Shoulders

Lift your shoulders and hunch them up tight around your neck. Let them drop, relaxed. Now pull each arm, in turn, down alongside the body, and relax.

Head

Tuck in your chin slightly and roll the head gently from side to side. Find a comfortable position in the center for the head to lie, and then relax.

Autosuggestion

After practicing the sequence shown, visualize your body in your mind's eye, and repeat this simple formula mentally: "I relax the toes, I relax the toes. The toes are relaxed. I relax the calves, I relax the calves. The calves are relaxed." Continue on up the body, applying the formula to each part along the way - the stomach, lungs, heart, jaw, scalp, brain, and soon. Feel a wave of relaxation rising up your body as you guide your awareness through each part. Each time you inhale, feel a wave of Oxygen flowing down to your feet; each time you exhale, feel the tension flowing out of your body, leaving your mind like a deep, still lake, without a ripple. Now dive deep into the center of this lake, deep within yourself, and experience your true nature.

Pranayama –

Pranayama is very important technique in yoga which is control and extension of Prana or Vital energy or Life force. Pranayama helps in management of this energy. Various techniques are available in yoga, which give interesting but good results.

The Pranayama can be classified in 2 types in terms

of physiology, Hypo ventilation or vitalizing Pranayama and Hyper ventilation or relaxing pranayama. Kapalbhati, Bhasrika and Fast breathing can be classified under Hyper ventilation (increases Oxygen and reduces carbon dioxide) and Deep breathing, Bhramari, Shitali, Sitkari can be classified as Hypo ventilation (oxygen level remains mostly same but the speed of respiration is lower, heart rate lower).

Kapalbhati, Bhasrika & fast breathing can be practiced by people suffering from obesity with good effects; these Pranayama techniques increase the lung capacity and help burning fats. Regular practice of Pranayama brings balance in the system in terms of Physical and Mental functions.

CLEANSING TECHNIQUES

Shankha Prakshalana or Master cleansing technique – Drinking 2 glasses of water, performing special asanas, again drinking the water, followed by asanas to evacuate the bowels is the process of cleansing of entire GI tract. The process is completed when one has completely cleansed the intestinal tract.

Agnisar – Fast movement of abdominal muscles in and out, is very good exercise to get rid of the accumulated fats in the abdominal region also it helps in streamlining Digestive system.

BANDHAS

Uddiyan Bandha

Mula bandha

Diet – More raw vegetables, fruits help in balancing the intake of the food. Reducing refined & processed food, fast food, non vegetarian diet helps in weight control. A special fasting program has shown promising results.

9

YOGA AND ITS BENEFITS

Yoga – Introduction

Quite a self contradictory statement it is: "Yoga - the new age fitness mantra", because Yoga is not new age at all. It's just that the benefits of the same are being discovered again. An ancient Indian philosophy, the principles of Yoga are timeless, holding true as much in today's time as it did centuries ago.

In Sanskrit, Yoga means "to unite". Primarily an exercise in moral and mental cultivation of poses and practices that aim towards harmonising your mind, body and soul to achieve a state of oneness with the universe. It's a spiritual practice that does not subscribe nor promote any particular faith; hence it can be practised by all. A lifestyle choice by many, the universally timeless philosophies of yoga can be incorporated into any belief system. Stress, anxiety, ill-health, unhappiness and anger can be transformed into peacefulness, vibrant health, service and love towards all creation. The techniques are important in this process but the goal should be kept firmly in mind.

The three main aspects of yoga are -

Asanas or Poses

The various yogic poses that give your body flexibility,

strengthen the muscles and even reduce fat build-up. More importantly many asanas or poses are aimed at improving the blood circulation and functioning of specific organs in your body. Keeping in mind your body's specific needs, you can work out a set of asanas for yourself.

Pranayama or Breathing

Pranayama can be called the singular most important aspect of yoga as they are means to purify the subtle energies flowing through the body. Yogic breathing techniques are an effective tool to calm, energize, harmonise and tranquillise the body and mind. All poses are to be properly coordinated with inhalation, exhalation and holding of breath. Breathing patterns if not followed correctly could result in the asana not having its desired effect.

Meditation

Mediation is a means to still the mind's restlessness. An invaluable tool in managing stress and anxiety. Regular meditation trains the mind to be calm, centred, relaxed and detached. This is extremely helpful while responding to stressful situations. It curbs overreaction, emotional outbursts and losing temper, thus giving the mind the time to rationalise and think about practical solutions.

BENEFITS OF YOGA

Unlike modern day exercises, which concentrate only on the body or on the mind, yoga techniques provide a holistic approach towards your welfare. Asanas help you to improve your strength and flexibility, so that you can carry out your daily activities unhindered. Deep breathing techniques help in removal of toxins in the body and aid in relaxation. Yoga can be a great weight loss and toning tool. It helps in healing and nourishing the body. Meditation calms your mind and gives you clarity of thought.

The major benefit of yoga is that it doesn't need any special place or equipment or clothes. All you need is mat and loose fitting clothes. Thus you can practice yoga even when you are away from your home.

Creating a Yoga Environment

Yoga can be practiced at any time of the day. Choosing to practice in the morning energizes you and the relaxed, soothing practice helps to wind up in the evening. The room should be airy, clean and well lit. Avoid air conditioners. Play soft music or yoga cassettes and keep incense sticks in the room to clean the air. If possible, keep some flowers in the room. Tips for great yoga practice

Yoga can be practiced at any time of the day. Choosing to practice in the morning energizes you and the relaxed, soothing practice helps to wind up in the evening. The room should be airy, clean and well lit. Avoid air conditioners. Play soft music or yoga cassettes and keep incense sticks in the room to clean the air. If possible, keep some flowers in the room.

Adopt a positive attitude. Set manageable goals. Start with simple exercises and as you progress, increase your intensity. Record your progress so that you can note down your experiences, thoughts and anything else. Practice yoga on an empty stomach or 3 hours after a meal. Avoid smoking, drinking, drugs, non-veg and fried foods. Keep your meals simple. Do your practice at the time convenient to you. But mornings till 9.00 am are preferable since they are neither too hot nor cold.

Yoga and Relaxation

Modern life is full of stress and problems. They put a lot of pressure on the human body. This causes a lot of life style problems like obesity, hypertension, high cholesterol, diabetes etc. People usually go to doctors and take expensive drugs for treatment. But these methods are not only expensive but also harmful in the long run. Yoga offers the cheapest and harmless solution to this problem in the form of relaxation

There are various types of relaxation vis-à-vis: physical, mental and spiritual. Physical relaxation is achieved by performing the asanas. The stretching and moving of your body during yoga practice releases the physical tension. Deep yoga breathing helps in mental relaxation. Spiritual relaxation is possible when both the mind and the body are relaxed.

Yoga and Meditation

Meditation is the one of the most important aspect of yoga. It helps in connecting the body, mind and spirit. Daily yoga meditation helps in mental purification and offers clarity of thought. It increases concentration and focus.

Meditation should be done in a clean, peaceful room at a fixed time. Sit cross-legged and keep your spine straight. Sit on the floor, a chair or on the yoga meditation cushion. Do not let anybody else use this room since your energy permeates this room and allowing others to

use this place might pollute the same. There is no need to keep eyes closed if you can concentrate with your eyes open.

Concentrate on your breath. Do not scold yourself if your mind wanders. Just bring your focus back onto your breath. If you can work with sounds better, use a sacred word or chant mantra. You can also view the image of your favourite deity in your mind's eye to help you focus.

Yoga and Lifestyle

Yoga develops a positive attitude amongst its practitioners. It teaches you the positive virtues like compassion, faith, trust and love. It makes you aware and receptive of your surroundings. It develops your strength and flexibility. Your health and complexion improves since all your body organs work to their maximum capacity. It teaches you to eat healthy, naturally produced, unrefined and unprocessed foods like fruits, vegetables etc. Yoga lays a great stress on elimination of unhealthy products like alcohol, smoking, non-veg and processed food, thereby decreasing toxic overload on your internal organs and thus they perform better.

Yoga and Pregnancy

Yoga eases many of the problems present during pregnancy like nausea, cramping, high blood pressure etc. It maintains good posture, and thus eliminates back pain. The deep yoga breathing and yoga meditation techniques cause mental relaxation and thus the pains during pregnancy and childbirth are minimized. The relaxation also aids in speedy recovery of the body after the childbirth.

However avoid poses on your back abdomen and inverted poses and back bends during this time since they can harm your baby. Also don't over stretch your muscles or increase the intensity of your practice.

Yoga and Children

A child's body is very flexible. Starting yoga at this tender age can help in increasing the height of the child. Yoga meditation aids in increasing the concentration. Since yoga concentrates on wholesome or static diet, the child learns the good eating habits and learns to love the different types of fruits and vegetables. Visualization helps in increasing the child's imagination. Try to make their session playful. Don't force them to exercise if they don't want to.

YOGA THERAPY

What is Yoga Therapy?

Yoga-chikitsa (Sanskrit) or Yoga Therapy has never been very easy to define, largely owing to the depth and breadth of the subject. And yet, simply stated, Yoga Therapy could be called a system of health care that helps treat human indispositions as naturally as possible, to alleviate pain and suffering through set of exercises, both physical and mental. Ideally, yoga therapy is preventive in nature, as is Yoga itself, while being curative in many instances, soothing in others, and restorative in most.

Yoga therapy is of modern denomination and represents man's first attempt to combine age-old concepts and techniques with contemporary medical and psychological know-how. So, where traditional Yoga was primarily concerned with spiritual transcendence, yoga therapy aims at holistic treatment of a variety of psychological or psychosomatic disorders ranging from sinusitis and asthma to emotional distress.

What is the principle of Yogic Therapy?

Yoga holds that a person's health condition depends on himself. It lays emphasis on physical, mental and emotional balance and development of a sense of harmony with all of life. There's nothing mystical about it. Nor is it external. Rather it is an inner faculty. Yoga endeavors to re-establish inner balance through a variety of ways, ranging from the gross to the subtle. Which is why it is considered a holistic art.

Rather than prescribe treatments, yoga therapy encourages awareness. Through age-old yogic techniques, we get to know ourselves better. From that knowledge, comes the ability to more easily accept and adapt to change, resulting in enhanced well-being in body, mind, heart and spirit. Hence its applicability to almost all chronic conditions.

What approach does yoga therapy take?

Contrary to modern medical science that tries to identify the pathogenic factor (be it a toxic substance, a micro-organism, or metabolic disorder) then eliminate it, Yoga takes a totally different point of view. It holds that if a person is sick there must be a deeper reason behind it – that illness doesn't arise by chance. It is the result of an imbalance, a disruption in the body-mind complex that creates the condition. Here the symptoms, the pathogenic factors, are not the issue. Yoga believes that the root cause lies somewhere else.

How is yoga therapy done?

The six steps of Yoga for overall well being:

1. Right Posture – Asanas

A set of postures that tone up the muscles and internal organs, revitalize the system, create overall awareness of the body and its function and help tranquilize the mind. they also energizes and stimulates the body's major endocrine glands. And by toning up the internal organs, they also prevent and cure many an illness.

2. Right Breathing – Pranayama

A set of simple breathing techniques that slowdown and normalize breathing while simultaneously exercising subtle influences on the entire system.

3. Right Cleansing – Kriyas

A set of easy and effortless hygienic procedures that draw the attention to the affected areas and buttress the body's own cleansing mechanisms.

4. Right Diet – Balanced Yogic Diet

Most, of not all, illnesses are in some way linked to wrong food habits. A slight modification in dietary habits can rehabilitate the entire system.

5. Right Relaxation – Shavasana

A relaxing asana done several times as part of the Yoga program. A process designed to soothe both mind and body. Yoga holds that tension is dis-ease (i.e a state if unease) and relaxation is health. To this end the whole eightfold path of Yoga is to purify the body mind complex.

6. Right Mindset – Meditation

Meditation is a technique used to stabilize the mind, increase concentration and will power, balance cellular and chakra energy and develop one-pointedness.

All these, if performed together and consistently, help rid oneself of a variety of psychosomatic disorders. Which is why, every yoga therapy session should include all these practices. They help eliminate the aggravated toxins from the system, balance the tri-doshas and stimulate the essential biochemical substances in the affected organs.

HEALTH ISSUES AND YOGA

The practice of Yoga helps bring about total relaxation of the mind and body. This, subsequently, brings about healing to occur at a deeper level of the human personality. Yoga's is a centuries-old tradition of healing practices for personal fulfillment and self realization. Even modern medical research recommends correct and regular practice of Yoga to help prevent as well as treat many types of ailments. What's more, Yoga also helps you live a healthful and stress free life.

Yoga has asanas (postures), pranayamas (breathing techniques), kriyas (cleansing techniques and special dietary recommendations for healing almost all health disorders, allergies, aches, pains etc. Most of the practices are simple yet have a magical effect on most ailments.

Practical hints on Yoga practice

With regard to Yoga Therapy for healing ailments we

suggest the following guidelines:

Become acquainted with your body and its limitations. Don't force, strain, or, least of all, judge yourself. If you experience any sort of pain, exhaustion, dizziness, shortness of breath, or any other discomfort slow down or stop, immediately.

Let go, relax, and transform yourself into a healthier, happier person, naturally. Practise at your own pace, starting with the easier asanas and pranayamas first. Slowly work up to other practices that are more challenging for you.

Never practice Yoga for 2-3 hours after meals. See that your stomach and bowels are empty. It is alright to have a few sips of water before, but not during Yoga practice. Always avoid practicing Yoga under direct sunlight.

Always wear loose and comfortable clothes, preferably cotton, to Yoga practice, to allow unrestricted movement. Keep your feet bare, use a large thick towel or Yoga mat.

Make it a point to relax for at least 10–15 minutes after each session It is always better to practise Yoga under expert guidance. Above all, consult your doctor before starting Yoga practice.

Like everyone else, we are sure that you too would be interested in doing the right set of Yoga practices. This is why we have brought out various Yoga practices specifically suited to individual ailments and needs.

Benefits of Yoga for Dancers

Whether it be Break-dance, Ballet, Burlesque, Belly

Dance, Tribal, or Hawaiian, every dancer relies on flexibility, confidence, and balancing or centering of the body. Yoga is beneficial to all dancers for these reasons and many others such as strength, posture improvement, improved circulation, and purifying the body from toxins.

Ashtanga Vinyasa Yoga or Power Yoga as it is referred to in the West is a form of Hatha Yoga. It focuses on linking the postures with the breathing exercises into a flowing Yoga practice. Because of these unique capabilities of Ashtanga Yoga, it warms up the body before deep stretching to stretch more safely. Also stamina is created; this is beneficial to the dancer's body for overall performance endurance.

In Ashtanga Yoga, the first half of the practice is a warm up (Sun Salutations) and standing asanas. The second half of the practice is a seated asana series and finishing sequence. The Sun Salutations are dynamic, getting the blood flowing, the heart rate up and using breath work to bring fresh oxygen to the blood improving circulation. The standing asanas are very beneficial for the dancer's body. They stress on balance, focus, strength, confidence, and equalizing/balancing both sides of the body. The seated asana sequence comprises many stretches for the hamstrings, hip openers, and core strengtheners. The seated asana series postures are very therapeutic for the dancer working out any remaining stress, tension, and toxins from the body.

One of the most precious gifts Yoga offers is the mind/body experience. It brings clarity and peace to the mind. At may dance classes, Yoga and Dance come together complementing each other bringing Eastern spirituality and movement to the west.

Yoga enables a dancer to attain the following physical abilities :

- Balance
- Clarity of the Mind
- Confidence
- Flexibility
- Improved Circulation
- Improved Hip Mobility/Flexibility
- Improved Lung Capacity
- Posture Improvement
- Purification of the Body
- Stamina
- Strength/Muscle Toning

- Stress Relief

Suggested Yoga Poses for Dancers

Baddha Konasana (Bound angle posture): This asana opens up your groins, opens up your hips, and stretches your spine. Overall it is great for dancers, particularly for body undulations/wave-ups thru the spine, hip figure eights of all kinds and isolations.

Padangusthasana (Foot and Big Toe Posture & Hand to Foot Posture): This asana purifies toxins that collect in your intestines and abdomen. This asana stretches the hamstrings and calves and is fantastic for all traveling steps such as camels and walking hip shimmy plus for footwork.

Vrikshasana (Tree pose):

This asana stretches the front of your chest and hips. It strengthens your quadriceps and spine, balances and tones up your spine. It also tones up your legs and feet. The Tree pose is also an excellent hip opener that works

you out for snake-

like arm movements, arm stamina and spinal ripples and undulations.

Utthita Trikonasana (Extended three angle posture)

This asana stretches the front and back of your legs. It strengthens your quadriceps. It also opens up your hips, chest, and elongates your spine. It realigns your skeletal system. Hip shimmies of all kinds can be achieved & improved with this asana.

Prasarita Padottanasana (Spread leg/foot stretching postures)

This asana stretches your low back, calves, and chest. It also strengthens your quadriceps and hip flexors. The benefits are that your hamstring and abductor muscles are stretched while your head is below the heart.

This series of postures also enhance hip flexibility and tone up your abdominal muscles. They also correct spinal abnormalities.

10

YOGA FOR MEN

As a general rule, men are supposed to be strong - physically and mentally. Besides, men are known to engage in more strenuous activities of life. They love to play sports and lift weights to keep a healthy figure. Besides, their jobs are usually more physically demanding such as carpentry and construction work. Add to that the pressure they have to undergo for being the head of the family and being a part of the so-called 'stronger sex' and men definitely have a strong case for practicing Yoga.

But it is important for each and every man to know that this stereotype of the 'stronger sex' may soon isolate them feel more from women. That is, if they continue to believe in it too much. However, through Yoga, particularly meditation, men will be able to look deeper into themselves, listen to their inner voice, and develop a more positive view on life. In this way they will also enhance their relations with other people.

As men are more into sports and other physical activities, the practice of Asanas will help offset any physical irregularities arising from such tasks. For example, in sports like golf or tennis, there is a tendency for some muscles to be used more than their respective symmetrical counterparts (i.e. right and left arms, legs, etc.) Asanas help by loosening tightness in the muscles, thereby bringing the body back into its natural alignment.

Yogasanas for Men:

Surya Namaskar – Sun Salutation, Sukhasana - Easy Pose, Headstand Pose – Sirsasana, Virasana – Hero Pose, Navasana – Boat Pose, Bhujangasana – Cobra pose, Shalabhasana – Locust Pose, Dhanurasana – Bow Pose, Chakrasana – Wheel Pose, Janu Sirshasana – Head to one knee pose, Paschimottanasana – Head To Knees Pose, Ustrasana – Camel Pose, Adho Mukha Svanasana – Downward Facing Dog, Garudasana – Eagle Pose, Viparita Karani – Legs Up the Wall, Sarvangasana – Shoulder Stand, Halasana – Plough Pose, Sethu Bandha Sarvangasana– Bridge Pose, Parsvottonasana – Pyramid Pose, Supta Padangusthasana – Reclined Big Toe Pose, Parivritta Parsva Konasana – Revolved Side Angle Pose, Parivritta Ardha Chandrasana – Revolved Half Moon Pose.

1. Sun Salutation (Surya Namaskar)

The Sun Salutation or Surya Namaskar is a Yoga Pose which limbers up the whole body in preparation for the Yoga Asanas. It is a graceful sequence of twelve Yoga positions performed as one continuous exercise. Learn how to practice Sun Salutation in this section.

The Sun Salutation or Surya Namaskar limbers up the whole body in preparation for the yoga asanas. It is a graceful sequence of twelve yoga positions performed as one continuous exercise. Each position counteracts the one before, stretching the body in a different way and alternately expanding and contracting the chest to regulate the breathing. Practiced daily it will great flexibility to your spine and joints and trims your waist.

One round of Sun Salutation consists of two sequences, the first leading with the right foot in positions 4 and 9 (as illustrated), the second leading with the left. Keep your hands in one place from positions 3 to 10 and try to coordinate your movements with your breathing. Start by practicing four rounds and gradually build up to twelve rounds.

Method 1. Stand erect with feet together and palms in the prayer position in front of your chest. Make sure your weight is evenly distributed. Exhale.

2. Inhaling, stretch your arms up and arch back from the waist, pushing the hips out, legs straight. Relax your neck.

3. Exhaling, fold forward, and press your palms down, fingertips in line with toes - bend your knees if necessary.

4. Inhaling, bring the right (or left) leg back and place the knee on the floor. Arch back and look up, lifting your chin.

5. Retaining the breath, bring the other leg back and support your weight on hands and toes. Keep your head and body in line and look at the floor between your hands.

6. Exhaling, lower your knees, then your chest and then your forehead, keeping your hips up and toes curled under.

7. Inhaling, lower your hips, point your toes and bend

#1

#2

#3

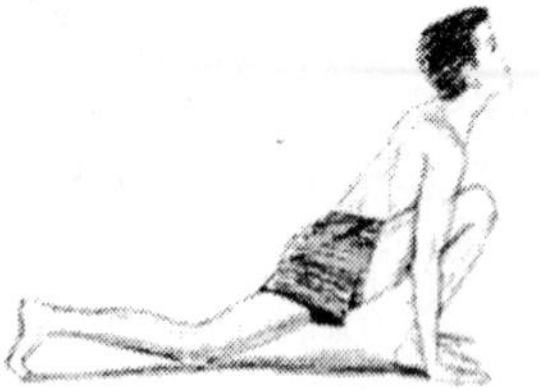

#4

#5

#6

#7

#8

#9

#10

#11

#12

back. Keep legs together and shoulders down. Look up and back.

8. Exhaling, curl your toes under, raise your hips and pivot into an inverted "V" shape. Try to push your heels and head down keep your shoulders back.

9. Inhaling, step forward and place the right (or left) foot between your hands. Rest the other knee on the floor and look up, as in position 4.

10. Exhaling, bring the other leg forward and bend down from the waist keeping your palms as in position 3.

11. Inhaling, stretch your arms forward, then up and back over your head and bend back slowly from the waist, as in position 2.

12. Exhaling, gently come back to an upright position and bring your arms down by your side.

2. Sukhasana (Easy Pose)

This is one of the classic Meditative Poses and is usually performed after doing the Corpse Pose. The Easy Pose helps in straightening the spine, slowing down metabolism, promoting inner tranquility, and keeping your mind still.

After relaxing in the Corpse Pose for a few minutes, come up and sit in the Easy Yoga Pose or Sukhasana for Pranayama and the neck, shoulder and eye exercises. This Yoga Asana is one of the classic Meditative Poses, which help to straighten the spine, slow down metabolism and still the mind. If you find that holding the Yoga Pose is uncomfortable, place a folded Yoga Blanket under the back of your buttocks.

In order to stretch the leg muscles evenly, be sure put each leg alternately on top in this Yoga Posture. When you are ready, substitute the Half Lotus or Lotus at this point.

Method: Sitting on the floor and bend your knees. Clasp your arms around them and press them to your chest to make the spine erect. Now, release your arms and cross your legs, letting your knees drop down toward the floor. Keep your head and body straight.

3. Headstand Pose – Sirsasana

Benefits:

Calms the mind. Strengthens the arms, legs, and spine. Improves balance.

Note: Wondering whether to invert while menstruating?

Instructions:

1. Come to your hands and knees with the wrists underneath the shoulders and the knees underneath the hips.

2. Bring your elbows to the floor forearm's distance apart.

3. Interlace your fingers, tucking the outermost pinky underneath.

4. Place the crown of your head on the floor cupped by your interlaced fingers.

5. Bring the hips up as if coming into Downward Facing Dog.

6. Walk the feet in towards your head until your hips are over your shoulders.

7. Kick up one leg and then the other.

8. Press down strongly into your forearms to keep all your weight from coming into your neck and head.

9. Reach up through the balls of your feet and rotate the thigh bones inward slightly. Hold for at least 10 breaths.

Beginners:

Look at the step-by-step illustrated guide for photos of each step. Practice the pose at the wall. Try to move further from the wall each time. Try removing one foot and then the other from the wall to practice balancing.

Advanced

Try the following variations: Bring both legs up at the same time keeping them straight. Lower down the same way, holding the pose with the legs at 90 degrees. Bring the legs into a lotus position. Release your interlaced fingers and bring the forearms flat on the floor. Lift your head off the floor coming into forearm stand.

4. Virasana – Hero Pose

Virasana is a balm for tired legs at the end of the day, as well as an alternative to Lotus for seated meditation.

(veer-AHS-anna)

vira = man, hero, chief

Technique

1. Kneel on the floor (on a folded blanket to pad your knees, shins, and feet if necessary), with your thighs

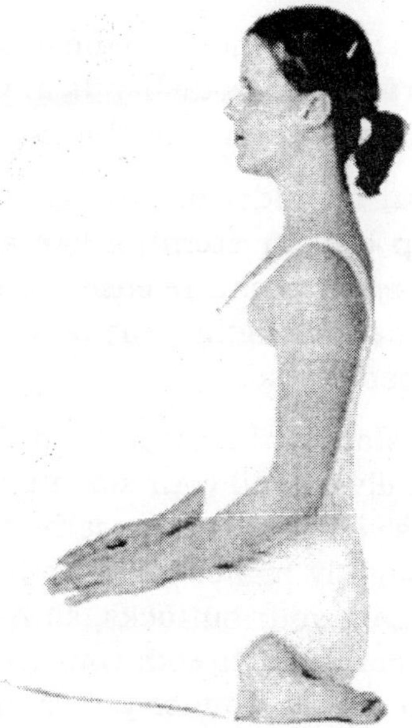

perpendicular to the floor, and touch your inner knees together. Slide your feet apart, slightly wider than your hips, with the tops of the feet flat on the floor. Angle your big toes slightly in toward each other and press the top of each foot evenly on the floor.

2. Exhale and sit back halfway, with your torso leaning slightly forward. Wedge your thumbs into the backs of your knees and draw the skin and flesh of the calf muscles toward the heels. Then sit down between your feet.

3. If your buttocks don't comfortably rest on the floor, raise them on a block or thick book placed between the feet. Make sure both sitting bones are evenly supported. Allow a thumb's-width space between the inner heels and the outer hips. Turn your thighs inward and press

the heads of the thigh bones into the floor with the bases of your palms. Then lay your hands in your lap, one on the other, palms up, or on your thighs, palms down.

4. Firm your shoulder blades against the back ribs and lift the top of your sternum like a proud warrior. Widen the collarbones and release the shoulder blades away from the ears. Lengthen the tailbone into the floor to anchor the back torso.

5. At first stay in this pose from 30 seconds to 1 minute. Gradually extend your stay up to 5 minutes. To come out, press your hands against the floor and lift your buttocks up, slightly higher than the heels. Cross your ankles underneath your buttocks, sit back over the feet and onto the floor, then stretch your legs out in front of you. It may feel good to bounce your knees up and down a few times on the floor.

Benefits

1. Stretches the thighs, knees, and ankles

2. Strengthens the arches

3. Improves digestion and relieves gas

4. Helps relieve the symptoms of menopause

5. Reduces swelling of the legs during pregnancy (through second trimester)

6. Therapeutic for high blood pressure and asthma

5. Navasana – Boat Pose

An abdominal and deep hip flexor strengthener, Boat Pose requires you to balance on the tripod of your sitting bones and tailbone.

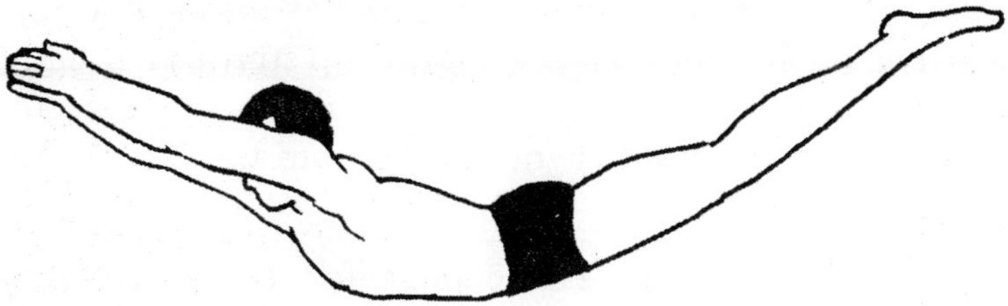

Technique

1. Sit on the floor with your legs straight in front of you. Press your hands on the floor a little behind your hips, fingers pointing toward the feet, and strengthen the arms. Lift through the top of the sternum and lean back slightly. As you do this make sure your back doesn't round; continue to lengthen the front of your torso between the pubis and top sternum. Sit on the "tripod" of your two sitting bones and tailbone.

2. Exhale and bend your knees, then lift your feet off the floor, so that the thighs are angled about 45-50 degrees relative to the floor. Lengthen your tailbone into the floor and lift your pubis toward your navel. If possible, slowly straighten your knees, raising the tips of your toes slightly above the level of your eyes. If this isn't possible remain with your knees bent, perhaps lifting the shins parallel to the floor.

3. Stretch your arms alongside the legs, parallel to each other and the floor. Spread the shoulder blades across your back and reach strongly out through the fingers. If this isn't possible, keep the hands on the floor beside your hips or hold on to the backs of your thighs.

4. While the lower belly should be firm, it shouldn't get hard and thick. Try to keep the lower belly relatively

flat. Press the heads of the thigh bones toward the floor to help anchor the pose and lift the top sternum. Breathe easily. Tip the chin slightly toward the sternum so the base of the skull lifts lightly away from the back of the neck.

5. At first stay in the pose for 10-20 seconds. Gradually increase the time of your stay to 1 minute. Release the legs with an exhalation and sit upright on an inhalation.

Benefits

1. Strengthens the abdomen, hip flexors, and spine.

2. Stimulates the kidneys, thyroid and prostate glands, and intestines.

3. Helps relieve stress.

4. Improves digestion.

6. Bhujangasana – Cobra pose

Technique

1. Lie prone on the floor. Stretch your legs back, tops of the feet on the floor. Spread your hands on the floor under your shoulders. Hug the elbows back into your body.

2. Press the tops of the feet and thighs and the pubis firmly into the floor.

3. On an inhalation, begin to straighten the arms to lift the chest off the floor, going only to the height at which you can maintain a connection through your pubis to your legs. Press the tailbone toward the pubis and lift the pubis toward the navel. Narrow the hip points. Firm

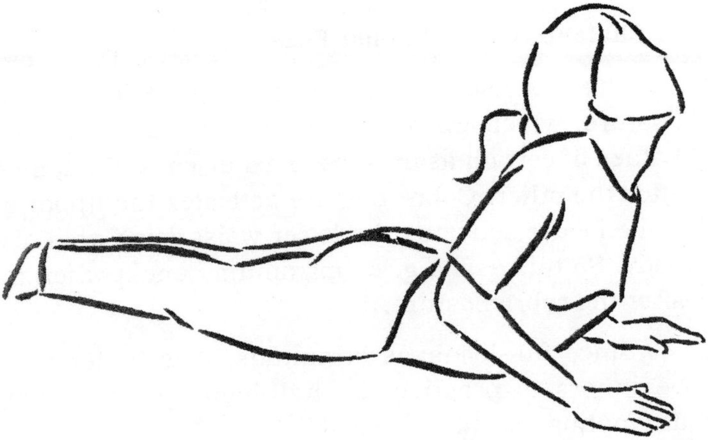

but don't harden the buttocks.

4. Firm the shoulder blades against the back, puffing the side ribs forward. Lift through the top of the sternum but avoid pushing the front ribs forward, which only hardens the lower back. Distribute the backbend evenly throughout the entire spine.

5. Hold the pose anywhere from 15 to 30 seconds, breathing easily. Release back to the floor with an exhalation.

Build up the exercise in a quiet way. When the lower back is stiff, this exercise may cause the lower back to feel a little painful and uncomfortable.

This is normal and will pass away as the stiffness decreases. In spite of the uncomfortable feeling that you may sometimes experience, this exercise is highly recommended for people with a stiff lower back or pain in the lower back.

7. Shalabhasana – Locust Pose

Salabha Asana is a reverse posture to the Cobra Posture, which gives a backward bend to the spine. Values of certain asanas are maximised when done one after the other. Cobra posture activates the upper area while locust activates the lower waist down area of the body. So this asana gives maximum benefit when done after the cobra posture.

Since full-locust is strenuous, it is better for the beginners to practice the half-locust posture before attempting the full-locust.

Full Locust Posture

Technique

1. Lie face down on the floor on your stomach, hands stretched backwards close to the body and the legs straight. Making fists of the hands bring them together beneath the thighs with the wrists touching.

2. Inhale as much air as you can. Holding your breath make your head straight and put the chin on the floor (on a folded blanket or towel). Tighten both the legs

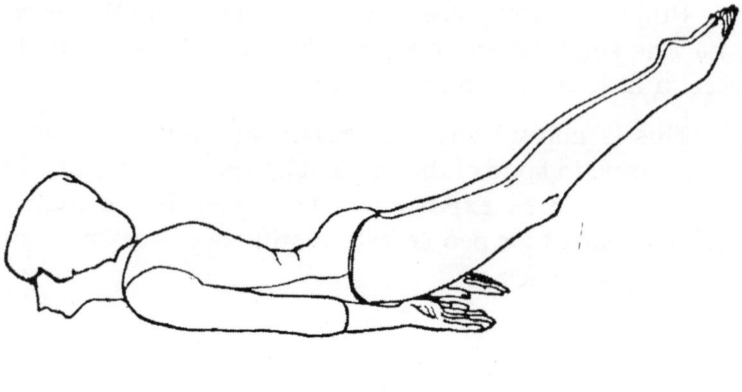

and lift them up as high as you can. Do not bend the knees.

3. Remain in the same posture for a few seconds.

4. Exhale and simultaneously lower the legs slowly to the floor. Do not drop the legs. By the time the legs touch the floor you should finish exhaling. You have completed one round of a most strenuous posture. Relax.

Restrictions :

1. Start with three rounds on the first day. Do not practice more than four rounds. While doing the asana special attention should be given for keeping the legs tight. Do not bend or fold on the knees. In the initial stage, do not try to retain in the same position excessively. Relax for about 6 10 8 seconds between each round.

2. For the beginners, it is always better to practice the half-locust posture before attempting the full-locust. When you first attempt the locust, you may be disappointed to find that your feet rise only slightly from the floor. Do not be discouraged. This will improve rapidly with practice.

Half - Locust Posture

For the half locust, the position, the breathing and the body conditioning are as same as the full-locust. The only difference is that you lift one leg up at a time. Lift legs alternatively. Do not twist the hips or bend the knee. Repeat lifting 2-4 times each.

Benefits :

The locust brings flexibility to the cervical (upper back) region and strength to the lower back. Brings a rich blood supply to the spine and the whole upper area. Favourably activates the kidneys, liver and all the organs of the lower part of the body. Increases abdominal pressure, regulating intestinal function and strengthening the abdominal walls and relieves back pain.

8. Dhanurasana – Bow Pose

Dhanur Asana gives a full backward bend to the whole of the spine and all the muscles of the back from the neck to the lower back or lumber region. Bhujanga, Locust and Dhanur forrns a series of exercises beneficial to the body when practiced together. As the forward bend flexes the spine, the bow extends it.

Technique

1. Lie on your stomach with your arms stretched on both sides. Place your right or left cheek on the floor. Bend the knees, bringing the feet up. Bring the heels close to the buttock area. Reach back to hold the ankles with your hands. The knees and the ankles should be closer to one another.

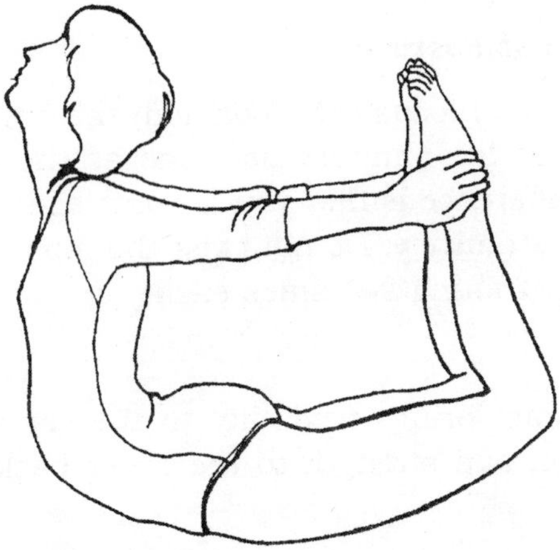

2. Inhale as much air as you can. Straighten up your neck and head. Holding the breath and keeping the arms straight, arch the entire body upwards. Lift the head, chest and thighs off the floor. Remain in this position for 5 to 6 seconds.

3. Exhale and return to the floor smoothly. Keep holding the ankles while you return to the first position. Put the cheek back on the floor and breath normally.

4. Leave the ankles and let the legs gradually return to the floor. Bring the arms and hands to the floor on both sides and relax for 6 to 8 seconds. You have completed one round of bow posture.

Note :

In this asana, all your efforts should be to give a backward pull with the legs and not a forward pull with the hands. Thus the knees remain on the floor and the only portion which is lifted and pulled upwards is the area above the abdomen, i.e. the chest and the head area.

Restrictions :

Start with two rounds on the first day and gradually to a maximum of four rounds. In the first position in case you find it difficult to hold the ankles then hold the toes.

Do not attempt the bow while pregnant, as these asana increases the pressure on the abdomen.

Benefits :

Activates and strengthen all the major and minor joints of the body. Strengthens all the abdominal muscles and organs. Develops digestive power and removes extra weight and fat from the stomach and waist areas.

Enhance the elasticity of the spine. Chest, lungs and neck are strengthened and activated, benefiting people suffering from asthma and other respiratory problems. For women, it corrects menstrual and other troubles related to reproductive organs.

9. Chakrasana – Wheel Pose

Technique

1. Lie on your back, feet apart

2. Bend both your knees and place your feet flat on the floor near your buttocks.

3. Place your palms under your shoulders with the fingers pointed towards the shoulders and the elbows shoulder width apart.

4. Inhale and press your palms into the floor

5. Straighten your arms to lift your shoulders and head off the floor.

6. Press your feet into the floor, inhale and lift your

hips up, rolling your spine off the floor to form a semi-circular arch or wheel.

7. Keep your legs and arms as straight as possible to lift your hips and chest up. Look behind.

8. Breathe normally and hold the pose for 2-4 breaths.

9. To release, exhale and slowly bend your elbows to lower your head, neck and then shoulders to the floor.

10. Bend your knees to slowly roll your spine and hips back to the floor.

11. It is very important to relax for a while after doing this pose.

10. Janu Sirshasana – Head to one knee pose

Technique

1. Sit on the floor with your legs out.

2. Bend one leg, bring the heel of your foot as close to your right groin as possible.

3. For comfort you may place a pillow under your bent knee. Ensure that your spine is straight.

4. Now exhale and begin to move forward slowly, keeping your back as straight as possible.

5. Breathing normally, stretch forwards and straighten your spine.

6. Maintain the position for as long as you can, breathing normally.

7. Move forward as far as you can, stretch your arms and try to hold your foot.

8. To return to an upright position, stretch forwards, inhale and stretch your arms up.

9. Repeat the pose with the next foot bent.

11. Paschimottanasana – Head To Knees Pose

Relax your body and mind, stretch your hamstrings, shoulders, and spine, relieve stress, and improve your posture and concentration by practicing the Seated Forward Bend. Learn how to do this properly and achieve maximum results.

This forward bend gives a complete stretching to the neck, the back, the hamstrings and calves. At the same time, it directs your attention inward. You stimulate the entire nervous system and learn to find stillness and relaxation during a period of effort or even discomfort when doing this stretching exercise.

Method

Tip 1: Sit down with your legs stretched. The legs lie side by side and the toes point upwards. Stretch your lower back and raise your arms. Look forward, lengthen

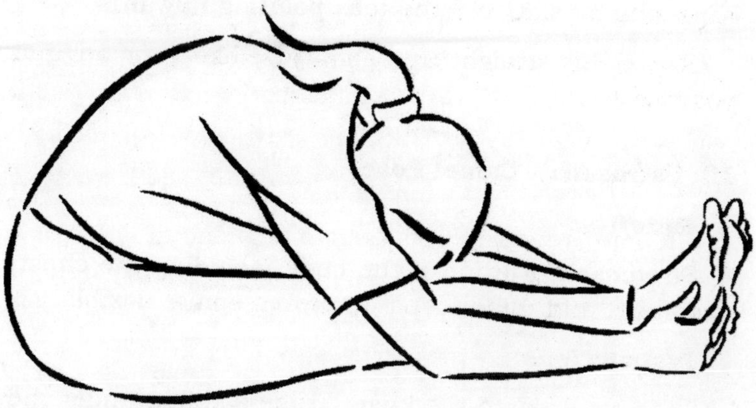

your back, and keep the chest and your breathing free.

Tip 2: Slowly bend forward, stretch your crown upward and try not to lose the supporting dynamism of the lower back. See to it that your legs do not move or tilt.

Tip 3: The moment you notice that you can only bend further by bending the lower back, move your hands to your lower legs, ankles or feet. Lightly pull your legs, ankles or feet and continue stretching.

Keep your shoulders down. Breathe in and out across the entire length of your spinal column deeply and in a relaxed way. Everytime you exhale, you should bend further towards your legs without losing the length in your back and the dynamism in the lower back. When you lose the dynamism in the lower back, you will notice that you lose a major part of the stretching and you will have a hard time breathing.

Step 4: Stretch out your arms forward.

Step 5: Slowly raise your upper body. Keep your legs

lying side by side and the toes pointing upwards.

Step 6: Sit straight up again, just like your original position.

12. Ustrasana – Camel Pose

Benefits:

Stretches the front of the body including the chest, abdomen, and quadriceps. Improves spinal flexibility.

Instructions:

1. Come up onto the knees. Take padding under the knees if they are sensitive.

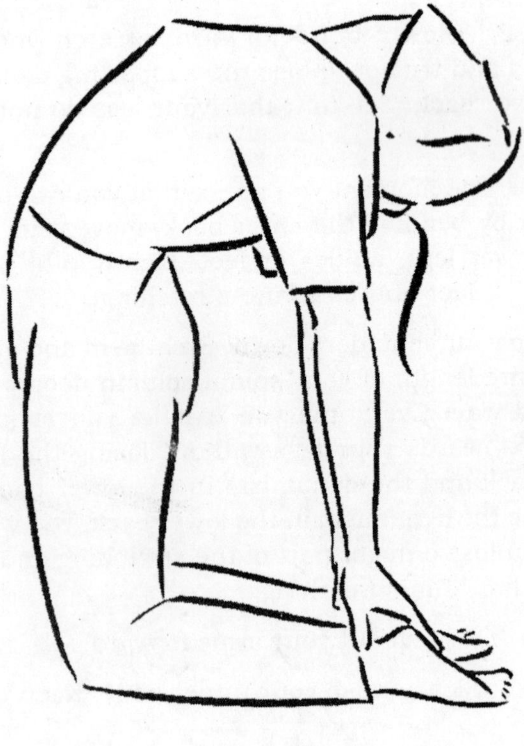

2. Draw the hands up the side of the body as you start to open the chest.

3. Reach the hands back one at a time to grasp the heels.

4. Bring the hips forward so that they are over the knees.

5. Let the head come back, opening the thoat.

Beginners:

Curl the toes under and come to the balls of your feet if you cannot reach the heels when the feet are flat. Or use blocks on either side of the knees.

13. Adho Mukha Svanasana – Downward Facing Dog

(AH-doh MOO-kah shvah-NAHS-anna)

adho = downward

mukha = face

svana = dog

Technique

1. Come onto the floor on your hands and knees. Set your knees directly below your hips and your hands slightly forward of your shoulders. Spread your palms, index fingers parallel or slightly turned out, and turn your toes under.

2. Exhale and lift your knees away from the floor. At first keep the knees slightly bent and the heels lifted away from the floor. Lengthen your tailbone away from the back of your pelvis and press it lightly toward the pubis. Against this resistance, lift the sitting bones toward the ceiling, and from your inner ankles draw the inner legs up into the groins.

3. Then with an exhalation, push your top thighs back and stretch your heels onto or down toward the floor. Straighten your knees but be sure not to lock them. Firm the outer thighs and roll the upper thighs inward slightly. Narrow the front of the pelvis.

4. Firm the outer arms and press the bases of the index fingers actively into the floor. From these two points lift along your inner arms from the wrists to the tops of the shoulders. Firm your shoulder blades against your back, then widen them and draw them toward the tailbone. Keep the head between the upper arms; don't let it hang.

5. Adho Mukha Svanasana is one of the poses in the traditional Sun Salutation sequence. It's also an excellent yoga asana all on its own. Stay in this pose anywhere from 1 to 3 minutes. Then bend your knees to the floor with an exhalation and rest in Child's Pose.

14. Garudasana – Eagle Pose

In Sanskrit Garuda means an eagle. This asans is difficult for beginners. But with regular practice and patience they can do it well.

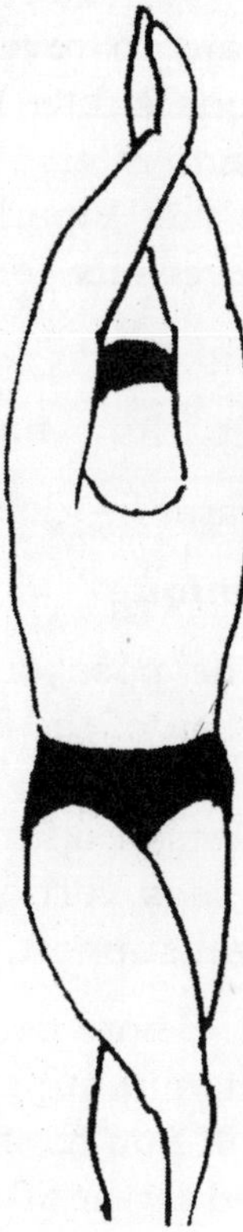

Technique

On a folded blanket stand upright. Bend the left knees slightly and twist the right leg over the left leg so that the right in step is touched behind the left calf. Remain in this pose for 20 seconds and breathe slowly. Gaze at a visible white spot or point. Come to the original position and relax.

15. Viparita Karani – Legs Up the Wall

Said to reverse the normal downward flow of a precious subtle fluid called amrita (immortal) or soma (extract) in the Hatha Yoga Pradipika, modern yogis agree that Viparita Karani may have the power to cure whatever ails you.

(vip-par-ee-tah car-AHN-ee)

viparita = turned around, reversed, inverted

karani = doing, making, action

Technique

The pose described here is a passive, supported variation of the Shoulderstand-like Viparita Karani. For your support you'll need one or two thickly folded blankets or a firm round bolster. You'll also need to rest your legs vertically (or nearly so) on a wall or other upright support.

1. Before performing the pose, determine two things about your support: its height and its distance from the wall. If you're stiffer, the support should be lower and placed farther from the wall; if you're more flexible, use a higher support that is closer to the wall. Your distance from the wall also depends on your height: if you're shorter move closer to the wall, if taller move farther from the wall. Experiment with the position of your support until you find the placement that works for you.

2. Start with your support about 5 to 6 inches away

from the wall. Sit sideways on right end of the support, with your right side against the wall (left-handers can substitute "left" for "right" in these instructions). Exhale and, with one smooth movement, swing your legs up onto the wall and your shoulders and head lightly down onto the floor. The first few times you do this, you may ignominiously slide off the support and plop down with your buttocks on the floor. Don't get discouraged. Try lowering the support and/or moving it slightly further off the wall until you gain some facility with this movement, then move back closer to the wall.

3. Your sitting bones don't need to be right against the wall, but they should be "dripping" down into the space between the support and the wall. Check that the front of your torso gently arches from the pubis to the top of the shoulders. If the front of your torso seems flat, then you've probably slipped a bit off the support. Bend your knees, press your feet into the wall and lift your pelvis off the support a few inches, tuck the support a little higher up under your pelvis, then lower your pelvis onto the support again.

4. Lift and release the base of your skull away from the back of your neck and soften your throat. Don't push your chin against your sternum; instead let your sternum lift toward the chin. Take a small roll (made from a towel for example) under your neck if the cervical spine feels flat. Open your shoulder blades away from the spine and release your hands and arms out to your sides, palms up.

5. Keep your legs relatively firm, just enough to hold them vertically in place. Release the heads of the thigh bones and the weight of your belly deeply into your torso, toward the back of the pelvis. Soften your eyes and turn

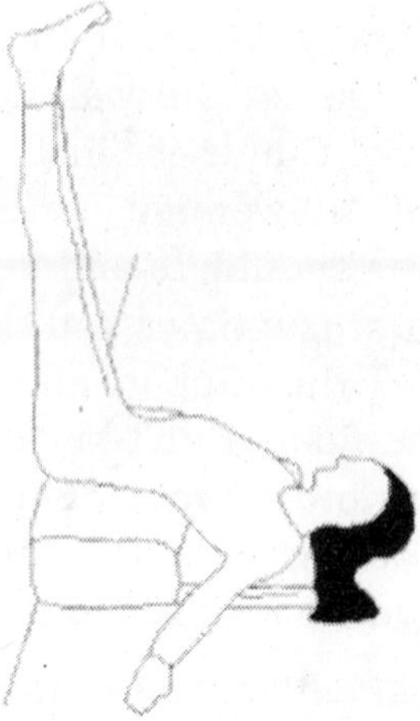

them down to look into your heart.

6. Stay in this pose anywhere from 5 to 15 minutes. Be sure not to twist off the support when coming out. Instead, slide off the support onto the floor before turning to the side. You can also bend your knees and push your feet against the wall to lift your pelvis off the support. Then slide the support to one side, lower your pelvis to the floor, and turn to the side. Stay on your side for a few breaths, and come up to sitting with an exhalation.

Benefits

1. Relieves tired or cramped legs and feet

2. Gently stretches the back legs, front torso, and the back of the neck

3. Relieves mild backache

4. Calms the mind

16. Sarvangasana – Shoulder Stand

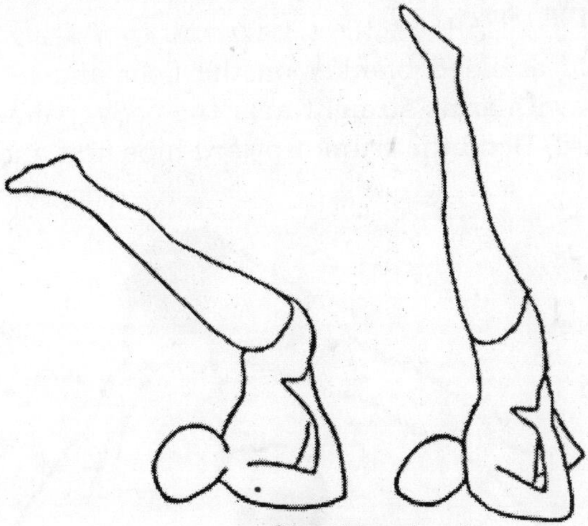

Shoulderstand

In Sanskrit "sarva" menas "All" or "entire" and "anga" means limb of body. Sarvang means the entire body or all the limbs. This is one of the most powerful and popular asans. The malfunctioning of thyrid gland can harm all other glands.

Technique

Spread a blanket on the floor and lie flat on your back. Then slowly raise the legs up lifting the trunk and hips vertically. The chin should be firmly pressed against the chest. Remain in this pose for a few minutes and breathe slowly and deeply and concentrate on the thyroid gland which is at the root of the neck.

17. Halasana – Plough Pose

In sanskrit "Hala" means "Plough". This pose is named so because it bears close resmbles to a plough (tool). It is one of the few asanas named after a tool. It is part and continuation of sarvangasan.

Technique

Spread a folded blanket on the floor and lie flat on the back with arms straight near the body, palms facing downward. Bend the trunk upward hips first and slowly

lower the legs over the head till the toes touch the floor. Remain in this pose for a couple of minutes. Return to the original position and relax.

18. Setu Bandha Sarvangasana—Bridge Pose

SET-too BAHN-dah)

setu = dam, dike, or bridge

bandha = lock

Technique

1. Lie supine on the floor, and if necessary, place a thickly folded blanket under your shoulders to protect your neck. Bend your knees and set your feet on the floor, heels as close to the sitting bones as possible.

2. Exhale and, pressing your inner feet and arms actively into the floor, push your tailbone upward toward the pubis, firming (but not hardening) the buttocks, and lift the buttocks off the floor. Keep your thighs and inner feet parallel. Clasp the hands below your pelvis and extend through the arms to help you stay on the tops of your shoulders.

3. Lift your buttocks until the thighs are about parallel to the floor. Keep your knees directly over the heels, but push them forward, away from the hips, and lengthen the tailbone toward the backs of the knees. Lift the pubis toward the navel.

4. Lift your chin slightly away from the sternum and, firming the shoulder blades against your back, press the top of the sternum toward the chin. Firm the outer arms, broaden the shoulder blades, and try to lift the space between them at the base of the neck (where it's resting

on the blanket) up into the torso.

5. Stay in the pose anywhere from 30 seconds to 1 minute. Release with an exhalation, rolling the spine slowly down onto the floor.

Benefits

1. Stretches the chest, neck, and spine

2. Calms the brain and helps alleviate stress and mild depression

3. Stimulates abdominal organs, lungs, and thyroid

4. Rejuvenates tired legs

5. Improves digestion

6. Helps relieve the symptoms of menopause

7. Relieves menstrual discomfort when done supported

8.Reduces anxiety, fatigue, backache, headache, and insomnia

9. Therapeutic for asthma, high blood pressure, osteoporosis, and sinusitis

19. Parsvottonasana – Pyramid Pose

Type of pose: Standing, forward bend

Benefits:

Stretches and strengthens the legs, especially the hamstrings.

1. From Downward Facing Dog – Adho Muhka Svanasana,bring the right foot forward next to the right hand.

2. Straighten the right leg as you step the left foot forward so that the feet are about three feet apart. The left foot is facing forward with sole flat on the floor.

3. Bring the body to an upright position and make sure the hips are squared towards the front of the mat.

4. Lengthen the spine on an inhale.

5. On the next exhale, deepen the right hip crease as you come into a forward bend bringing the hands to the floor or onto blocks if they don't reach the floor.

6. On each inhale, lengthen the spine.

20. Supta Padangusthasana – Reclined Big Toe Pose

Benefits:

Gently stretches the hamstrings and calves. Can help reduce back pain by addressing Flat Low Back Posture.

Technique

1. Come to lie on your back with the legs outstretched.

2. Bend the right knee and hug it into your chest.

3. Place a yoga strap around the ball of the right foot. Hold the ends of the strap with each hand.

4. Straighten the right leg up toward the ceiling while holding tightly to the strap.

5. Stretch the right leg upwards with the foot flexed, but keep the ball of the hip joint resting in the socket and both sides of your butt equally pressing into the floor

6. Keep the left foot flexed and the left leg pressing towards the floor.

21. Parivritta Parsva Konasana – Revolved Side Angle Pose

Since most students can't easily keep their back heel down in this pose, a modified version will be described here with the back heel raised off the floor. See Deepen the Pose below for a brief description of the full pose.

(par-ee-vrt-tah parsh-vah-cone-AHS-anna) parivrtta = to turn around, revolve

parsva = side, flank

kona = angle

Technique

1. Stand in Tadasana. With an exhalation, step or lightly jump your feet 3½ to 4 feet apart. Rest your hands on your hips. Turn your right foot out to the right 90 degrees and turn your left foot in slightly to the right. Align the right heel with the left heel. Firm your thighs and turn your right thigh outward, so that the center of the kneecap is in line with the center of the right ankle.

2. Exhale and turn your torso to the right until you're facing directly out over the right leg; as you do this, lift your left heel off the floor and spin on the ball of the foot until the inner left foot is parallel to the inner right foot. Then exhale again and bend your right knee. If possible,

bring the right thigh parallel to the floor. Keep your left leg active by pressing the thigh up toward the ceiling and extending strongly through the left heel. At the same time, resist the lift of the left thigh by pressing the tailbone toward the pubis.

3. With another exhale turn further to the right and lean the torso down, placing the left hand on the floor inside the right foot. Dig your right thumb into the right hip crease and push the thighbone down toward the floor. Firm the shoulder blades into the back ribs and lean the torso back slightly, away from the inner thigh. Stay

in this position for a few breaths.

4. If this position seems challenging enough, stay for the recommended time. If you want to go further, bend your left elbow and bring it to the outside of the right knee. Resist the knee and elbow against each other. If possible, straighten your left elbow and reach the hand toward the floor (if you can't reach the floor, support your hand on a block). You can keep your right hand on your hip, or stretch it over the back of the right ear with the palm facing down. Then turn your head to look at the right arm. As in all twists lengthen and soften the belly, extend the spine with each inhalation, and increase the twist as you exhale.

5. Stay for 30 seconds to 1 minute. Inhale to come up, exhale to release the twist. Reverse the feet and repeat for the same length of time to the left. Then return to Tadasana.

Benefits

1. Strengthens and stretches the legs, knees, and ankles

2. Stretches the groins, spine, chest and lungs, and shoulders

3. Stimulates abdominal organs

4. Increases stamina

5. Improves digestion and aids elimination

6. Improves balance

22. Parivritta Ardha Chandrasana – Revolved Half Moon Pose

Type of pose

Standing, balancing, twisting

Benefits:

Strengthen the ankles, and thighs, improves balance, cleanses the organs

Technique

1. From Trikonasana, soften the right knee and bring the right hand to your hip.

2. Place the left hand flat on the floor about a foot in front of the right foot.

3. Begin to straighten the right leg while simultaneously kicking up the left leg parallel to the floor.

4. Twist the torso towards the right, bringing the right arm up toward the ceiling and the gaze up to the right fingertips.

5. Keep both hips squared towards the floor.

Beginners

Take a block underneath the left hand. Do the pose near a wall and bring the left foot to the wall when you kick up the left leg.

SUGGESTED PRANAYAMAS FOR MEN:

Kapalabhatti, Anuloma-Viloma, Ujjayi, Brahmari, Bhastrika.

1. Kapalabhatti

Make sure your stomach is empty (do not eat for two hours prior to practicing kapalabhatti.) Sit in a comfortable cross-legged position, with a straight spine. This allows your energy to circulate more freely in your body. Keep your eyes closed and mentally gaze at your third eye center, the point in between your eyebrows.

Inhale fully. Exhale all the air out.

Inhale to a comfortable level and begin a round of short, sharp and forceful exhalations through the nose,

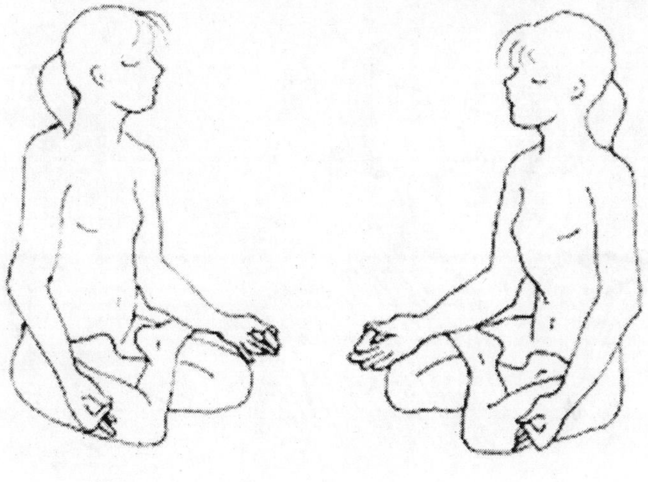

forcefully contracting your abdomen on every exhalation. Inhalations happen automatically, don't pay attention to them. Concentrate on the exhales. Draw your diaphragm in and up on every exhalation and make sure that every exhalation is twice as long as every inhalation. Count fifty sharp exhalations, then exhale the remaining air out of the lungs, inhale deeply and exhale slowly and completely. You can repeat another round if you wish.

Kapalabhatti clears the stale air out of the lungs, it increases the oxygen supply in the blood , which leads to blood's purification,. Kapalabhatti clears the brain and tones the diaphragm muscle.

2. Anuloma-Viloma

Adopting the Padmasana (pose) the yogi should draw in breath through the Candra (left nostril) and having retained it to capacity, should exhale through the Surya (right ostril).

Then he should again fill in the (thoracic) cavity by taking in breath through the Surya (right nostril) and exhale through the Candra (left nostril) after performing Kumbhaka in a systematic manner. Inhaling through that nostril by which he had exhaled and having retained the breath so long as it can be done without suppressing the impulse to exhale, one should exhale by the other one slowly - never rapidly.

Note :-

Swatmarama called this, a Nadisodhak Pranayama. 'Suddha nadigana bhavanti yaminam mastray-adurdhvatah' practising like this for three months, purifies the nadis. The popular name for this Nadisodhana Pranayama is 'Anuloma-Viloma.'

Technique :-

1. Sit in Padmasana.

2. Fold your index and middle finger of right hand towards palm. Now thumb should remain towards right nostril and ring finger and little finger should be towards

left nostril.

3. Closing the right nostril with the thumb inhale (prolonged) through the left nostril.

4. Now closing the left nostril with the ring finger and the little finger, exhale slowly through right nostril removing the thumb. (The time should be double than the time taken for inhaling i.e. the ratio should be 1 : 2).

5. After exhalation, inhale (prolonged) through the same nostril (right).

6. Now closing the right nostril with thumb exhale through left nostril (removing the ring finger and the little finger) as per previous practice. This completes one round of easy Anuloma-Viloma.

Technique (with Kumbhaka):-

1. Sit in Padmasana.

2. Fold your index and middle finger of right hand towards palm. Now thumb should remain towards right nostril and ring finger and little finger should be towards left nostril.

3. Closing the right nostril with the thumb inhale (prolonged) through the left nostril.

4. After completing inhalation close the left nostril also with little and ring finger and hold the breath inside (i.e. practise Kumbhaka).

5. After retention, keeping the left nostril closed with ring and little finger, exhale slowly through right nostril.

6. After exhalation inhale (prolonged) through the same nostril (right).

7. After complete inhalation close both the nostrils and practise Kumbhaka.

8. Retaining the breath according to the capacity exhale slowly through the left nostril (removing ring finger and little finger from it). This completes one round of Anuloma-Viloma with Kumbhaka.

Remember:-

1. This is a Nadisodhaka Pranayama.

2. If you cannot adopt Padmasana, adopt any comfortable sitting posture; sit erect.

3. In the beginning (at least for 6 months) practise easy technique of Anuloma-Viloma (i.e. without Kumbhaka).

4. When you inhale or exhale through one nostril, other should be kept closed.

5. While inhalation, the abdomen should not bulge out. Lungs along with chest should be expanded. Keep the abdomen little pressed carefully.

6. While practising Pranayama with Kumbhaka give equal time for inhalation and Kumbhaka, i.e. begin with the ratio of 1 : 1 : 2.

7. Time for exhalation should be double from that of inhalation.

8. While closing the nostril with the fingers do not press them so hard that the nose is bent.

9. Always remember that on completion of Pranayama if ther is an obstruction in respiration or it is fast it means that you have retained the breath more than your capacity which is not desirable.

10. Pranayama with Kumbhaka should always be practised under the guidance of a qualified teacher.

3. Ujjayi (The "Loud Breathing")

This consists in drawing air in through both nostrils with the glottis held partially closed. Ujjayi translates as "what clears the throat and masters the chest area." This partial closure of the glottis produces a sound like that heard in sobbing, except that it is continuous and unbroken. The sound should have a low but uniform pitch and be pleasant to hear. Friction of air in the nose should be avoided; consequently no nasal sounds will be heard. A prolonged full pause should begin, without any jerking, as soon as inhalation has been completed. Closure of glottis, use of chin lock and closure of both nostrils are standard. Prolong the pause as long as

possible; but it should be terminated and exhalation commenced smoothly and slowly. When properly performed, exhalation proceeds slowly and steadily through the left nostril with the glottis partially closed as in inhalation. One may begin to exhale with release of air pressure by lifting the finger from his left nostril, loosening his chin lock and then partially opening his glottis. Exhalation should be complete.

Ujjayi breathing has many variations. For example, we can breathe in through the throat, then completely close one nostril and breathe out through the other nostril, which is only partly closed. This technique is called an anuloma ujjayi. In a pranayama technique called viloma ujjayi, we breathe in through the nostril and breathe out through the throat. This technique is used to lengthen the inhalation. In ujjayi pranayama it is important to follow this rule: when we regulate the breath through the nostril, we never breathe through the throat at the same time.

Although the total length of time required for a single cycle of breathing will vary with different persons, certain ratios of the periods needed for inhaling, pausing and exhaling are recommended. The period occupied by exhaling should be about twice as long as that occupied by inhaling. Practice inhaling and exhaling without a full pause. Then, when you feel ready, hold your breathing for a pause which is comfortable. With continued practice, this pause can be extended to a duration which is double that of the inhalation or equal to that of the exhalation. Advanced practitioners of yoga hold their pauses to four times the duration of inhalation and double the duration of exhalation.

4. Brahmari (The Bee)

Like many yoga practices, this breathing practice is taken from nature, in this case by mimicking the sound of a buzzing bee.

The Bee is very useful preparation for meditation, and is a simple, straightforward tool that can be used to relax the autonomic nervous system. For teachers and health professionals, this is a gentle, extremely useful practice that can easily be taught to virtually anybody.

1. Sit up erect in a chair, such that your abdomen and chest are "open" (rather than slouching). Allow your eyes to close. Relax your body.

2. Close your lips throughout the practice, but leave your mouth cavity open in the back, in the area of the throat.

3. Then, simply make a sound like a buzzing bee, as you exhale through the nostrils, pushing in at the upper abdomen, while allowing the chest to remain relatively still.

4. Be aware of the feel of the vibration in the throat, the mouth, the cheeks, and the lips. You will hear the sound from within.

5. After the buzzing exhalation, then silently inhale through the nostrils, leaving the lips closed, and allowing the lower ribs to flare out slightly as the diaphragm muscle contracts. Again, be aware of the feel and listen to the sound.

Do the practice aloud for about two minutes.

Then do the practice silently, only in your mind for about two minutes, making no external sound, and not allowing the vocal cords to vibrate. Just imagine internally that you are hearing the sound. (To continue the practice silently, for an even longer period of time can lead to a very pleasant meditation)

As an alternative to measuring an amount of time, you may want to internally count a certain number of breaths (such as 15-20) to do aloud, rather than watching a clock.

Then, internally count the same number of breaths, but doing it silently, making no audible sound nor moving your throat or vocal cords.

You will notice that this practice of "the bee" easily brings a calmness to the body, the breath, and the mind:

1. Body is easily relaxed.

2. Breath is automatically smooth, slow, and with no jerks or pauses.

3. Mind is free from chatter.

While you do the practice, allow your mind to be wide awake, clear, and gently focused. This is a practice of being alert and calm, not of going to sleep or entering into a trance.

You can easily have the benefits of this practice at any time, in any public place. All you have to do is leave your eyes open and make no audible sound as you sit quietly. Internally, you are gently practicing "the bee."

Take the peacefulness, calmness and clarity with you into your daily life after completing the practice.

5. Bhastrika

Bhastrika (Bellows) is the most powerful of all Breathing Exercises for raising Kundalini Bhastrika. Bhastrika or Bellows consists a series of pumping followed by the retention of breath like Kapalabhati.

Warning in Performing the Bhastrika (Bellows)

You should exercise caution against the temptation of pushing too far in your initial practice of Bellows. If you have the tendency to push the limit, lie down when doing this exercise since there is a risk for you to lose consciousness and fall on the floor. Forced breathing makes you relaxed and revitalized. Excess in practice may induce dizziness, drowsiness and loss of consciousness. No harm can come from hyperventilation

as long as you are in bed. If you happen to lose consciousness, your breathing pattern will tend to rectify itself and return to normal. Excessive ventilation results to lightheartedness, giddiness or a feeling that you are floating in the air.

Bhastrika (Bellows)

Bhastrika is primarily consists of forced rapid deep breathing which serves as a basis for many varieties of exercises, all of which may be described by the same name. Although air is forced both in and out, the emphasis is placed upon the expulsion or explosion of air. A series of such expulsions, each following the other in quick succession without either Full or Empty Pause, is called "A Round". Beginners should limit a round to about five explosions, though the number may be increased to ten, or even more if needed to obtain the desired effect. The desired effects range from increased ventilation, increased Blood Circulation, clearing of the

Nasal Passages and increased thinking capacity to eliminating of all Mental Disturbances. Please be warned against generating such powerful explosions since it can cause injuries to lung tissues. Extending a series for so long can also cause dizziness. Comfort and not reckless excess should guide your motives and manner of doing the Bhastrika or Bellows.

Although you can breathe through your mouth or both mouth and nose, regular breathing is limited to either both or one nostril. The breath-stroke in the rapid succession of breaths may or may not be very deep, but it is customary to finish or follow a round by the deepest possible inhalation and exhalation. A series of normal breaths should occur before undertaking a second round. A deepest possible inhalation and exhalation may, and perhaps should, introduce each round. Some nasal hissing can be expected but avoid unpleasant sound and fluttering of the nasal skin surfaces. You may perform the Bhastrika exercise while standing but it is advisable to do it in a Seated Position in order to allow maximum Relaxation of the abdominal muscles and easy diaphragmatic breathing. Variations include using a full pause after each round, partial glottis closures and Alternation of Nostrils.

MEDITATION FOR MEN

Preferably concentration on rhythmic breathing. Or else try mantra incantation

Combining their weight training with Yoga isn't bad. In fact, it can produce even better results. Asanas allow for better flexibility and relax the muscles. Pranayama helps maintain vibrant health. It also improves response

from the nervous system. Meditation will help keep their focus and concentration. It will also clear the mind, reducing stress resulting from repetitive actions of weight lifting and work.

YOGA FOR STRENGTH

A lot of people wonder whether Yoga can improve their strength and muscle fitness. Almost everyone acknowledge that Yoga helps reduce stress and increases flexibility and overall health. However, when it comes to increasing muscle fitness folks think it might not be the most appropriate physical fitness culture. then again, going by expert opinion, Yoga can definitely make you stronger.

If you really wish to get better results your daily fitness routine, you should really consider adding Yoga asanas and pranayama to your workout sessions. Contrary to traditional weight building exercises, in Yoga your body provides the resistance. Even if you don't produce bulked up muscles, you will definitely increase your muscle strength. Further, some balancing postures call for a lot of muscle control to prevent you from falling over. This helps build up and strengthen the muscles. Yoga goes even far beyond aerobics and weight training; it can benefit you both physically and mentally.

Besides all other benefits, Yoga can help you improve muscle fitness and make you actually feel and be stronger. Whether or not you decide to use it as your primary means of strength training or supplement your other exercises, Yoga definitely helps your muscles grow fit, balanced, and strong. As a matter of fact, many asanas are performed very slowly. Or you are required to retain a specific pose for several breaths. Those who have experienced it, support the theory that it is far more challenging to the muscles to retain a pose or do it slowly than to let momentum move you through an action.

Further, in weight training, you isolate specific

muscles as you perform an exercise. This leads to short, tightened muscles. On the other hand, the muscles you develop in Yoga training are more likely to be elongated; since as you are strengthening them, you are simultaneously lengthening them, as well. Above all, Yoga practise helps realign the muscles so that they are better balanced. You truly work your whole body when you practice Yoga. This is because in Yoga you don't focus on isolated muscles, but actively recruit smaller muscle groups too.

Finally, you are less likely to get injured practising Yoga, since you are not overworking any specific muscle group.

YOGA FOR LEGS

Here are some Yogasanas and exercises that will help improve the flexibility and blood circulation of your legs. But remember to keep your breathing pattern normal. Don't hold a posture for more then 10-30 seconds. Do only up to three repetitions at a time, depending upon your own level of strength and fitness.

 # 1

Stretch both your legs out

Stretch both your arms up and slowly stretch forward, dropping your head onto your knees

Hold the pose for 10-25 seconds then release

Repeat this movement 5 times.

 # 2

Hold your arms of the chair, keeping your back straight

Raise one leg and stretch your toes forwards and then bend them inwards

Hold on to the posture for 10-25 seconds then release

Repeat this action with the other leg

Repeat this movement 5 times

 # 3

Holding the arms of a chair, raise both your legs

Bend your toes inwards

Hold the pose for 10-25 seconds then release

Now keep your legs in the same position and stretch your toes and foot outwards

Repeat this movement 5 times

 # 4

Keeping one leg on the ground, raise one of your knees up towards your chest keeping your back straight.

Hold your leg with both your arms; gently pull towards your chest for 10-25 seconds then release.

Repeat this action with your other leg.

Repeat this movement 5 times.

11

YOGA FOR WOMEN

Emotional pressure and stress can have a profound effect on a woman's health more so because women tend to be more emotional than men. It's been proven time and again that emotional distress can lead to a number of psychosomatic ailments. Factor like hormonal changes also affect women's health. This is why many women find Yoga an solution to health problems.

A lot of women suffer from premenstrual syndrome and menstrual cramps. Menopause brings with it considerable hormonal changes that often lead to increased stress levels in women. Pregnancy is another major change a woman undergoes in life. It brings with it changes and stress to her body. During pregnancy it is also possible that the mother's health problems can reflect in the health of the baby, as well. Naturally the mother has to be as healthy as possible during the whole pregnancy.

YOGASANAS FOR WOMEN

It is quite common for women to prepare for the last months of pregnancy and labor through Yoga. All mothers wish to deliver their babies without complications. Certain yogasanas, including the cat pose and the fish pose, are excellent in helping the mother develop both physical strength and mental focus so necessary for labour.

Yoga is also known to reduce the effects of other pregnancy issues. These include morning sickness, dizziness, fatigue, so on and so forth. A number of Yoga stretches help relax and strengthen the pelvic muscles.

Then again, having a young baby can be very tiring; hence women in the postnatal period often turn to Yoga to increase their vitality and energy levels. The fish pose is great for increasing oxygen supply to the body and enhance relaxation. If you want to spend some time in meditation, the hero pose is ideal.

Another popular yogasana is the cat pose, regardless of one's age or physical condition. This is particularly due to the fact that it is good to increase flexibility of the spinal column, as well as relax lower back muscles. These muscles carry the weight of the whole upper body, particularly when you stand for long.

This pose is often followed by the headstand. It can be difficult to master, but it also has great benefits. Reversing gravity in the body lets many parts rest and relax in a way they normally never do. The headstand is also great for relieving lower back muscle pressure and back pain.

Please note that all pranayamas, particularly Kapalabhatti, Anuloma-Viloma and Ujjayi are excellent for all women, throughout their lives, regardless of all health conditions. Yoga breathing techniques are particularly effective in childbirth as they help the mother focus on the delivery rather than the pain.

YOGA FOR MENSTRUAL CRAMPS

Menstrual cramps - the blight of many a woman's monthly cycle - come in many different types. Gentle yoga can benefit women with this problem.

Yoga teaches balance - balance of the body with relation to gravity; balance of the mind between action and observation and balance of the neuro-endocrinal system between stress and relaxation. Through regular Yoga practice you learn which poses help re-establish balance in every aspect of your existence. In this ancient discipline, there are asanas that are particularly useful during the menstrual period. These asanas ease menstrual cramps, heavy bleeding, pelvic discomfort and the low back pain associated with menses. They also help smoothen out the emotional rough edges some women encounter at this time of their cycle.

Yoga poses during menstrual period :

1. FORWARD BENDS

1. Janu Sirshasana

2. Paschimottanasana

These are calming poses. Lower abdominal and pelvic compression further aids cramps and heavy bleeding.

1. Janu Sirshasana (Head to One Knee Pose)

Technique

1. Sit on the floor with your legs out.

2. Bend one leg, bring the heel of your foot as close to your right groin as possible.

3. For comfort you may place a pillow under your bent knee. Ensure that your spine is straight.

4. Now exhale and begin to move forward slowly, keeping your back as straight as possible.

5. Breathing normally, stretch forwards and straighten your spine.

6. Maintain the position for as long as you can, breathing normally.

7. Move forward as far as you can, stretch your arms and try to hold your foot.

8. To return to an upright position, stretch forwards, inhale and stretch your arms up.

9. Repeat the pose with the next foot bent.

2. Paschimottanasana – Head To Knees Pose

Relax your body and mind, stretch your hamstrings, shoulders, and spine, relieve stress, and improve your

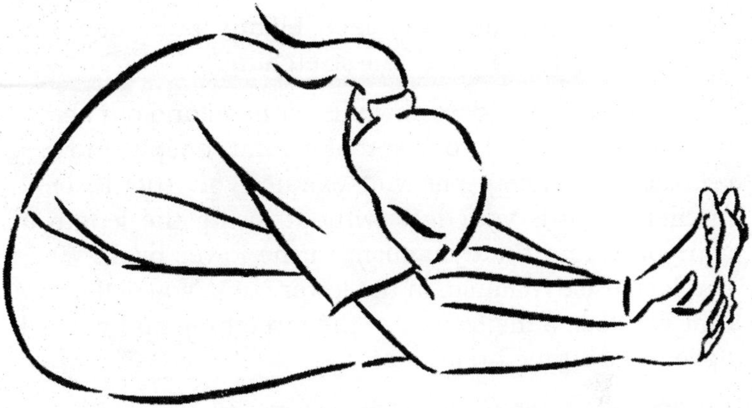

posture and concentration by practicing the Seated Forward Bend. Learn how to do this properly and achieve maximum results.

This forward bend gives a complete stretching to the neck, the back, the hamstrings and calves. At the same time, it directs your attention inward. You stimulate the entire nervous system and learn to find stillness and relaxation during a period of effort or even discomfort when doing this stretching exercise.

Method

Tip 1: Sit down with your legs stretched. The legs lie side by side and the toes point upwards. Stretch your lower back and raise your arms. Look forward, lengthen your back, and keep the chest and your breathing free.

Tip 2: Slowly bend forward, stretch your crown upward and try not to lose the supporting dynamism of the lower back. See to it that your legs do not move or tilt.

Tip 3: The moment you notice that you can only bend further by bending the lower back, move your hands to your lower legs, ankles or feet. Lightly pull your legs, ankles or feet and continue stretching.

Keep your shoulders down. Breathe in and out across the entire length of your spinal column deeply and in a relaxed way. Everytime you exhale, you should bend further towards your legs without losing the length in your back and the dynamism in the lower back. When you lose the dynamism in the lower back, you will notice that you lose a major part of the stretching and you will have a hard time breathing.

Step 4: Stretch out your arms forward.

Step 5: Slowly raise your upper body. Keep your legs lying side by side and the toes pointing upwards.

Step 6: Sit straight up again, just like your original position.

2. STANDING POSES

1. Parivrtta Trikonasana (Revolved Triangle Pose)

(par-ee-vrit-tah trik-cone-AHS-anna)

parivrtta = to turn around, revolve

trikona = three angle or triangle

Technique

1. Stand in Tadasana. With an exhalation, step or lightly jump your feet 3½ to 4 feet apart. Raise your arms parallel to the floor and reach them actively out to the sides, shoulder blades wide, palms down. Turn your left foot in 45 to 60 degrees to the right and your right foot out to the right 90 degrees. Align the right heel with the left heel. Firm your thighs and turn your right thigh

outward, so that the center of the right kneecap is in line with the center of the right ankle.

2. With an exhalation, turn your torso to the right, and square your hip points as much as possible with the front edge of your sticky mat. As you bring the left hip around to the right, resist the head of the left thigh bone back and firmly ground the left heel.

3. With another exhalation, turn your torso further to the right and lean forward over the front leg. Reach your left hand down, either to the floor (inside or outside the foot) or, if the floor is too far away, onto a block positioned against your inner right foot. Allow the left hip to drop slightly toward the floor. You may feel the right hip slip out to the side and lift up toward the

shoulder, and the torso hunch over the front leg. To counteract this, press the outer right thigh actively to the left and release the right hip away from the right shoulder. Use your right hand, if necessary, to create these two movements, hooking the thumb into the right hip crease.

4. Beginning students should keep their head in a neutral position, looking straight forward, or turn it to look at the floor. More experienced students can turn the head and gaze up at the top thumb. From the center of the back, between the shoulder blades, press the arms away from the torso. Bring most of your weight to bear on the back heel and the front hand.

5. Stay in this pose anywhere from 30 seconds to one minute. Exhale, release the twist, and bring your torso back to upright with an inhalation. Repeat for the same length of time with the legs reversed, twisting to the left.

2. Ardha Chandrasana (Half Moon Pose):

This is best done with the support of a wall or a chair.

Half Moon deeply stretches and opens the sides of the body and improves core body strength, balance and concentration. Half moon strengthens the ankles and knees, improves circulation and energizes the entire body.

1. From the mountain, interlace the fingers, pointing the index finger up over the head, press the feet into the floor and reach the fingers and crown up while relaxing the shoulders down and back.

2. Exhale and press the right hip out to the side,

arching over to the left. Keep the feet grounded and the legs and buttocks engaged. Reach up and out through the fingers and crown.

3. Breathe and hold for 2-6 breaths.

4. To release: inhale and press into the feet as you reach the fingers back up towards the ceiling.

5. Repeat on other side.

3. OTHER IMPORTANT YOGIC POSES

1. Supported Sethu Bandha (Supported Bridge Pose)

SET-too BAHN-dah)

setu = dam, dike, or bridge

bandha = lock

Technique

1. Lie supine on the floor, and if necessary, place a thickly folded blanket under your shoulders to protect your neck. Bend your knees and set your feet on the floor, heels as close to the sitting bones as possible.

2. Exhale and, pressing your inner feet and arms actively into the floor, push your tailbone upward toward the pubis, firming (but not hardening) the buttocks, and lift the buttocks off the floor. Keep your thighs and inner feet parallel. Clasp the hands below your pelvis and extend through the arms to help you stay on the tops of your shoulders.

3. Lift your buttocks until the thighs are about parallel to the floor. Keep your knees directly over the heels, but push them forward, away from the hips, and

lengthen the tailbone toward the backs of the knees. Lift the pubis toward the navel.

4. Lift your chin slightly away from the sternum and, firming the shoulder blades against your back, press the top of the sternum toward the chin. Firm the outer arms, broaden the shoulder blades, and try to lift the space between them at the base of the neck (where it's resting on the blanket) up into the torso.

5. Stay in the pose anywhere from 30 seconds to 1 minute. Release with an exhalation, rolling the spine slowly down onto the floor.

Benefits

1. Stretches the chest, neck, and spine

2. Calms the brain and helps alleviate stress and mild depression

3. Stimulates abdominal organs, lungs, and thyroid

4. Rejuvenates tired legs

5. Improves digestion

6. Helps relieve the symptoms of menopause

7. Relieves menstrual discomfort when done supported

8.Reduces anxiety, fatigue, backache, headache, and insomnia

9. Therapeutic for asthma, high blood pressure, osteoporosis, and sinusitis

2. Supported Viparita Dandasana (Upward Turned Staff Pose) or Dwi Pada Viparita Dandasana (Two-Legged Inverted Staff Pose)

This advanced backbend strengthens and invigorates the whole body.

At first glance, this may seem like a strange way to prepare for active asanas. Bolsters are more commonly used in restorative practices or, occasionally, to prepare for backbends. But work with bolsters can provide deeper gifts.

Bolstering Your Practice

To practice this supported backbend, you'll need a bolster. You can buy a prefabricated bolster, but it is recommended to use blankets because they are adaptable. You will need to experiment a bit to find the right bolster for you.

If your back is stiff, start modestly by rolling a single blanket into a firm cylinder. If you are more experienced or flexible, try a bolster rolled from two blankets. Sit on the floor in front of the bolster and lie back over it, positioning it under your middle and lower back. Relax your legs and melt backward over the bolster, lowering your upper shoulders and resting your head on the floor. Relax your arms on the floor at about the level of your shoulders.

As you begin, your body will probably grab your attention first. Your sensations may range from complete

ease to significant discomfort. Seek an experience that is difficult enough to make you aware of places where you are tight, but which allows you to coax those tense areas into the state of alert relaxation that is essential in a hatha yoga practice.

If your lower back is in pain, your breathing strained, your neck crunched, or your head doesn't reach the floor, your position needs to be modified. Reposition the bolster by moving it slightly higher or lower. If that adjustment does not help, place a smaller blanket roll under your shoulders and neck or reduce the size of your roll. If your back totally rebels, remove the bolster and consider trying it again later in your practice. (When you first try this approach, you may find it easier to warm up by practicing more active asanas first.)

Once you have found a position that feels right, challenging but not too uncomfortable, begin to turn your attention inward. Though you have already made some adjustments to become more comfortable, the sheer physical challenge of adapting to this unfamiliar position may still overshadow the more subtle inner landscape of the pose. Now your real work begins as you seek a way to dive beneath the strong sensations on the surface to an inner place where there is room for you to breathe smoothly and be both mentally and physically calm. The support of your bolster may allow you to create more ease and spaciousness than you can when you have to support all your weight with your muscles.

As you lie on the bolster, respond to areas that feel tight or uncomfortable by trying to stretch and move them. Use your hands to gently pull your head and lengthen your neck. To lengthen the lower back, tuck your tailbone and slide your hips farther away from the bolster. Enhance your fine tuning by turning your attention to your breathing. Initially, your breath may reflect the discomfort in your body by being slightly ragged. Consciously slow it down and slightly extend each exhalation. As your breathing steadies, notice how it develops a rhythm that expands beyond the chest to resonate through your whole body. Coaxing that pulse into your tightest areas is your goal.

Facing the Challenge

As you lie over the bolster, you may at first reflexively tighten in reaction to the strong back arch. However, it is critical that you consciously soften and make more room inside your body. Continue to modify your position (even reshape your bolster if necessary) until you are at your "edge"—that place where you feel yourself physically challenged, but still able to maintain a steady breathing rhythm.

Though you are letting go, your body should not collapse. Just flopping is not letting go. In fact, undoing resistance should be a highly conscious process with distinct and tangible sensations. Tension must be faced, dissolved, and finally recycled into true expansion. As your surface grows quiet, become acquainted with the inner movement that pulsates through your body on the beat of each breath. Observe this "undoing" process closely: You are learning to recognize resistance and transform it into renewal, a skill that will mature until it can support even the most challenging asanas.

When you feel ready to take on more challenge, cup your hands behind your head and bring your elbows in so they are shoulder-width apart. Pause for a moment to feel how broad your upper back becomes when you do this, and then, as you exhale, slowly begin to spread your elbows wider without narrowing your upper back. This will open your chest and thoracic spine even more. Keep your elbows wide for a few breaths before relaxing your arms out at your sides and on to the floor at shoulder level.

Letting yourself completely fall back into the bolster, close your eyes and allow the rhythm of your breathing to draw you inward. Depending on how comfortable and absorbed you are, the time you spend here may vary from several minutes to half an hour or more. At the end, in your clean slate of a body, you will be ready for the renewal that comes from practicing asanas.

When you are ready to leave the bolster, put your feet flat on the floor. Removing any props you've placed under your neck, lift your hips and slowly push yourself over the bolster onto your shoulders. Move the bolster under your hips and hug your knees into your chest for a minute or so. You may feel mild discomfort in your lower back that should subside quickly, to be replaced by heat that spreads throughout your back.

You are now ready to progress to a more active yoga practice informed by the skills you have developed over the bolster—a practice more likely to find the balance of physical action, internal focus, and conscious breathing that form the core of hatha yoga.

Stepping It Up

If you know your practice will include backbends, you can save your bolster work until you come to the point where backbends loom. If you find the bolster work already described easy, consider adding this even deeper version. It is wonderful at the beginning of your practice, but is especially effective when preparing for backbending.

Place a double blanket roll on top of a stool or milk crate. Sit on the bolster and slide your hips down just enough so that you can lie back and position the bolster in the small of your back. Lie back, letting your back melt into the bolster, and allowing your arms, legs, and head to hang. You may be tall enough or flexible enough so that your head reaches the floor. In that case, try folding one or two blankets between the crate and bolster for more height.

Hanging in this position may not be easy at first because your spine must be flexible enough to tolerate the weight of your hips and shoulders. You may reduce any strain by placing a block under your head and resting your hands on your chest—or you may even have to bail out for now. Don't be discouraged. This does not mean you won't ever go further, only that there is enough of an obstacle that you must temporarily retreat. The work on the lower bolster is plenty of challenge and will eventually prepare you to go deeper.

If this deeper position is within your capacity, take several minutes to relax into the pose just as you did with the lower bolster. Letting yourself trust the support of the bolster, slow your breath and extend your exhalation as you adjust, lengthening and broadening your back into a deep, even, comfortable arch—a prelude to the malleable spine that is desirable in all backbends. You can deepen the arching action further by either stretching your arms overhead or bending them and sliding your hands past your ears to hold the stool. In either case keep your elbows shoulder-width apart: With this alignment, you'll properly direct the bending action to your thoracic spine, instead of arching by hyperextending your shoulders. To open your chest even more, roll your top shoulder blades back toward the stool.

Approach this higher bolster with the mindfulness you have honed by working with the lesser bolster. Do not sacrifice the pumping rhythm of your breath, as it will help you stay over the bolster longer and in more comfort. Stay as long as you feel you can continue to replace tension with relaxation and expansion. To come off the bolster, slide your hips to the floor and iie back against your props. At this point, your spine should feel warm, your breath steady, and your focus sharp. You're prepared to respond with sureness to the challenges that will arise in the upcoming backbends.

Dwi Pada Viparita Dandasana

Before going further toward Dwi Pada Viparita Dandasana, you should be able to practice Urdhva Dhanurasana with straight arms and Sirsasana I (Headstand) without strain. If you meet these prerequisites, you're ready. Here we go!

Prepare as for Urdhva Dhanurasana: Lie on your back, feet on the floor, heels under the knees, and step your feet a little wider than your hips. Bend your arms and place your palms on the floor by your ears, fingertips facing the shoulders, shoulder-width apart. Pause for a moment to focus and tune in to your breathing. As you exhale, extend your calves and back thighs to pull your hips, shoulders, and head from the floor as you straighten your arms. As before, rotate your upper shoulder blades toward your tailbone to lift your shoulders and lighten the load on your arms.

Since you probably won't be able to hold this asana for very long, corrective actions need to be done quickly and decisively. Bend your arms and place the crown of your head on the floor between your hands and feet, keeping your elbows shoulder-width apart and directly over your wrists. To ensure that your neck does not become compressed, exhale, press your hands into the floor, and again rotate your top shoulder blades toward your tailbone. Keep your chest open and lifted. On your next exhalation, slide one hand past your ear to cup the back of your head, bringing your weight onto your forearm. Repeat the same action with the other arm, interlacing your fingers behind your head. (You may be more successful in these arm movements if you lift onto your tiptoes.)

With a powerful exhalation, press down through your elbows and lift your chest to raise your head off the floor. As your head lifts, bring your heels down. Of course, your head may seem glued to the floor; if that's the case, continue to hold the pose where you are. If you do manage to lift your head, the pose may actually become easier, since this movement allows your upper arms to directly support your weight, easing the demand on your muscles. But be careful not to strain the shoulder joints by pushing them beyond your elbows. Avoid this overextension by keeping your weight evenly distributed between your elbows and wrists, and by not allowing your elbows to drift more than shoulder-width apart. It is absolutely fine to remain in this position, with your head raised and your feet directly below your knees. In the full pose, however, you walk the feet away from your hands until your legs are nearly straight; then you plant your feet and exhale as you stretch down through your calves and push to straighten the legs completely. Place the crown of your head back on the floor inside the cup of your hands, extend your elbows into the floor, and rotate your top shoulder blades toward your tailbone to help your shoulders stay lifted. Your middle back will be asked to bend more deeply.

Now is the time to fully incorporate the inner quality you found during your time over the bolster. Don't lose your internal focus in the challenge of the moment. Do your best to maintain a steady breath rate. Use your breath, like a heart, to pump movement that reverberates through you, extending on your inhalation, opening on your exhalation, and softening hard edges to create a pose that is strong and peaceful.

Come out of this asana with great attention. First, walk your feet back under your knees. Continuing to balance on your head and to lift your shoulders, return your palms to the floor next to your ears. Again check to make sure your hands are directly under your elbows. Push with your hands to lift the head and tuck your chin and tailbone in as you roll your spine back down to the floor, tailbone touching last. Consciously slow your breathing down until you are once again at rest and can feel the powerful calm that is the product of balanced backbends.

Of course, such a dynamic pose as this will make you aware—perhaps painfully so—that asking the body to be flexible and strong simultaneously is a tall order. Difficult as these demands may be, they present an opportunity to maintain an asana using the skills of introspection, breathing, and surrender—skills that eventually transform a pose from an impossibility or an exercise in brute strength into a lucid, precise, poised asana. Practicing with this focus leads to sthira sukha ("steady comfort," Patanjali's definition of asana), a state in which the fluctuations of the mind have stilled and one finds a state of immense clarity that shines forth from within.

Yoga poses to avoid during menstrual period :

Inversions:

Poses like Sirshasana, Viparita Karani and Sarvangasana are not recommended during the menstrual period. This is for both philosophic as well as physiologic reasons.

However, the most important thing to do to minimize menstrual problems is to take good care of yourself, to honor your body, all month long. If you know, for instance, that coffee or Coke brings on premenstrual headaches, find a non-caffeinated substitute. Those tasty ic cream sodas offer a little more sinful treat without doing much harm. In general, if you avoid greasy foods and sugary desserts, if you cut down on alcohol and caffeinated beverages, and substitute home-cooked meals for processed foods, you could alleviate much of your physical and emotional discomfort.

Suggestions for Women

Get lots of rest. Even if you don't do anything else for yourself, at least rest, during the first day or two, of your periods. You will be amazed at how much better you feel the rest of the month.

Beware food cravings. If you crave sweet or junk food don't turn to chips and salsa. Instead, cook something seasoned with salt. That should satisfy you longer. If you still crave sugar, we recommend a cup of lukewarm water sweetened with honey.

Eat only pacifying foods

Try to modify your routine. Treat yourself to a warm oil massage or a facial to balance the nervous system and soothe your mind. Or, rub warm sesame oil into your hair, leave it in for a few hours (or overnight), and shampoo it out.

YOGA FOR PREGNANT WOMEN

A pregnant woman who does not know the mechanics of labor will, naturally, be tense and frightened. This only increases the pain. Yoga is a simple technique that strengthens the body and enables it to tackle new developments with maximum ease and comfort. Yoga makes people look within and understand the body mechanism. It is a great preparatory technique to help pregnant women cope with what has to come. Here are a few tips for pre-natal (pregnancy) care:

The general Yogasanas can, if you wish, be done only for the first 2 months.

Suggested pranayamas for pregnant women :

- Vajrasana
- Padmasana
- Sukhasana
- Shavasana

1. Vajrasana

Technique

Sit on the folded blanket with the feet stretched backward and big toes crossed. The knees should be kept together but heels apart. Lower the buttocks inside the feet. The heels should touch the sides of the hips. Place the hands on the knees, palms downward.

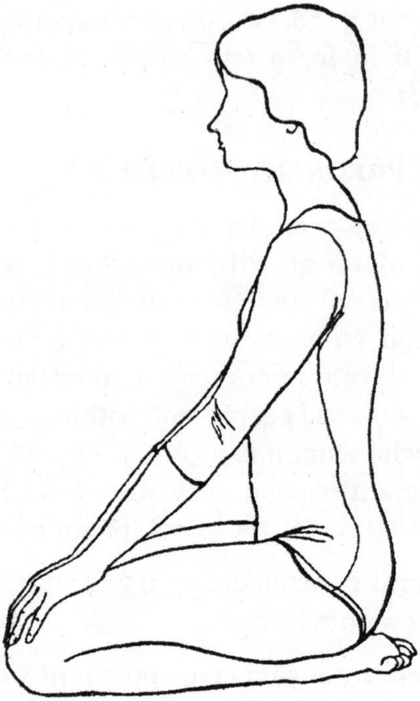

2. Padmasana

Technique

Sit on the folded blanket with your legs outstretched, bend each leg and place each foot on the opposite thigh, soles turned upwards. Pull the foot as high as you can. Keep the palms of the right and left hand on the right and left knees, touching the thumbs with tips of index fingers and gaze at the tip of the nose. Keep the head, neck and spinal column straight and erect, and breathe slowly.

3. Sukhasana

This is one of the classic Meditative Poses and is usually performed after doing the Corpse Pose. The Easy Pose helps in straightening the spine, slowing down metabolism, promoting inner tranquility, and keeping your mind still.

After relaxing in the Corpse Pose for a few minutes, come up and sit in the Easy Yoga Pose or Sukhasana for Pranayama and the neck, shoulder and eye exercises. This Yoga Asana is one of the classic Meditative Poses, which help to straighten the spine, slow down metabolism and still the mind. If you find that holding the Yoga Pose is uncomfortable, place a folded Yoga Blanket under the back of your buttocks.

In order to stretch the leg muscles evenly, be sure put each leg alternately on top in this Yoga Posture. When you are ready, substitute the Half Lotus or Lotus at this point.

Method: Sitting on the floor and bend your knees. Clasp your arms around them and press them to your

chest to make the spine erect. Now, release your arms and cross your legs, letting your knees drop down toward the floor. Keep your head and body straight.

4. Shavasana

Technique

On a soft carpet or blanket of folded rug lie full length on back with arms away from the body with palms facing upward and feet slightly apart. Finally keep the mind free, start breathing deeply, slowly and rhythmically. The practitioner at the final stage of this asana should feel that his body is motionless as the dead body sinking in the ground. Rhythmic and deep breathing are absolutely necessary for concentration which gives complete relaxation.

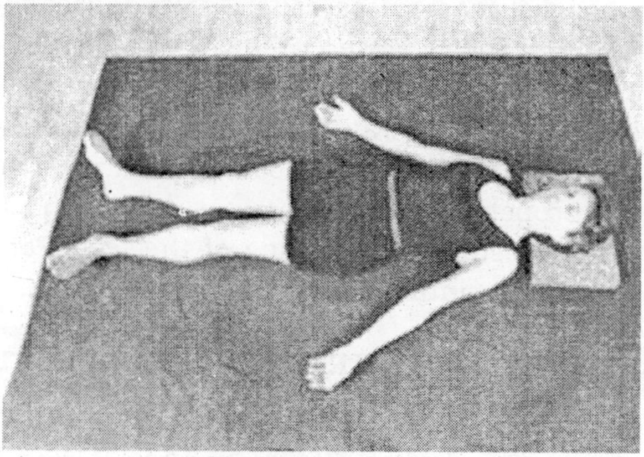

Always end your Yoga session with this asana to relax your body. The meaning of relaxation is undoing tensed muscles and hence it is synonymous to reduction of pain.

'Pranayama' or breathing exercises should be done twice daily. This is to facilitate complete expulsion of carbon dioxide that will give way for fresh intake of oxygen.

Suggested breathing exercises are:

- Mild kapalabhatti
- Lots of anuloma-Viloma
- Brahmari

Deep or free breathing at the rate of 5 breaths per minute also contributes to relaxation as compared to the normal rate of 18-20 breaths per minute. We also advise an enema once a week to make way for proper elimination from the intestine. Regular morning and evening walks are compulsory.

As far as diet goes, spices, salts, sweets and fat should be drastically reduced. Have starchy foods in moderation and plenty of fruits, vegetables, juices, curd, buttermilk and sprouts. Preferably, avoid foods that take a long to digest such as non-vegetarian food and dairy products. Due to the property of salts to retain water, it can lead to high blood pressure and swelling of the feet. For this reason, minimum intake of salt is recommended.

YOGA POSTURES FOR FERTILITY AND CONCEPTION

The regular and determined practice of Hatha Yoga helps you stay fit by preserving and expanding your physical and mental faculties. It slows down the ageing process and helps you remain strong and active, right up to old age.

YOGA ASANAS FOR FERTILITY:

The following asanas, including one mudra and Bandha, are recommended for fertility, for fostering reproduction and combating impotence and sterility :

1. Sirshasana
2. Sarvangasana
3. Matsyasana
4. Viparita Karani
5. Halasana
6. Bhujangasana
7. Dhanurasana
8. Salabhasana
9. Paschimottanasana
10. Janu Sirshasana
11. Supta-Vajrasana
12. Ardha-Matsyendrasana
13. Baddha-Konasana
14. Yoga-Mudra
15. Uddiyana-Bandha

1. Sirshasana

Benefits:

Calms the mind. Strengthens the arms, legs, and spine. Improves balance.

Note: Wondering whether to invert while

menstruating?

Instructions:

1. Come to your hands and knees with the wrists underneath the shoulders and the knees underneath the hips.

2. Bring your elbows to the floor forearm's distance apart.

3. Interlace your fingers, tucking the outermost pinky underneath.

4. Place the crown of your head on the floor cupped by your interlaced fingers.

5. Bring the hips up as if coming into Downward Facing Dog.

6. Walk the feet in towards your head until your hips are over your shoulders.

7. Kick up one leg and then the other.

8. Press down strongly into your forearms to keep all your weight from coming into your neck and head.

9. Reach up through the balls of your feet and rotate the thigh bones inward slightly. Hold for at least 10 breaths.

Beginners:

Look at the step-by-step illustrated guide for photos of each step. Practice the pose at the wall. Try to move further from the wall each time. Try removing one foot and then the other from the wall to practice balancing.

Advanced

Try the following variations: Bring both legs up at the same time keeping them straight. Lower down the same way, holding the pose with the legs at 90 degrees. Bring the legs into a lotus position. Release your interlaced fingers and bring the forearms flat on the floor. Lift your head off the floor coming into forearm stand.

2. Sarvangasana

In Sanskrit "sarva" menas "All" or "entire" and "anga" means limb of body. Sarvang means the entire body or all the limbs. This is one of the most powerful and popular asans. The malfunctioning of thyrid gland can harm all other glands.

Technique

Spread a blanket on the floor and lie flat on your

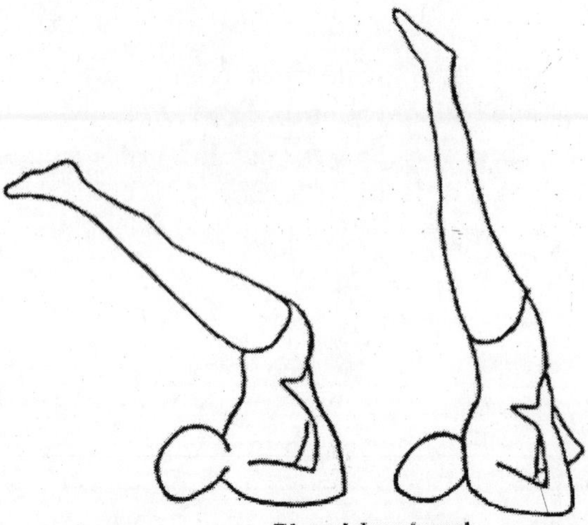

Shoulderstand

back. Then slowly raise the legs up lifting the trunk and hips vertically. The chin should be firmly pressed against the chest. Remain in this pose for a few minutes and breathe slowly and deeply and concentrate on the thyroid gland which is at the root of the neck.

3. Matsyasana

Technique

1. Lie on your back with your knees bent and arms at your side.

2. Arch your back as much as you can while raising

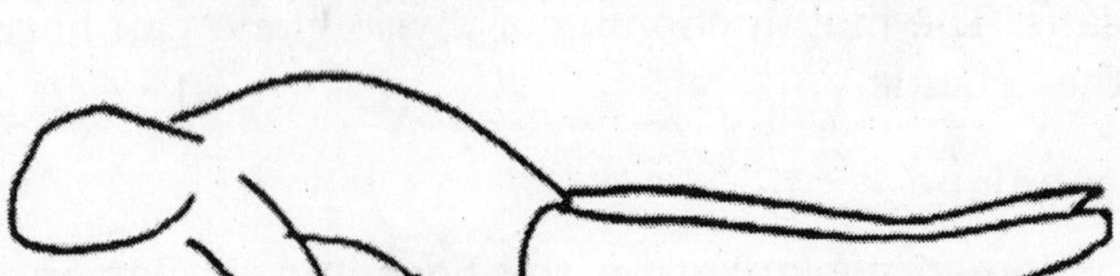

Fish Posture

it off the ground by pushing the floor with your elbows. At the same time, throw your head backwards, resting the crown of your head on the floor. Use your forearm and elbows to support you.

3. Expand your chest. Breathe deeply with the abdomen and concentrate on the thyroid gland.

4. Stay in this position for about one minute. Slowly come back to the starting position.

Benefits

1. The fish posture normalizes the function of the thyroid, pituitary, pineal and adrenal glands. It limbers and stretches the neck, strengthens and tones the nervous system, the kidneys, the stomach and intestines, the pelvic organs, and the nerves connected with the sex functions.

2. This is the only posture in this sequence which bends the spine (including the neck) backwards. This is essential, to counteract the preceding asanas which bend the spine forwards. The result is to give a healthy stretch to the muscles and ligaments of the spine in the opposite direction.

3. This posture benefits people with asthma.

4. Viparita Karani

Viparita Karani is a Sanskrit term that refers to the "action of inverting." Thus it is more of a general action rather than an asana and hence the name does not end with "-asana." In Iyengar Yoga, Viparita Karani is the name we tend to give specifically to the feet-up-the wall position, although any inverting action is technically

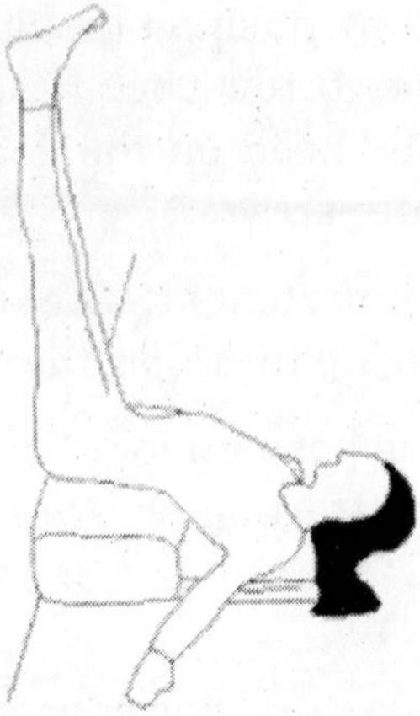

Viparita Karani and some texts will use this term to refer to Sarvangasana, for instance. It is often called the "fountain of youth pose" because of its profound restorative effects. Viparita karani is an inversion in the shoulderstand family and confers benefits similar to Sarvangasana, but it is easier to hold for extended periods of time for maximum rejuvenating benefits. Few asanas have both the soothing and energizing effect of Viparita Karani.

Some poses are for doing, this pose, like Savasana, is for UN-doing. This pose is for just being and observing. In the restorative poses, "you don't do, you just view." You become as acutely aware as possible of the processes of your body, your breathing, your tensions and how to realease them, and your mental fluctuations. This pose is extremely cooling for your nervous system. The spirit of surrender that we learn in these restorative poses is something that we should carry into our active asana work as well.

It is good to devote one entire session each week to doing nothing but this one pose. Any fatigue, anxiety, or depression will be alleviated with Viparita Karani. When you're exhausted from your day, it's time to go upside-down. Aim for about 20-30 minutes in the pose if you are doing it as an entire session, but do not exceed that length of time as a general rule.

You should use a bolster or about three folded blankets for this pose, and you should be very slightly backbending over the support, not using it just to support your hips. Mr. Iyengar had originally designed a "Viparita Karani" wooden box for this pose, though we rarely use that prop for this pose anymore (although we still use it for other poses). Have your support about 3-4 inches away from the wall so your buttocks hang downward just slightly off the support. This slight backbending action should not be so much that it brings any tension into your abdomen. You want your front lower ribs at about the same height as your front hip points (anterior iliac crests) or a little lower. You want the sensation of a lifting in your front rib and floating rib area, while your abdomen should be relaxed and sinking. Another support you can use is two blocks (on their flat sides, end to end), with one or two 1/2 folded blankets on top of them. This is a slightly firmer support.

It is good to do this pose on a sticky mat to allow you to tuck your shoulders a little underneath as in Sarvangasana and keep them there in a relaxed way. This action will help open your chest. Also lengthen the back of your head (the occiput) away from your shoulders before you begin to relax into the pose.

If you choose not to use a sticky mat, one good idea

is to place a block between your bolster or blanket support and the wall to keep your support from sliding toward the wall when you are coming into and out of the pose.

If you want more support for your shoulders, you can use a folded blanket just in front of the bolster for your shoulders to rest on and allow your head to be off the blanket onto the floor (just as with the blankets in Sarvangasana). Make sure the blanket extends to support your cervical spine, just touching the tops of your shoulders. Without this sensory contact (Skt. "sparsa") under the neck it is more difficult for the body as a whole to release.

It helps to strap a belt around your thighs just above your knees before you go into the pose to bind your legs together so you can relax more completely in the pose without your legs falling apart. Try to fasten the belt so the buckle is not directly on your skin. You never want the belt buckle on your skin in a restorative pose if you can help it since that can be a distraction that inhibits deep relaxation. In fact, when doing any restorative work, make every effort not to have your body touching anything unnecessary or uncomfortable in any way (even if it's not really painful), because that contact will generate mental fluctuations (Skt, "cittavrtti") and disturb your mind, even if only subtly. That contact will act like a bridge to lead your focus outside your body whereas what we are aiming for in the restorative poses is to move inward.

The standard way of entering this pose is to sit on the bolster or support, lie down on your side and take both your sitting bones to the wall, and then roll onto your back, taking your legs up the wall. Just as in Halasana, you can also roll forward into this pose from Adho Mukha Svanasana by keeping your chin well tucked and setting yourself down onto your shoulders, then rolling forward to take your legs gently to the wall. Take care not to set yourself down on your head or neck. To come out of the pose, you can reverse this process back out into Halasna, then back into Adho Mukha Svanasana and then relax in child's pose. You should be quite comfortable and grounded in Halasna before attempting these variations. Also, the main focus of this pose is relaxation, so these variations are more for just occasional practice or, for instance, for entering the pose in a crowded class where you are shoulder-to-shoulder with other students.

There are several variations for positioning your arms in this pose. Experiment with them and find how they affect you differently and if one allows you to relax more deeply.

(1) along your sides as in Savasana

(2) straight out to your sides at shoulder level

(3) in the "stick 'em up position" with your hands overhead. If you choose this position, keep your upper arms at about the same level as your shoulders, not much higher over your head because that position can cause some tension in your throat and neck area.

(4) resting on your abdomen. Sometimes in a class situation, this may be your only option if there are others close around you due to a lack of wall space.

If your arms are overhead, from your feet to your

hands, all the way should be downhill. This is an inversion.

When doing any restorative pose, focus on softening your sense organs (eyes, ears, nose, tongue, and skin) -- the "organs of perception." Your mouth should be almost open, your lips touching very slightly. Have the sensation of unhinging your jaw so that your teeth do not touch. Your tongue should relax onto your lower palate, not press on your upper palate, and descend back and downward. This tongue position is key in all the restorative poses and in pranayama. Though it may feel awkward at first, practice it until it feels natural. Soften your throat.

One particularly restorative way to end this pose is to slide your legs down the wall and cross them in Sukhasana on the wall for a while, changing the cross of your legs mid-way through, and then to slide your tailbone back onto the floor and allow your legs to rest on the bolster crossed in Sukhasana for a while, again changing the cross of your legs. This position is especially useful for allowing your abdomen to recede and relax.

5. Halasana

Technique

Spread a folded blanket on the floor and lie flat on the back with arms straight near the body, palms facing downward. Keeping the legs straight raise them slowly above the head. Only stomach abdominal muscles should be used to raise the legs. Bend the trunk upward hips first and slowly lower the legs over the head till the toes

touch the floor. Keep the legs straight. Now interlock the fingers and stretch the arms. The legs and hands are stretched opposite direction. Breathe slowly without any strain. Remain in this pose for a couple of minutes. Return to the original position and relax.

6. Bhujangasana

Technique

1. Lie prone on the floor. Stretch your legs back, tops of the feet on the floor. Spread your hands on the floor under your shoulders. Hug the elbows back into your

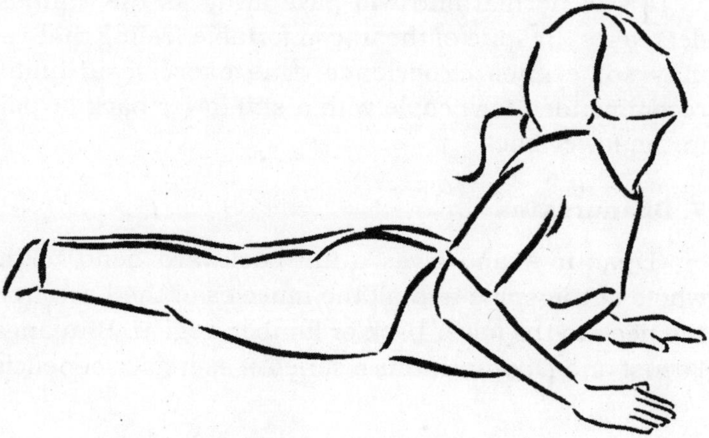

body.

2. Press the tops of the feet and thighs and the pubis firmly into the floor.

3. On an inhalation, begin to straighten the arms to lift the chest off the floor, going only to the height at which you can maintain a connection through your pubis to your legs. Press the tailbone toward the pubis and lift the pubis toward the navel. Narrow the hip points. Firm but don't harden the buttocks.

4. Firm the shoulder blades against the back, puffing the side ribs forward. Lift through the top of the sternum but avoid pushing the front ribs forward, which only hardens the lower back. Distribute the backbend evenly throughout the entire spine.

5. Hold the pose anywhere from 15 to 30 seconds, breathing easily. Release back to the floor with an exhalation.

Build up the exercise in a quiet way. When the lower back is stiff, this exercise may cause the lower back to feel a little painful and uncomfortable.

This is normal and will pass away as the stiffness decreases. In spite of the uncomfortable feeling that you may sometimes experience, this exercise is highly recommended for people with a stiff lower back or pain in the lower back.

7. Dhanurasana

Dhanur Asana gives a full backward bend to the whole of the spine and all the muscles of the back from the neck to the lower back or lumber region. Bhujanga, Locust and Dhanur forms a series of exercises beneficial

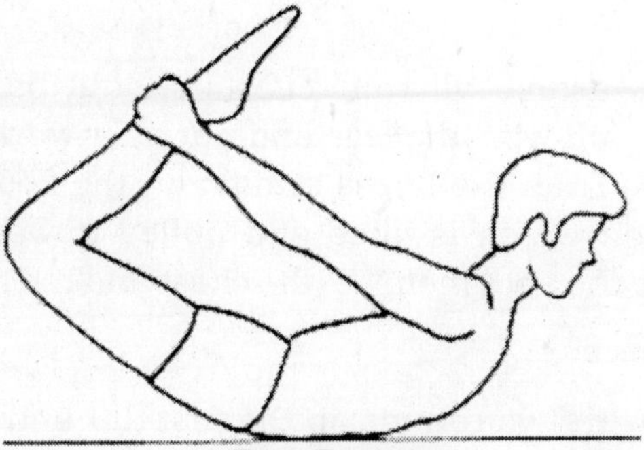

Bow Posture

to the body when practiced together. As the forward bend flexes the spine, the bow extends it.

Technique

1. Lie on your stomach with your arms stretched on both sides. Place your right or left cheek on the floor. Bend the knees, bringing the feet up. Bring the heels close to the buttock area. Reach back to hold the ankles with your hands. The knees and the ankles should be closer to one another.

2. Inhale as much air as you can. Straighten up your neck and head. Holding the breath and keeping the arms straight, arch the entire body upwards. Lift the head, chest and thighs off the floor. Remain in this position for 5 to 6 seconds.

3. Exhale and return to the floor smoothly. Keep holding the ankles while you return to the first position. Put the cheek back on the floor and breath normally.

4. Leave the ankles and let the legs gradually return to the floor. Bring the arms and hands to the floor on both sides and relax for 6 to 8 seconds. You have completed one round of bow posture.

Note

In this asana, all your efforts should be to give a backward pull with the legs and not a forward pull with the hands. Thus the knees remain on the floor and the only portion which is lifted and pulled upwards is the area above the abdomen, i.e. the chest and the head area.

Restrictions

Start with two rounds on the first day and gradually to a maximum of four rounds. In the first position in case you find it difficult to hold the ankles then hold the toes.

Do not attempt the bow while pregnant, as these asana increases the pressure on the abdomen.

Benefits

Activates and strengthen all the major and minor joints of the body. Strengthens all the abdominal muscles and organs. Develops digestive power and removes extra weight and fat from the stomach and waist areas. Enhance the elasticity of the spine. Chest, lungs and neck are strengthened and activated, benefiting people suffering from asthma and other respiratory problems. For women, it corrects menstrual and other troubles related to reproductive organs.

8. Salabhasana

Salabha Asana is a reverse posture to the Cobra Posture, which gives a backward bend to the spine. Values of certain asanas are maximised when done one after the other. Cobra posture activates the upper area while locust activates the lower waist down area of the body. So this asana gives maximum benefit when done

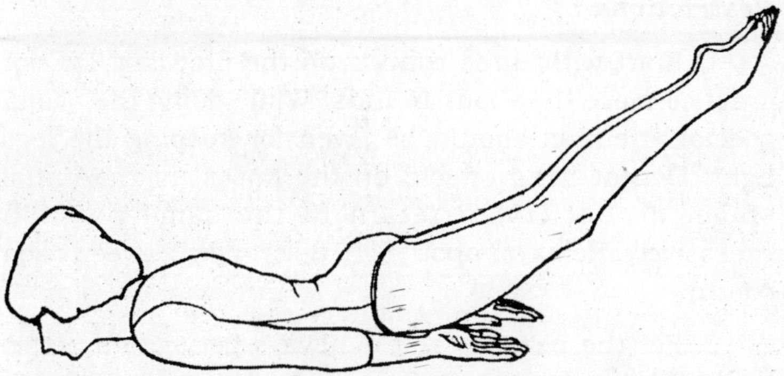

after the cobra posture.

Since full-locust is strenuous, it is better for the beginners to practice the half-locust posture before attempting the full-locust.

Full Locust Posture

Technique

1. Lie face down on the floor on your stomach, hands stretched backwards close to the body and the legs straight. Making fists of the hands bring them together beneath the thighs with the wrists touching.

2. Inhale as much air as you can. Holding your breath make your head straight and put the chin on the floor (on a folded blanket or towel). Tighten both the legs and lift them up as high as you can. Do not bend the knees.

3. Remain in the same posture for a few seconds.

4. Exhale and simultaneously lower the legs slowly to the floor. Do not drop the legs. By the time the legs touch the floor you should finish exhaling. You have completed one round of a most strenuous posture. Relax.

Restrictions :

1. Start with three rounds on the first day. Do not practice more than four rounds. While doing the asana special attention should be given for keeping the legs tight. Do not bend or fold on the knees. In the initial stage, do not try to retain in the same position excessively. Relax for about 6 10 8 seconds between each round.

2. For the beginners, it is always better to practice the half-locust posture before attempting the full-locust. When you first attempt the locust, you may be disappointed to find that your feet rise only slightly from the floor. Do not be discouraged. This will improve rapidly with practice.

Half - Locust Posture

For the half locust, the position, the breathing and the body conditioning are as same as the full-locust. The only difference is that you lift one leg up at a time. Lift legs alternatively. Do not twist the hips or bend the knee. Repeat lifting 2-4 times each.

Benefits :

The locust brings flexibility to the cervical (upper back) region and strength to the lower back. Brings a rich blood supply to the spine and the whole upper area. Favourably activates the kidneys, liver and all the organs of the lower part of the body. Increases abdominal pressure, regulating intestinal function and strengthening the abdominal walls and relieves back pain.

9. Paschimottanasana

Relax your body and mind, stretch your hamstrings, shoulders, and spine, relieve stress, and improve your posture and concentration by practicing the Seated Forward Bend. Learn how to do this properly and achieve maximum results.

This forward bend gives a complete stretching to the neck, the back, the hamstrings and calves. At the same time, it directs your attention inward. You stimulate the entire nervous system and learn to find stillness and relaxation during a period of effort or even discomfort when doing this stretching exercise.

Method

Tip 1: Sit down with your legs stretched. The legs lie side by side and the toes point upwards. Stretch your lower back and raise your arms. Look forward, lengthen your back, and keep the chest and your breathing free.

Tip 2: Slowly bend forward, stretch your crown upward and try not to lose the supporting dynamism of

the lower back. See to it that your legs do not move or tilt.

Tip 3: The moment you notice that you can only bend further by bending the lower back, move your hands to your lower legs, ankles or feet. Lightly pull your legs, ankles or feet and continue stretching.

Keep your shoulders down. Breathe in and out across the entire length of your spinal column deeply and in a relaxed way. Everytime you exhale, you should bend further towards your legs without losing the length in your back and the dynamism in the lower back. When you lose the dynamism in the lower back, you will notice that you lose a major part of the stretching and you will have a hard time breathing.

Step 4: Stretch out your arms forward.

Step 5: Slowly raise your upper body. Keep your legs lying side by side and the toes pointing upwards.

Step 6: Sit straight up again, just like your original position.

10. Janu Sirshasana

Technique

1. Sit on the floor with your legs out.

2. Bend one leg, bring the heel of your foot as close to your right groin as possible.

3. For comfort you may place a pillow under your bent knee. Ensure that your spine is straight.

4. Now exhale and begin to move forward slowly, keeping your back as straight as possible.

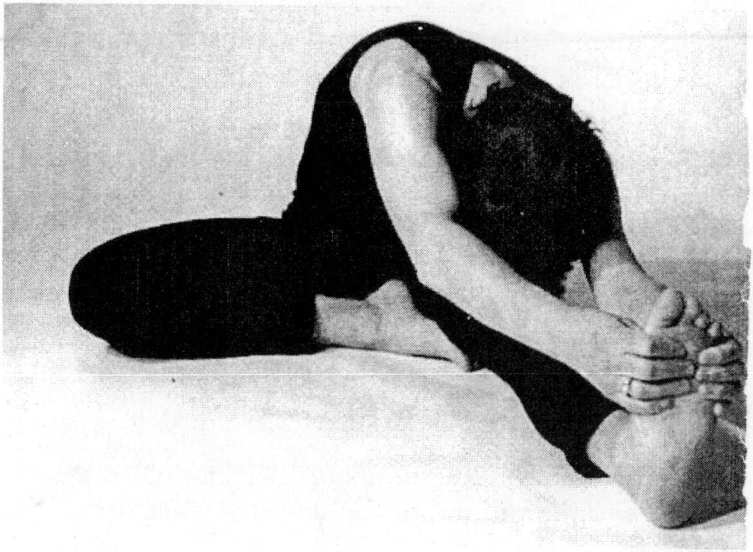

5. Breathing normally, stretch forwards and straighten your spine.

6. Maintain the position for as long as you can, breathing normally.

7. Move forward as far as you can, stretch your arms and try to hold your foot.

8. To return to an upright position, stretch forwards, inhale and stretch your arms up.

9. Repeat the pose with the next foot bent.

11. Supta-Vajrasana

Technique

1. Kneel, with the knees together, the feet about 12 inches apart, soles upward, and sit between the feet.

Supta - Vajrasana

2. Begin with the spine upright (vajrasana) and then bend backwards until the spine rests on the floor with the arms stretched back.

3. Retain the position for 2 minutes. Regain the normal position by reversing the process.

Caution:

There should never be more than normal pressure on the back, arms, and the ankle joints while doing this exercise.

Benefits

1. This stretches the thigh muscles and the abdomen.
2. The stomach is stimulated.
3. It strengthens the thighs.
4. Helps those suffering from constipation.

12. Ardha-Matsyendrasana

Placing the right foot at the root of the left thigh, encircling the (right) knee by the left leg, holding (the two feet by the opposite hands), twisting the body and staying in this posture is the Asana declared by Sri Matsyanatha.

Notes:- For the beginners this Asana is made easy and named Ardha-Matsyendrasana. The only difference is that in Matsyendrasana the folded leg is placed at the

root of the thigh below abdomen, in Ardha-Matsyendrasana it is placed by the side of the opposite buttock.

Technique :-

1. Sit extending both the legs together in front, hands by the side, palms resting on the ground. Fingers should remain together pointing forward.

2. Fold the right leg at knee.Slowly set the right heel at the perineum.

3. Now folding the left leg, bringing it from above the right knee, place it by its side on the ground. The knee of the left leg should remain towards sky.

4. Now bring the right hand on the left side of the left knee. The left knee should remain at the left side of the right armpit.

5. Now straighten the right hand and hold the toe or ankle of the left leg.

6. Twisting the body to the left side, look backwards,

place the left hand bringing it from the back on the right thigh. Gaze should be towards back.

7. While returning to the original position first release the hand from the thigh and turn head forward.

8. Now bring the back to normal position after loosening the right hand.

9. Bring the left leg in original position.

10. Now bring the right leg also original position.

11. Repeat it similarly from the other side by folding the left leg first.

Remember :-

1. Some persons may experience difficulty in practising it. If they cannot hold the toes of the left by right hand they should hold the ankle.

2. If that also is not possible then hold the knee.

3. While twisting backward twist the backbone turning well.

4. Before resorting to the practice of this Asana pracitse Vakrasana.

Benefits and Limitations :-

1. It is very much useful in constipation and dyspepsia.

2. This Asana improves liver efficiency and removes debility of kidney.

3. It is very useful in diabetes.

4. It is very beneficial for the muscles of shoulder and back.

5. Those suffering from stiffness in spine should practise it very carefully.

13. Baddha-Konasana (Bound Angle Pose)

Bound Angle Pose, also called Cobbler's Pose after the typical sitting position of Indian cobblers, is an excellent groin- and hip-opener.

(BAH-dah cone-AHS-anna)

baddha = bound

kona = angle

Technique

1. Sit with your legs straight out in front of you, raising your pelvis on a blanket if your hips or groins are tight. Exhale, bend your knees, pull your heels toward your pelvis, then drop your knees out to the sides and press the soles of your feet together.

2. Bring your heels as close to your pelvis as you comfortably can. With the first and second finger and

thumb, grasp the big toe of each foot. Always keep the outer edges of the feet firmly on the floor. If it isn't possible to hold the toes, clasp each hand around the same-side ankle or shin.

3. Sit so that the pubis in front and the tailbone in back are equidistant from the floor. The perineum then will be approximately parallel to the floor and the pelvis in a neutral position. Firm the sacrum and shoulder blades against the back and lengthen the front torso through the top of the sternum.

4. Never force your knees down. Instead release the heads of the thigh bones toward the floor. When this action leads, the knees follow.

5. Stay in this pose anywhere from 1 to 5 minutes. Then inhale, lift your knees away from the floor, and extend the legs back to their original position.

Benefits

1. Stimulates abdominal organs, ovaries and prostate gland, bladder, and kidneys

2. Stimulates the heart and improves general circulation

3. Stretches the inner thighs, groins, and knees

4. Helps relieve mild depression, anxiety, and fatigue

5. Soothes menstrual discomfort and sciatica

6. Helps relieve the symptoms of menopause

7. Therapeutic for flat feet, high blood pressure, infertility, and asthma

8. Consistent practice of this pose until late into

pregnancy is said to help ease childbirth.

9. Traditional texts say that Baddha Konasana destroys disease and gets rid of fatigue.

14. Yoga-Mudra

Technique

1. From a position sitting on your heels, press your sitz bones downward.

2. Press the crown of your head away from your shoulders and feel the elongation of your spine.

3. Bring your hands behind your back, interlacing your fingers. Press your hands away from your shoulders, allowing your arms to elongate, your shoulder blades to come together, and your chest to expand.

4. Lift your tailbone and allow the lifting to extend your torso forward over your knees, bringing your forehead to rest on the ground.

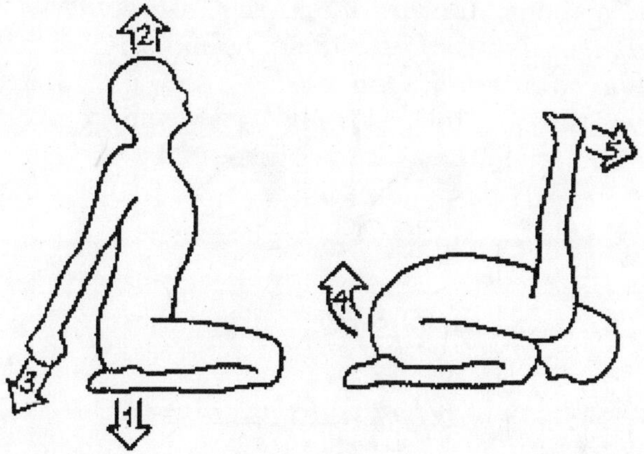

5. Allow your arms to come over your head, pressing your little fingers toward the ground in front of you.

Stay in the posture. Breathe.

To release, press your shins downward and drop your tailbone as you return to the starting position. Release your hands and feel them rise.

Benefits:

1. Tones and irrigates the kidneys
2. Stimulates digestion

16. Uddiyana-Bandha (Upward Abdominal Lock)

"Of all the Bandhanas, this is the best. The complete practice of this makes emancipation easy" (Gheranda-Samhita 3.1).

"Even an old person can become young when [Uddiyana Bandha] is done regularly" (Hatha-Yoga-Pradipika 3.58).

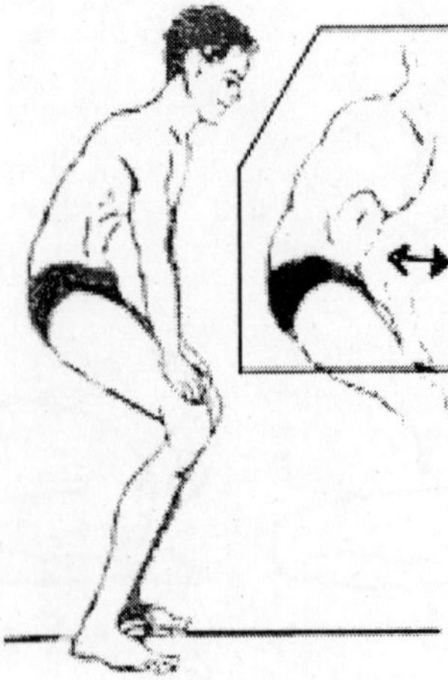

(oo-dee-YAH-nah BAHN-dah

uddiyana = upward (cf. ud = "up, upwards")

bandha = binding, tying a bond, fetter; putting together, uniting, contracting, combining; mundane bondage, attachment to this world (as opposed to emancipation, mukti or moksha).

There are a few important points to remember when beginning the practice of Uddiyana Bandha: perform it only on an empty stomach, and only after an exhalation, never before an inhalation. During the time you hold the bandha, also perform Jalandhara Bandha. Most teachers recommend that you learn this bandha in a standing position, and only move to sitting after you've gained some experience. Similarly, wait until you've been sitting for a while before using this bandha during pranayama. T.K.V. Desikachar suggests that Uddiyana can also be learned in a supine reclining position (see the Variation section below).

Technique

1. Stand with your slightly feet apart, eyes open. Different teachers have different ideas about the proper way to perform this bandha. Here are four possibilities:

a) Practice with your torso rounded forward, knees bent, hands resting on your knees.

b) Learn the bandha first with your torso rounded forward and then, after getting some experience, practice the bandha standing upright, hands on hips.

c) Practice throughout with your torso upright.

d) Start the practice with your torso rounded forward,

perform Uddiyana Bandha, and then stand upright, with your hands on your hips (Iyengar).

2. Inhale deeply through your nose, then exhale quickly and forcibly, also through your nose (or pursed lips). Contract your abdominal muscles fully to push as much air as possible out of your lungs. Then relax your abdominals.

3. Perform what's called a "mock inhalation"; that is, expand your rib cage (thorax) as if you were inhaling, but don't actually inhale. The expansion of the rib cage

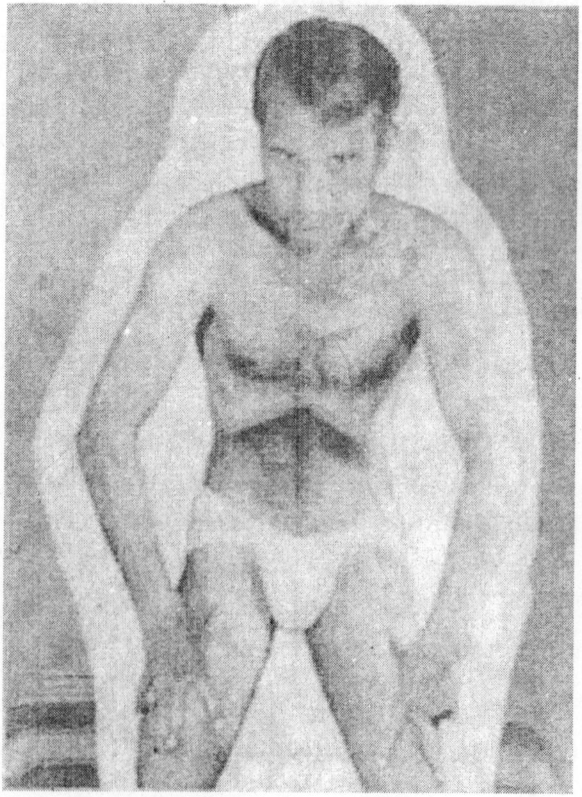

(without the inhalation) sucks the abdominal muscles and viscera up into the thorax and hollows the belly (some teachers say to actively but slowly lift abdominals, or navel, toward the spine). Because you should always perform Jalandhara Bandha along with Uddiyana Bandha, come into Jalandhara Bandha at this point.

4. Hold the bandhas for five to 15 seconds. Then slowly release the abdominal grip and inhale normally. Perform three to 10 rounds, depending on your capacity, with one or more normal breaths between each round.

Benefits

1. Strengthens the abdominal muscles and diaphragm

2. Massages abdominal viscera, the solar plexus, and the heart and lungs

3. Increases gastric fire; improves digestion, assimilation, and elimination; and purifies the digestive tract of toxins

4. Stimulates blood circulation in the abdomen and blood flow to the brain

5. Stimulates and lifts the energy of the lower belly (apana vayu), to unite it with the energies localized in the navel (samana vayu) and heart (prana vayu).

All of them should be practiced during a complete Yoga session.However, the asanas indicated above could prove be harmful if they are performed incorrectly and without the guidance of a qualified instructor. Before accepting a student, the Yoga instructor should be informed about the student's state of health and should be able to offer necessary advice on how to perform the asanas correctly.

Some asanas should not be done by menstruating women – like those marked with an asterisk (*) – by those suffering from spinal problems or from hyper or hypotension. Likewise, those with various other problems such as asthmatic and heart problem or orthopedic ailments like arthritis, osteoarthritis, muscle spasms etc. The asanas in question could be modified or replaced by more suitable Yogic practices.

Further, the asanas should not be practiced during the period of digestion. They should be done either before meals, or at least 4 1/2 hours after a substantial meal. The duration and number of repetitions for each asana should gradually be increased, in strict adherence to the instructor's guidance. Ideally, at the end of a Yoga session, you should not feel tired, but fresh and full of energy.

YOGA POSITIONS FOR OLDER WOMEN

For older women, Yoga offers a primary form of therapy that can help them adjust to hormonal changes and cope with a wide range of problems. Yoga practice can be an effective antidote to the stiffness and fatigue that tends to settle into the body with the passage of time. Even a short Yoga session helps replenish energy reserves, especially when practised with the help of Yoga props.

When periods stop, some women say that Yoga is their menopause medicine. If you practice Yoga prior to menopause, all the poses that are especially useful for coping with uncomfortable symptoms will already be familiar to you. You will be able to reach for them like a nurturing and supportive friend.

ESSENTIAL YOGA POSITIONS FOR OLDER WOMEN

Yogasanas for Older Women

- Supported Lying Down Bound-Angle Pose – Supta Baddha Konasana)
- Supported Child Pose – Adho Mukha Virasana
- Supported Downward Facing Dog Pose – Adho Mukha Svanasana
- Supported Bridge Pose – Sethu Bandhasana
- Supported Legs-Up-the-Wall Pose – Viparita Karani
- Supported Deep Relaxation Pose – Shavasana
- Always place your props for these poses on a Yoga mat so that they don't slide.

YOGA BOLSTERS FOR OLDER WOMEN

Yoga bolsters provide a firm support for the entire length of the spinal column, from the lower back to the head, when you are lying down. The abdominal muscles, chest and back release their tension, lengthen and relax deeply. Bolsters are specifically designed so that the sides of the rib cage may open and expand and move downward toward the floor.

When your rib cage expands laterally like this, naturally your breathing capacity deepens. The bolster leaves a vital and lasting impression on the body of what it feels like to have the chest open and free. Then again, two or three firm blankets, neatly folded similar to the shape of a yoga bolster, can also be used.

Yoga Poses for Flat Abs

We have all heard about the abs and the need for strengthening them. Most folks also have the desire to have well-toned, strengthened and flat abdominal muscles. So they go to the gym. But did you know even Yoga has a set of cleansing kriyas, physical exercises, postures and breathing exercises that will literally crush the bulge?

Poses that target excess weight in the abdominal region:

- Surya Namaskar – Sun Salutations
- Dhanurasana – Bow pose
- Mayurasana – Peacock pose
- Padahastasana – Standing forward bend
- Kakasana – Crow pose

Eka Pada Baka Dhyanasana – One legged crane meditative pose

Of course there are many other poses that could be very useful for toning the abs such as the Shoulder Stand (Sarvangasana), the Plough (Halasana), Wheel (Chakrasana), so on and so forth.

In addition, keeping in line with Yoga's insistence on a cleaner colon as the first step to abdominal weight loss or tone, we suggest that you perform cleansing kriyas.

Suggested Cleanising Kriyas for abdominal weight loss :

- Vaman dhauti (every day for a month)

- Shanka Prakshalana (once a week for a month)

Breathing exercises to burn abdominal fat:

- Kapalabhati

- Anuloma-Viloma

- Bhastrika

- Suryabhedana

Together with these cleansing techniques, the Yoga poses are excellent for detoxifying the body. They cleanse and exercise the abdominal region. ·Further, a set of simple push-up to gain wrist strength or practicing it against the wall. Jhula asana (swinging lotus) is also known to produce great results.

We would also include other basic exercises such as the use of the Ab-wheel, windmills etc. They offer a bit of variety sometimes. However, that is just on occasion. The aforementioned Yoga Poses are excellent in themselves for exercising the abdominal region thoroughly. Coupled with a customized diet, those of you seeking abdominal weight loss would find success in using these Yoga practices.

12

THE PHILOSOPHY OF YOGA

In the context of the ancient Vedic culture of India, the knowledge that takes one forward and liberates one from the limited experience of body consciousness or the name and form consciousness, the ultimate knowledge that bestows upon one cosmic consciousness, is known as the higher knowledge or the greater knowledge, Para Vidya. This higher knowledge is clearly differentiated from the lower or the lesser knowledge, which pertains only to things that are within the confines of time, space and causation, that are limited by time, space and causation. This latter knowledge of things that are limited within time and space is therefore finite and temporary. It is non-eternal. It is the lesser knowledge, and at best it can help you to have a comfortable life of physical conveniences, sense satisfaction, and temporary, partial desire-fulfilment. It has not the power—limited, finite things have not the power—to liberate you from fear and sorrow, to liberate you from all the limitations and imperfections that pertain to this limited life bound by birth and death, hunger and thirst, joy and sorrow, and the ever-changing experiences of sense contacts. Those who seek a knowledge that is beyond this relative knowledge are, therefore, the aspirants for Para Vidya or the higher knowledge which ultimately bestows upon you freedom from bondage, fear and sorrow. This higher knowledge bestows upon you ultimately the experience of your real identity, your true Self which is beyond the apparent, limited self. It ultimately confers upon you spiritual illumination and perfection, the peace that passeth understanding, freedom from all limitations and absolute bliss.

Practice—The Keynote of the Science of Yoga

Para Vidya is not only for knowing, but also for doing. It is not simply for acquiring information, but more importantly, for putting that information to use by translating it into action, into practice. Because, Para Vidya or the science of Yoga is a practical science that is to be applied in living your life. This vital fact, this important point, in relation to the knowledge of Yoga should not be lost sight of. There should be in you the desire and the determination to start applying the instructions contained in the science of Yoga to your own life and conduct—to your mental actions and verbal actions, as well as to your outer physical actions. That is the very essence of this study that it is acquired with the specific intention and objective of simultaneously translating it into action, of simultaneously applying it to your daily life. Thus, every part of Yoga, right from the very start, is knowledge imparted for conversion into Abhyasa, because it is Abhyasa only that will ultimately bring to you the fruit of your knowledge in the form of rare experience that nothing else in this world can give. Therefore, always remember this term, this word, this concept, of Abhyasa, because Yoga is a practical science of Self-realisation and Abhyasa is the very essence of this science. You learn in order to live, to do.

The Afflictions that Beset the Human Being

The philosophy of Yoga puts forward, in non-technical or non-metaphysical terms, the thesis that you are essentially an all-perfect entity totally free from any imperfection and not subject to any undesirable, imperfect, negative experience whatsoever. What are the undesirable, imperfect, negative experiences within the range of human knowledge? They are all those things which you are commonly engaged in trying to avoid by so many devious methods. Every day, from the time of your birth, you keep trying to avoid the discomfort and pain that is brought about by hunger. You do not want to remain on an empty stomach even for an hour or two beyond your usual time of breakfast or lunch. If the lunch is missed, you are very, very perturbed, very much disturbed, very much distressed. You become very morose and irritable also. Your whole mood changes. You become a different person. You are no longer a pleasant person. All the days of your life you are engaged in trying to avoid the unpleasant experience of not getting your food. If you do not get your morning breakfast or morning tea, or if you are deprived of your lunch, or if you have to miss your supper, you become a different person. You do not like that experience. So, you try to avoid that circumstance by somehow or the other trying to get something to eat. Have you ever thought about this? This is such a daily and common experience, and such a routine experience, that no one pays any attention to it from the philosophical angle, from the analytical metaphysical angle.

What is it that happens to you if you have to miss your meal just once? You whole interior changes. You become a different person. You are no longer a pleasant person. You are inclined to give a sharp answer. You are displeased. Your peace is lost. You do not feel happy and you manifest your unhappiness in the form of a sharp answer or an irritated reply or aggravating conduct. This is an affliction that constantly keeps plaguing the human individual. When he wakes up in the morning, he has this affliction of the desire for taking food. One may call it hunger. Many naturopaths have a different opinion on whether this desire for food is really hunger or not. They have their own opinion. But normally, when you wake up in the morning, the desire that arises for taking something is regarded as the sign of hanger. So, this experience that bothers you, which if it is not satisfied distresses you, changes your personality for the time being, and makes you a different person to your own wife and to your brothers and sisters and even to your mother, is an affliction.

The same is the case with thirst, sleep, fatigue and other emotions also. Various sentiments and emotions bother you, disturb you, throw you out of gear and make you restless. They have the power to agitate you, to make you feel distressed. Unfulfilled desire, anger, a little failure on the part of someone to show respect to you, unkindness from someone, some sharp word from someone, or the failure on the part of someone to recognise your presence—all these immediately put you in a turmoil. Thus, physically, you are subject to the afflictions of hunger, thirst and fatigue and heat and cold. And mentally, emotionally and sentimentally, you are always subject to the affliction of varying states of mind. In this way, you are constantly falling a prey to varying states of mind, not all of which are pleasant. Some are pleasant, many are distressing. Yoga philosophy says that this is an unnatural condition, that this is not your natural condition. You are not a creature subject to such afflictions. You are not a being who has any one of these distressing experiences and symptoms. You are above them, you are beyond them, you are really free from them. They do not really form a part of your actual, true nature. This is very fine for Yoga philosophy to say! But this is not your experience. Your experience contradicts the possible validity or truth of this fine philosophy. Your experience is directly the contrary of what Yoga philosophy says about you. Every day you are in a state of distress only. Every day you suffer. The afflictions of hunger, thirst and discomfort, heat and cold, pain and pleasure are your daily experience. If a little attention is not paid to you when you ask something, your mind is thrown into a state of distress, agitation and turmoil; and it brings about physical changes also. Your blood pressure goes up, your face is flushed, you feel hot and uncomfortable all over, and you want to blurt out something. You want to express your feeling of displeasure and distress and give vent to it so that you can relieve yourself of this inner buildup. You are altogether in an upset condition if someone somehow fails to pay due attention to what you try to bring to his notice, if your request is not regarded, if your presence is not recognised, or if something which you put forward is not properly attended to. So, your experience is an ever-fluctuating, ever-changing experience of constant contraries and constant opposites swinging between hope and despair, joy and sorrow, elation and depression—not only depression, but also a great deal of agitation caused by unfulfilled desires and cravings for things, agitation caused by irritability, annoyance, anger, fear, worry, anxiety and jealousy.

The Real Status of Man

Yoga philosophy says, "No. You are really free from all these things. You have no afflictions. You have no hunger, no thirst, no sleep, no fatigue. You have no pain, no pleasure. You have no distress, no agitation, no worry, no anxiety. You are a being full of perfection, complete in yourself, lacking nothing, full of joy, full of peace, full of bliss". Then, if that is the fact, how come that your entire life, your entire experience from morning till night, contradicts this fact? What is the explanation? What is the reason for this? Why is this complication there? Whence has this problem arisen?

Yoga philosophy offers the analogy of a perfectly clear crystal which is transparent and pure, but becomes filled as it were with some colour if some coloured object is brought forth near it. The object thus brought forth may be a green-coloured ball or a little red-coloured flower or a blue-coloured cork and the whole crystal becomes green or red or blue. This proximity of something having some characteristic brings about a seeming transference of that characteristic from that something into the pure, transparent, clear crystal. So, it is the proximity to something that is the cause for the apparent change in the otherwise attributeless crystal ball. Now, Yoga philosophy says that you are also in a similar state of proximity to something, you have become involved with something, and therefore, states and conditions that exist in that factor seem as though they have come and taken possession of you.

In the ease of the crystal, if you want it to become clear once again, what is the method to bring it about? You have to bring about once again a separation between the crystal and its proximate object. You have to bring about a cessation of the proximity that is there between the crystal and the object by separating the two. If the proximate object is taken away and the crystal is once again isolated from that object which has been superimposing all its qualities upon it, then, once again the crystal is pure, clear and transparent. Once again it stands in its own nature; it regains its own nature. It is no more modified and qualified by the something else which is not part of its essential being. This is the analogy that you have to consider and keep in mind.

Prakriti and Its Play of Superimposition

Now, what is it that has thus become involved in a state of proximity with you that is seemingly transferring its imperfect nature upon you, upon your perfectly pristine native condition, which is sorrowless, painless, without any limitation, without any blemish? Yoga philosophy tells you that it is phenomenal nature. Nature, in all its variations, acts as the factor which limits you into a certain range of experience which is its own area, which is its own territory; and, by its proximity and by its close association with you, it transfers its varying experience into you as it were, and this cosmic nature with its different variations is termed Prakriti. And in your own physical personality, in your own individual personality, this Prakriti comprises all those factors other than your essential pristine identity, other than your eternal unchanging nature. Your eternal, unchanging nature is an identity independent of this cosmic nature, called Prakriti, and therefore, perfectly free from all the limitations that are part of Prakriti. But your present experience does not seem to reflect that essential identity of pristine awareness, where you are totally independent of any changeful experience whatsoever, where you are ever in a state of unchanging experience of fullness, peace and joy. On the other hand, your present experience seems to be the very contradiction of your pristine experience. Why? It is precisely because of your being associated with Prakriti in all its variegated modes, because of your being involved with it in a state of identification, taking upon yourself and your consciousness factors that do not really pertain to your eternal pristine native state. These factors are foreign to you, but you have taken them upon yourself. Or, they have become somehow like creepers twining into a tree due to close association. This association and this close proximity is the root cause of your being deprived of that experience of fullness and perfection, of peace and joy, which is your native state, and of your being caught in the trammels of a complicated pattern of experience which is the very contradiction of your pristine state. This is the problem. Your experience is not, therefore, your normal and natural experience. It is an unnatural, abnormal experience; and the cause, the main source or cause, the reason for this experience, is your having got into this bad company, having got into this embroilment or entanglement in Prakriti; and your true native state, your true identity in the state of Purusha, of Self, of Real Being, is lost. And as long as this involvement in the ever-changing Prakriti—which is full of contradictory experience, full of complication, full of fluctuation—is going to continue, your problem also is going to continue. As long as this state of association and entanglement with phenomenal nature is going to continue, your problem also is going to continue. The only way of putting an end to this problem, of brining about a cessation of this hotchpotch of ever-changing experience—pleasant, unpleasant and neutral—is once again to regain your isolation, to go back to your normal and native pristine position, where you are not associated with any other factor, where you are not entangled or embroiled in any other factor, where you are independent. In that independent state, you are by yourself in a state of grand isolation, untouched by anything, beyond anything. In that pristine state, you are yourself as you are, as you eternally are, independent of any other factor, grandly isolated, free from any other association. If you regain that state which is your normal state, native state—now you are in an abnormal state—then all problems vanish. There is no more weeping and wailing, there is no more swinging between contrary experiences. You regain your pristine, ever-stable, unchanging state of fullness, of perfection. So, when this association with Prakriti or cosmic nature has precipitated this unfortunate state of affairs, to put an end to it, there is only one way and that is the right royal way—stop this association, terminate this association with the imperfect Prakriti, and be yourself. Establish yourself in your pristine isolated position. This is the philosophical thesis which is at the basis of the science of Yoga.

The Spiritual Reality of Man and the Psychological Situation in which He is Caught Up

How to bring about this separation so that you once again regain your independent status where you are not caught up in the factor called Prakriti? How to bring about this breaking of your unfortunate association with Prakriti? That is what the science of Yoga is concerned about. How to give back to you your independence, how to give back to you once again that pristine state in which you are always there—that is the subject-matter of the science of Yoga.

The imperfect-experience condition which is distressing, going up and down, has arisen due to your association with Prakriti or Nature that is ever unsteady. This association has to be broken if you are to regain your independent status of everlasting joy. So, the problem and the solution are provided for you by the philosophy of Yoga and the working out of the solution is gradually elaborated in a systematic manner in the practice of Yoga. But, this practice has to recognise the present reality. The present reality is that you are a very-much harassed being subject to a great deal of distress, of limitations. Whatever the truth of your identity may be, you have lost the awareness of your identity. Now you are not in that state of identity. So, we have to start from where you are. We cannot start from the other end, whatever you might be. That seems to have no relevance at all, because that experience is lost. It is no longer there. You may be told theoretically about it; you may believe it. But now you find yourself in a totally different position, and so we have to start from the position in which you are, where you are completely involved in thought, in mind, in the mental process, in sentiments, emotions—in short, involved in all the variations of all the physical as well as the psychological factors which make up Prakriti. Prakriti is made up of many things—the five elements, the Prana, the senses, and the mind in its different modes, each mode having its own variations. One single mode of the mind has got so many variations—Vasanas, Samskaras, imaginations, anger, passion, greed, hatred, envy, jealousy, worry, selfishness, attachment. The intellect has its own variations—clear perception, unclear perception and wrong perception. So, it is a complicated maze in which your consciousness is caught at present. And, in any practice that has to bring about the liberation of your Self, you must take count of the actual present position and start from there, and hence the need to get a clear idea of the psychology of Yoga.

The practice of Yoga rests upon the present situation of the individual being and the present situation of the individual being is the psychological situation. The spiritual reality of the individual being is totally hidden and overcome by his psychological situation, like the sun or the moon overcome by an eclipse or a big piece of cloud. The practice of Yoga is thus based upon the realistic recognition of the present psychological position of the individual. As such, a clear knowledge of the present psychological situation of the individual is very essential. Herein comes the necessity of knowing about the psychology of Yoga. Based upon the psychology of Yoga, they have formulated a certain set of practices which form the practice of Yoga.

So, you are the Purusha, totally free from all sorts of negative experiences and afflictions. You are self-sufficient, independent, complete, of the nature of absolute peace and joy. But, that stage which the philosophy of Yoga clearly declares to be your authentic and genuine identity seems to be a far cry from where you now find yourself. You are very much dependent, not independent, very much full of experiences which you are always trying to get rid of somehow or the other, which you are always trying to replace by a more satisfying condition. So, it is not a very flattering position to find yourself in. Yoga science tries to explain to you why you are in this condition. Is there a way out of this condition? If so, what is it? Based upon the knowledge supplied by the science of Yoga as to why your present condition has been brought about, the way out of it also has been formulated. And if you seriously start applying this knowledge of the way out in the form of Abhyasa or personal practice, gradually it gives you back your state of independence or fullness—independence from all limitations, from all afflictions.

To sum up: your true identity is a state of absolute independence and freedom from any negative or painful or undesirable experience. You are a perfect being, free from all afflictions, independent. But, your present state does not seem to be anywhere near that pristine state and this is due to your association with another cosmical factor called phenomenal nature which Yoga philosophy calls Prakriti.

Your proximity to, and association with, Prakriti has brought about this vitiation of your own Self-experience and replaced it by a very unsatisfactory, contradictory and mixed-up experience. And therefore, this association has to be terminated. Once again separating yourself from Prakriti, you have to establish yourself in your original independent status. And the practical aspect of the science of Yoga tries to give you a certain systematic method by which this can be achieved.

13

THE PSYCHOLOGY OF YOGA

The philosophy of Yoga and the psychology behind its practice—the two are bound up together in such a way that any consideration of the one inevitably has to simultaneously take into account the other, because the practice of Yoga is laid upon the basis of a psycho-philosophical background. The philosophy of Yoga and the psychology of Yoga are present not only as a background to this science of Yoga, but also as the basis for the practice of the Yogic processes. It is upon this basis that the different practices have been formulated and presented and this point should be borne in mind always, not only when we make a study of Yoga, but also when we actually practise the different Angas of Yoga. Only then will the practice become more meaningful to us and only then can the practice itself be done in a right way and in a rational way. If this Yoga practice is to be effective, you must know why you are engaging in this practice, what this practice is supposed to achieve for you, what you are expected to gain out of this practice, and what the effect of this practice is supposed to be upon your own nature, upon your own spiritual state. Otherwise, there would be no terms of reference by which you can ascertain whether the practice is actually proceeding in the right direction or not, whether it is bearing fruits step by step or not. Upon what hypothesis, upon what thesis will you judge whether your Yoga practice is progressive or stagnant, whether it is fruitful or sterile? How can you make out? It is only when you have a certain frame of reference with which you can tally your practice from time to time that you will be in a position to engage in your practice meaningfully, in an effective and satisfactory manner. And that is why it is necessary to bear in mind the psycho-philosophical basis of these Yoga practices even while you are engaged in them.

Warding off Painful Experiences—The Main Motivation Behind All Human Activity

Every yoga enthusiasts are familiar with the broad outline of the philosophy behind Patanjali's Yoga Darshana. An analysis of the present condition of the individual shows that he is subject to many afflictions and painful experiences, many limitations and imperfections, upon the physical level and upon the psychological level—hunger and thirst, pleasure and pain, elation and depression, what they call Harsha-Soka, Sukha-Duhkha. So, bodily and mentally, the pattern of experience of the common individual does not seem to be very, very satisfactory, very desirable even, not at all beautiful. Most human beings are constantly engaged in an endless struggle of warding off painful experiences, of keeping at bay experiences that are distressing, that cause great discomfort and inconvenience. If you analyse human activity, you find that it is inextricably interconnected and interwoven with human experiences; and most of the activities are a reaction called up or thrown forth to counter these experiences, to try to change them, to try to overcome them, to try to nullify them, to try to eliminate them. So, we cannot say that human activity is in a large measure anything creative, anything gainful. It is all negative. Nothing comes out of it, except that you try to escape from bad experiences and manage to get rid of something here and something there which you do not want. It is not that you have brought forth something wonderful. So, it is neither constructive nor creative, neither gainful nor really meaningful. But, it is seen to be petty, Alpa. The Upanishad calls it Alpa. Constantly, a vast aggregate of the human race on this earth is engaged in a never-ending process of trying to ward off painful experiences, try to get rid of suffering and pain, that which it does not want. Duhkham Ma Bhuyat: Let no sorrow befall. That is the motivation. That is the idea behind most human activity. "I do not wish sorrow; I do not wish pain; I do not wish discomfort; I do not wish to have inconvenience and suffering." So, it is not a gainful process. It is not a creative or a constructive process. Life goes on like this in this struggle.

When you consider this aspect of human activity and endeavour, you find that it is not so much an original activity, due to human will or human initiative, but something forced upon the human individual. Willy-nilly he is compelled to engage in these activities, not out of his own volition, but due to the force of circumstances or outer conditions. In the light of this situation, the ancient seers tried to find out what was the cause of this. They asked themselves: "Why has this situation arisen? How has this situation come about?".

And as a result of their intuitive discoveries, they came out with this knowledge that these experiences stem from an unfortunate involvement of a being who really is not subject to these experiences, who is in a pristine state, who is in his own independent native state, who is always in a state of perfect bliss, freedom and joy. So, this is an unnatural condition, an abnormal condition, resulting from an involvement in a factor which Yoga Shastras call the phenomenal nature or Prakriti. And, due to involvement in this Prakriti, the Purusha, who is a perfect being, independent, free from all afflictions, weeps and wails. So they said: "We shall try to formulate a method by which there may be brought about once again the isolation of the Purusha from this involvement, by which there may be brought about once again a separation of these two factors—Purusha and Prakriti—the coming together of which has resulted in all sorts of suffering".

The Nature of Purusha's Involvement in Prakriti—The Interplay of the Three Gunas

What is the form of this involvement of the Purusha in Prakriti? In what way is Purusha involved in Prakriti? What is Prakriti? In what way is it present? Advaita Vedanta uses the term Maya also with reference to this phenomenal nature and the Gita gives a certain extent of information, a certain hint that this Prakriti is made out of three Gunas—they call it qualities for want of a better term—or three states of being, namely, Sattva, Rajas and Tamas. This divine cosmic illusory power called Prakriti comprises three Gunas. And Prakriti herself is present in the form of the gross physical body, the vital power that manifests as the living breath, the senses that are situated in the physical body with their natural urges towards their respective sense-objects, and the inner man, the inner being, in the form of thinking and feeling, in the form of remembering and recollecting, in the form of reasoning and willing. It is due to your involvement in this Prakriti that you are experiencing this present state of a mixture of joy and sorrow, a constantly fluctuating mixed state, like a person tasting in the mouth an equal mixture of sand and sugar. One moment you feel the sweetness; another moment the teeth grind upon the sand particles and you feel very bad about it. When it is said that the Purusha is involved in Prakriti in its variegated modes as the gross physical body, the senses, the inner Prana, mind, intellect, memory and ego, all these go to make up the sum-totality of your individual human personality. All these represent the Prakriti in its various aspects. And the involvement of the Purusha in these aspects of Prakriti necessarily affects their manifestation or expression. It affects the way in which your mind expresses itself, your feelings express themselves, your thoughts express themselves. It affects the way in which your senses manifest their nature and your body displays its dynamics in its various movements in the form of restlessness, in the form of wanting to be active, in the form of hunger, in the form of various desires to eat, drink and rest, to sleep and to move about. These manifestations constantly keep you in a state of restlessness and agitation, and also drag you out of your innermost centre and forcibly bring you out into contact with the external universe of names and forms, of temporary things. And Prakriti being a composition of the three Gunas, the manifestations and movements of these various aspects of Prakriti—inner and outer, psychological and physical—also tend to fall under one or the other of these Guna categories. All this came in for the study of the ancient seers. They observed the human individual, observed his nature, in just the same way as a modern scientist would observe an ants' colony in a glass case, day after day, keeping the ants some food and observing them by day and by night, how they go after food, what their activities are, what their nature is, what code of conduct they have got, what their laws of behaviour are and so on. In a like manner, the ancient seers, the great scientists of the inner man, observed the human individual, his nature, his behaviour and his experience. And they studied the various manifestations of the different modes of Prakriti in the human individual within the area of framework of his nature. They made a study of how Sattva manifested in man, how Rajas manifested and how Tamas manifested.

An urge to activity, a constant restlessness, a tendency to movement, was the effect of the Rajas in Prakriti. Everything ugly, negative, anti-social and destructive was the result of the manifestation of the Tamas in Prakriti. Everything beautiful, sublime, elevating, refined and subtle was seen to be the effect of the manifestation of the Sattva in Prakriti. When we say "Prakriti", you should not have in your mind the picture of some goddess or some lady creating a lot of trouble. It is not like that. Prakriti is only a word to indicate a cosmic principle which is in the form of a force. It is not so much a power as a force. Power is exercised or wielded, whereas force just manifests itself, carries everything before it. Prakriti is therefore a cosmic force, a cosmic principle which is in the form of a force, manifesting upon different levels. When this force manifests upon one level, it is said to be Tamasic. When this force manifests upon another level, it is said to be Rajasic. And when this force manifests upon yet another level, a third level, it is said to be Sattvic. And, on all these three levels, it keeps on manifesting. How this goes on has been hinted at in the famous Bhagavad Gita which is both a Brahma Vidya and a Yoga Shastra. They have hinted at a cyclic manifestation of this Prakriti wherein sometimes Sattva predominates overriding Rajas and Tamas, sometimes Rajas predominates overriding Sattva and Tamas, and sometimes Tamas predominates overriding Sattva and Rajas.

Svabhava—The Individual's Pre-acquired Pattern of Samskaras and Vasanas

Quite apart from this aspect of the movement of the three Gunas of Prakriti, there is another even more important aspect of the presence of these three Gunas of Prakriti in human nature, and that more important aspect is also to be grasped only upon the basis of philosophy. Philosophy behind and beyond Yoga has expounded the presence of recurring embodiments for the Purusha as long as the Purusha has not succeeded in dissociating himself from Prakriti and regaining his splendid isolation, his pristine independent condition. As long as that is not achieved, there is ever-recurring embodiment for the Purusha, and in each new embodiment the Purusha comes with a pre-acquired background condition. What is this pre-acquired background condition? When you have completed one page in an accounts book and you have to start upon a fresh page, you bring forward to the beginning of the fresh page the last entry that is at the end of the previous page. That will be the basis of commencement of fresh entries upon the new page. Thus, the fresh page is not a blank page. It already commences with a starting background condition. It is already there. Whether it is a credit or a debit or whatever it is, it is there. In a similar manner, at the time of each embodiment, you come into this world with a certain pre-acquired pattern of Samskaras and Vasanas, of impressions and innate tendencies, latent tendencies, which already have set the pattern of your nature in this fresh embodiment. So, this condition in which you start your life, commence your career, human career, with a certain set pattern, with an intermixture of Rajas, Tamas and Sattva in a certain ratio, is the state of Prakriti in you, is your inborn Prakriti, your built-in Prakriti state. And this is an even more important aspect of the presence of Prakriti in you than the cyclic manifestation of the three Gunas in Prakriti continuing in a sort of an ever-recurring movement within you. This condition in which you come into the world with a certain set pattern of the Prakriti with its three Gunas is indeed a very vital factor, because this decides the exact form in which the cyclic manifestation of the three Gunas will take place in you.

Will Prakriti keep on manifesting in you as the truthfulness of Harischandra or Yudhishthira or George Washington who, as the story goes, cut down an apple tree in the garden and confessed it to his father? Or, will the three Gunas manifest in you as a compromising attitude—an attitude where if it is not too inconvenient, you will stick to truth, but if it is likely to bring suffering to you, you will not mind uttering a falsehood? Or, will Rajas and Tamas manifest in you as a downright lying habit, so much as to say that you are born with a tendency to speak only false, never to utter truth? What decides the nature of manifestation of the three Gunas of Prakriti in you? The deciding factor is the background nature which you have already acquired and brought along with you when you have come into this present embodiment, into this fresh page of your account book. It is your background nature that decides the exact form, the exact Rupa-Rekha, the exact blueprint, of the dynamics of the recurring manifestation of the three Gunas in you—the precise form in which Prakriti will manifest in your particular character, in your particular individuality. And this background nature brought forward from previous births will differ from person to person. In a family there may be seven children, say, two daughters and five sons. In each one, the cyclical manifestation of the three Gunas will be there, the ever-changing pattern of their manifestation will be there. But the exact form in which this changing pattern will express itself in actuality may be completely different in each one of the children, though they are born of the same parents, brought up in the same home and environment, fed with the same food. It will be completely different, because of this other aspect of each one's involvement in Prakriti, namely, the ratio in which the three Gunas of Prakriti happen to be present in the background nature, in the foundation, in the pre-acquired built-in born nature. We call this foundation nature by the name "Svabhava". Svabhava will never change. The foundation will never change. One can go on altering the building, the superstructure, demolishing and remodelling and all that, but the foundation is unalterably there, and upon that foundation only all the remodelling will have to be done. So, the foundational aspect of your involvement in Prakriti is a very important factor.

The Animal in Man—The Problem of the Unregenerate Human Individual

The ancient Rishis, having known both these aspects of Purusha's involvement in Prakriti, namely, the presence of Prakriti in man and the manifestation of Prakriti in his nature, went on studying the two aspects. For the purpose of this study, they went deep within themselves, directed the attention of their concentrated mind upon each subject, and performed a certain very, very unique spiritual exercise upon that subject to know all the ins and outs about that subject. That spiritual exercise was called Samyama. As you proceed in Raja Yoga, you will come across this Samyama, which is an inner spiritual process made up of concentration and meditation and an intense superconscious state of cognition, of perception. A simultaneous practice of all these three put together, namely, concentration, meditation and Samadhi, directed upon a particular subject, is Samyama. Through such Samyama upon human nature, upon human behaviour, upon the inner man, the Yogis of old discovered various truths. Through such Samyama, through intuitive experiences, through a direct vision of man and things, they studied and learnt about the manifestations of the different aspects of Prakriti in different subjects. In man they discovered that the manifestations of Prakriti were sublime in some cases, neutral in some, and very degenerate and very ugly in others. Upon the very lowest end of the scale, they found that the involvement of Purusha in Prakriti resulted in Tamasic manifestations like cruelty, violence, a tendency to cause suffering, to injure, to hurt, to destroy, a dire propensity of inhuman nature. And they said that this was also a part of human nature. In common terminology, we say, "He is a very devil, he has got the devil in him, he is a devilish person". So, there is a devil in man. But, in metaphysical terminology, they call it the animal in man, because this propensity to attack, injure, hurt, destroy, cause pain and suffering, this violence is the law of the jungle. It is a common feature of the animal state of existence. So, within the human being, the involvement of Purusha with Prakriti, upon the lowest gross level, resulted in the unfortunate expression of animal propensities.

Also, an animal leads, through the whole of its life, a gross body-bound existence; its life is confined to the satisfaction of hunger, thirst, sex and sleep. That is animal life. Sex is there, because the law of biological evolution requires that the species should not become extinct. Therefore, for the continuity of the species, reproduction is indispensable, and for the process of reproduction, sex activity becomes an inevitable part of the biological, physical animal. It is because of sex that over millions of years different species have continued to exist. They are still there, and in spite of so much in nature that tries to destroy them, they continue to be there, thanks to this in-built sex mechanism, this reproductive process in the biological, evolutionary scheme of things for life on earth ordained by some mysterious superconscious being. So, these characteristics of sex, hunger, thirst and sleep form the root nature of life on earth. The whole life is nothing but a constant effort to satisfy hunger, thirst, sex and sleep and this is present in the animal man. So far, it is all right. Its presence is no dire calamity or disaster. But, if it becomes the more dominant part of your life-style, then it becomes a dangerous predicament, because you have reached a level where the biological evolution has brought you to the peak point, where quite another aspect of evolution is supposed to commence. From the peak point of the biological evolution, ethical and spiritual evolution is about to start, and as long as you allow the brute nature in you to become the dominant factor in your life-style, this will never commence, this will never be launched—this other evolution at the commencement of which you have arrived, from where you have to ascend higher and higher ultimately to become God. You are, after all, the Purusha, divine, eternal, all-perfect. But, as long as your whole nature is only a manifestation of violence, destruction, sex satisfaction, cunningness and devious dishonesty, the necessary process of ascent will never start. That will never start. So, it becomes a great calamity.

So, what happens? The human personality becomes

the unfortunate playground for the qualities of violence, carnal passion, untruth, falsehood, deception, dishonesty, acquisition and an ever-expanding process of sense satisfaction. No satiation. The more you have, the more you want, and in more ways you want to satisfy your senses, in more ways you want to give satisfaction to the animal in you. You want to go on satisfying the senses of sight, taste, sound, touch and smell. There is no end to this ever-progressive, ever-expanding sensuality, to this unsatisfied desire to grab and accumulate and acquire by hook or by crook, to this type of dishonest life-style. So, this is the problem of the unregenerate human individual and the science of Yoga sets about tackling this basic problem of the unregenerate human individual personality dominated by the animal level of his nature. And the first liberation of man from Prakriti has to be from this direct manifestation of Tamo-Guna, the grossest state of Prakriti's threefold nature. And so, Patanjali commences the Yoga discipline by saying that the first and foremost task is to come to grips with the animal in you, to get involved in a tussle with the animal in you and try to overcome it. Refuse to give in to the urge for violence, for injury, for hurting others, the urge for causing destruction either by thought, word or deed, by any movement of your personality. Refuse. Make a strong determination that from you nothing but humanity will manifest, never the animal. Tell yourself: "Now I have awakened to the fact that there is the animal in me. I am no more going to be a stage for the manifestation of the animal in me. I have determined that the stage will be cleared of the animal in me and only the human will manifest". This is the first Yogic determination, the first Yogic vow. You take a vow in order to make a strong determination. You take a Pratijna. In this manner, in Yoga, where philosophy and psychology form the basis of practice, the commencement of practice is to counter man's involvement in Prakriti in its grossest aspect. This is the Abhyasa of Yama, the first Anga of Yoga.

14

ASANA AND PRANAYAMA

In Patanjali's Yoga, Asana does not mean a specific posture, but means sitting. It means, mainly, sitting for meditation. Asana means a meditative seat. The way in which you sit for meditation should be such that the body is motionless and steady, and also, it should not cause any discomfort to the body; otherwise, it cannot be maintained for a long time. It is only when the posture is comfortable that you can maintain it for a long life. Maintaining the Asana for a long time is of paramount importance to facilitate proper meditation. The whole science of Yoga is only to prepare the person for meditation physically, vitally and mentally. So, a comfortable posture is a very important thing. The factor of comfort is very important. This is emphasised by the very terse definition of "Asana" in Patanjali's Yoga, namely, "Sthira Sukham Asanam". Therefore, Asana in Raja Yoga does not imply the different postures of the science of Hatha Yoga. They say that there are 84 lakhs of different postures. Researchers have dug up many of them. Each Yoga teacher likes to think that he has discovered many of these forgotten postures and so there are Yoga teachers who have produced books containing 200 postures, 250 postures and so on. This process is going on. However, our Master, beloved and worshipful Gurudev Swami Sivanandaji, has made it clear that out of these 84 lakhs 84 are most important. So, in his basic Yogasana book which was brought out nearly fifty years ago in Madras, titled "Yogasanas Illustrated", he has mentioned this fact and outlined the 84 important Asanas. They belong to Hatha Yoga and are mentioned in Siva Samhita, Gheranda Samhita, Hatha Yoga Pradipika and such other Hatha Yogic texts. People belonging to the Nath sect also have got some of these Asanas. In the case of Pranayama also, the Pranayama of Raja Yoga lays emphasis mainly upon Kumbhak or retention of the breath, and not upon the different types of Pranayama which are a part of the science of Hatha Yoga. In Raja Yoga, steadiness and comfort are the most essential factors of Asana; and the ability to restrain the breath, the ability to hold the breath or retain the breath, is the most important feature about Pranayama. By thus maintaining a steady unshaken posture for a long time, several things accrue to the Raja Yogi. One is that the mind gradually begins to get into a state of steadiness. This is not however due to the steadiness of the body, because in this Yogic framework, the body and the mind are not directly connected.

The Body and the Mind in Western Psychology and in Yoga

In the Western medical and psychological framework, the body and the mind are directly connected—and here by 'mind' is indicated only the lower mind, the emotional mind, mind as thought and emotion, as imagination and emotion. Mind reacts upon the body, creates various conditions in the body. Contrariwise, body conditions do affect the mental moods. If you have got a nagging pain somewhere in the body, you are depressed, you cannot keep cheerful. If you have got a toothache or a stomachache, or if you suffer from general indisposition or fever, then you become irritable, you become morose, you become cheerless. Certain types of diseases, especially those where pain is involved, affect the mind. The other way round, the mind being in a state of anxiety, the mind being in a state of stress, the mind being in a state of depression or deep conflict, it also creates tensions in various parts of the body leading to different kinds of conditions. It may lead to over-secretion of certain hormones and juices or it may inhibit the secretion of certain essential juices and bring about spasms of the muscles, causing constipation, causing various conditions.

The field of study which deals with the interaction between the body and the lower mind is called by the Westerners "Psychosomatics". "Somos" is body; "Psycho" is mind. And Psychosomatics deals with the connection between mind and body, deals with the effect of the mind upon the body. Psychosomatics is now being very much studied within the framework of medical science in the West.

Whereas, in the Yogic framework, the body is not directly connected with the mind. But then, it is indirectly connected, the interim factor that brings about the connection between the body and the mind being Prana. If the body is kept perfectly still and steady, what happens is that gradually the Prana is brought into a state of harmony, the Prana is brought into a state of stability. And when the Prana is thus established in a state of stability and harmony, the mind also is gradually brought into a state of stability and harmony, because of the link or the communication that subsists between Prana and the mind. The condition of the Prana thus influences the condition of the mind. Prana is the vital key to the control of the mind, to the control of all thoughts. Thus, by stilling the body and keeping it steady for longer and longer periods in a progressive way through daily Sadhana, daily Abhyasa, what happens is that ultimately the Prana assumes a state of stability and steadiness. This steadiness is communicated to the mind and this has the salutary effect of gradually quietening the mind. At least during the time when you are seated in the Asana, the mind also tries to become quiet. The mind also becomes a little steady. This is the benefit.

An Experiment with Asana

And then, by cultivating the practice of sitting continuously in one steady posture, the practitioner develops Titiksha, the power of endurance. And frequently, there is an urge within the mind to move, but in spite of that, you do not move. You overcome that impulse, which means, your will power is developed by habituating yourself, by compelling yourself, to sit steady and unshaken for a long time in a single posture. Thus, Atma-Bal, Mano-Bal, is developed in the practitioner. And gradually, when you are well established in the Asana, the effect of heat and cold do not have the power to affect and disturb the body as much as is generally the case. You may be perspiring, it may be very hot; but once you have got the habit of sitting steadily, you will not care. You will not want to fan yourself. You become impervious to heat and cold, even cold. I have experimented on this personally in my early days. Sometimes we used to go the Ganges bank in mid-December and January, when it is coldest in Rishikesh. In those early years of development of the Sivananda Ashram, there was no Ghat, no steps, no cement, nothing. The Ganges bank was a wild terrain of just rock and shrubs sloping down to the river. One had to step carefully. We would go at night around 10 p.m. or 11 p.m. fully dressed in sweater, flannel shirt, blanket and all that and sit upon a bare rock. We would sit on out favourite Yogic posture or Asan, and then divest ourselves of all clothes one by one, till only the Kaupin was left, and we would just put a folded towel on the rock and sit. As we removed the clothes one by one, we would feel a little chill because of the intense cold outside. But once we sat in the Asana, there was no sensation of cold at all. There was no sensation of cold and soon the body reaction set into motion and the outer skin became sensationless. It became rough like sandpaper. All the pores of the skin stood up like thorns, and in that condition, we sat for half an hour, one hour, till midnight and there was no sensation. We would be feeling hot in the armpits and perspiration would be dripping down, but the outer body would be completely ice-cold. All the same, we would have no sensation. But if we moved or started moving, then we would begin to feel the cold. As long as we sat motionless, the connection between the mind and the body got broken and the mind was away from the body. And until the time of our unlocking the Asana and getting out, there would be absolutely no sensation of cold. I have not experimented this with heat. But with cold it has been proved by personal experimentation that if one goes and sits in a certain steady Asana, especially if it is Padmasana or Siddhasana, there is no sensation outside. And sometimes during this experiment, wind would blow, biting cold wind would come from the Laxmanjhula side, but then the body would not feel it, would not mind it. It would be aware of the cold, but it would not relate itself to the cold; which is why the Yoga Darshana says that one goes beyond heat and cold if one is established in the Asana.

And I have seen this fact proved in extreme cases also. There used to be a Paramahamsa Yogi called Paramanand, a Punjabi Sadhu, in Badrinath. In Badrinath, even in the midsummer month of June, you cannot sit in the shade, because the altitude is about 10,500 feet and the place is surrounded by perennially snow-capped mountains. But, if you move into the sun, then it is bearable. After taking bath in the hot-water spring, you can go about in a banian or with a single towel thrown across your shoulder. This, only if there is bright sunshine and a blue sky, but even then, if you came under a tree, immediately you would start feeling cold.

That is the atmosphere in Badrinath. And all the twelve months this Paramanand used to live barebodied. He had only a Kaupin and long hair. He kept no vessel with himself; so he could not take a bath dipping the vessel and pouring the water over his head. But there are two or three little waterfalls, little streams—they call it Dhara—coming down from the mountainsides. This

Yogi's method of bathing was to go and sit near the stream, hold the water in the cup of his palms, and then put it over his body. His skin used to be dark black and rough like a buffalo's hide. I have heard of an even greater Titikshu, though I have not seen him. He was called Sri Krishnashram. He used to live in icy Gangotri. So, these are all advanced stages of Titiksha, but even while practising Asana as the third Anga of Raja Yoga, a stage comes when you are able to sit for a long enough time in a single posture without motion. You forget the body. The body becomes impervious to heat and cold and thus you develop the power of endurance as well as the will power of the mind.

Theory of Health and Disease in Ayurveda and Yoga

And then, by sitting in a meditative pose, you obtain a great deal of internal health benefits. Even though Asana is not a physical exercise—it is not any movement of the body—the meditative pose is such a balanced pose that by sitting in it, the Prana becomes equally distributed to all parts of the body.

According to Ayurveda, any disease, any discomfort, or anything wrong in any part of the body, is due to an upsetting of the balance between the three humours. In Ayurveda, they believe in the theory of the Tridoshas—Vata, Pitta and Kapha—wind, bile and phlegm. These three are common constituents of the human body, and if they are in a certain proportion and balance, the body is in normal health.

But if this balance, this ratio, is disturbed due to any reason, then there comes about an abnormal condition of the body. It may manifest in different ways with different symptoms. And each set of symptoms is given a label and is called by the name of a particular disease. But they say that disease is due to the imbalance of the Tridoshas—Vata, Pitta and Kapha. And most of the approach of the Ayurvedic physicians is to give some medication which will restore the balance between the Tridoshas. When this balance is restored, the person is back to normal. Whereas, in the Yogic interpretation of health and disease, they say that disease is due to the upsetting of the balance in the distribution of Prana. If the Prana becomes unevenly distributed, if it does not go to a particular place, a diseased condition can manifest in that place. Or, if the Prana accumulates too much in some place, then also a certain abnormal condition can arise. Equal distribution of Prana all over the body, throughout the body, in a balanced way, diffused—that is the condition desired. And this equal distribution means the presence of as much Prana as is required in each part. Equal distribution does not mean that Prana should be equally distributed all over the body. No. Prana is required in different proportions, in different degrees, in different parts of your body. And, if it is present in that natural state, then it is called equal distribution of the Prana. Little variations do occur in this distribution during the course of the day. When you eat food, the Prana is more concentrated over the region of the stomach. When you do intellectual work, the Prana is more active in the area of the brain. And Yogasanas bring about equal distribution of the Prana throughout the body in the desired proportion for the normal state. It is interesting to note that the Yogic interpretation of disease and the Ayurvedic theory of disease do not contradict each other. It is only one statement from two angles of vision, from two approaches. When the three humours are thrown into an imbalance, the predominance of any one of them in a particular place may draw Prana there in an abnormal quantity or may inhibit Prana from entering that particular place. From the Ayurvedic point of view, it is imbalance of the Tridoshas; and from the Yogic point of view, this imbalance of the Tridoshas brings about a disharmony in the distribution of the Prana. So, the two viewpoints are not contradictory. They are expressions of a condition from two different angles.

Take the case of a husband and a wife with one child. The husband has a certain income and he is able to look after the family with that income. As years go by, a second child comes, and the mother becomes widowed too. She now comes to live with her son and so the family grows and now they are in great financial difficulty. They are not able to look after the family. Now, why has this condition come about, this difficulty, this economic problem? We may say that it is because of the growth of the family beyond its capacity to look after itself. Or, we may say that the income is not enough, that it is not proportioned to the expenditure. From the point of view of monetary resources, the problem has arisen because the income is not sufficient. From the point of view of the family, the problem has cropped up because the members have become too many, the number of people have become too many. It is stating the same problem from two different angles. Likewise, in the case of health and ill health. When you are healthy, the Tridoshas are in balance; or you may say that the Prana is equally distributed. And when you are ill, the balance of the

Tridoshas is upset; or you may say that the Prana's even distribution is upset. So, inner health ensues out of the practice of the Asana. Due to the practice of the Asana for a long time, the Prana tends to become equally distributed throughout the body, and gradually, the normal health condition is restored to the body. This is important. And here, it is the inner health which is more vital, more important. Asana brings about inner health. It makes you impervious to heat and cold. Power of endurance is increased. Will power of the mind becomes increased. These are the benefits of the practice of Asana. And, indirectly, through the medium of the Prana, the steadiness of the body gradually brings about a certain stability of the mind, a certain steadiness of the mental activity, a certain harmony of the mental activity.

Then we come to the fourth Anga of Raja Yoga, namely, Pranayama. Pranayama is a way of controlling the Sukshma Prana within to which you have no direct access. Prana is a subtle invisible force. It is the life-force that pervades the body. It is the factor that connects the body and the mind, because it is connected on one side with the body and on the other side with the mind. It is the connecting link between the body and the mind. The body and the mind have no direct connection. They are connected through Prana only and this Prana is different from the breathing you have in your physical body. Prana is not Svasa. The respiratory breath that moves within your nostrils is not Prana. It is called Svasa Vayu. Svasa-Prasvasa, inhalation and exhalation, is of air. But then, why is the regulation of the inner breath and the outer breath of the nostrils given the name of Pranayama, when they do not constitute Prana, when they constitute only Svasa Vayu? The process of regulation of breath is given the name Pranayama, because this is the way to ultimately gain control over the subtle life-force that is present within as Prana.

How Pranayama Controls Prana?

Having no direct access to Prana, the ancient Rishis evolved this method, because the outer manifestation of the inner Prana is present in the human system in the form of breath. Breath is the outcome of the movement of Prana. Breath is the outcome of the most vital and important movement of Prana. It is the Prana that moves the lungs and makes the lungs expand and contract, expand and contract, expand and contract, from the moment you are born until the moment you give up your body in death. It is Prana, the great life-principle, which keeps on this movement. It is that which pumps the heart. It does various other functions as well, pervading the whole body and being present in different ways. In performing different functions, the same Prana assumes distinct names—Prana, Apana, Vyana, Udana, Samana. Besides these, there are five Upa-Pranas or subsidiary Pranas also.

In this way, this life-principle is working all the time; and whether you are awake or asleep, whether you are conscious or unconscious, automatically this Prana keeps up all the indispensable essential life-movements within you. If these life-movements are not kept going, life will not last. You will not be able to live; the body will not be kept alive. So, the Prana functions involuntarily. You do not exert to make the lungs move. It is not you who are keeping up the pumping motion of the heart. It is not you who are keeping up the bellow-like contracting and expanding movement of the lungs. You are not even aware of the movement of the lungs, not even conscious of it. It is only when something happens to you that you are aware; otherwise, you are not even conscious of it. It is this Prana, this great manifestation of Divinity, this great manifestation of the Cosmic Energy, that keeps going all these essential, vital movements in your body. The expansion and contraction of the lungs manifests in the body as the ingoing and outcoming breath. And the ingoing and outcoming breath is the symptom of the movement of the Prana, which keeps the lungs in a constant state of indispensable vital activity. So, this breath in the nostrils is due to the movement of the subtle Prana within your body, just as the movement of the second-hand, the minute-hand and the hour-hand are due to the hidden or undiscerned inner movement of the hairspring within the mechanism of the timepiece or the watch. It is because there is the constant unbroken movement of the hairspring inside that on the surface of the visible dial, the hour-hand and the minute-hand are able to move round and do their work.

Now, if you want to bring about a slowing down or a cessation of the movement of the hairspring within the timepiece, you have no means of doing it, because you have no access to it. It is somewhere inside covered over by the structure of the watch or the timepiece. You cannot get at it. The only way of trying to get at it is through its outer symptom or outer manifestation. So, if you place your finger on the second-hand of the timepiece moving round in one little corner of the dial and stop it, if you arrest the second hand, gradually the movement of the hairspring also becomes arrested. Similarly, if you stop the minute-hand of the timepiece, then also, the movement of the minute-hand being the ultimate result and outcome of the movement of the inner hairspring, the movement of the hairspring gradually slows down and then comes to a stop. It is in this reverse fashion, this remote and indirect fashion, that the regulation and stoppage of the outer breath of the nostrils achieves the ultimate result of controlling and even bringing to a stop certain aspects of the movement of the subtle Prana, because the Prana is connected with the outer breath.

The outer breath is connected with the subtle Prana as the latter's ultimate outer effect. Thus, Pranayama takes you within.

Kumbhak and Its Benefits

Pranayama in Raja Yoga is retention of the inhaled breath. Later on, it assumes the form of the retention of breath—retention of the inhaled breath as well as retention of the exhaled breath or outer breath. The latter is called Bahya Kumbhak. You stop breathing when the breath is out, when the lungs are empty. This is Bahya Kumbhak. And as you advance in the practice of Kumbhak, you go into the stage of Dhyana. When you are practising Pranayama, all the emphasis is upon the practice of Pranayama. When, after having successfully practised that stage, you start taking up Pratyahara and Dharana, what happens? The stress or emphasis upon this Abhyasa, namely, your practice of Pranayama, becomes lessened, and more emphasis begins to be laid upon Dharana. Then Pranayama is done automatically and it becomes a secondary or an auxiliary process in relation to Dharana. And in this condition, the Kumbhak comes about spontaneously. It is called spontaneous Kumbhak or Kevala Kumbhak. You are not bothered, you are not considering whether it is breath in the state of exhalation or breath in the state of inhalation; you are not thinking about it at all. When the mind is in a state of good concentration, you take hold of the opportunity—you make hay while the sun shines and immediately stop the breath, because the moment you stop the breath, immediately the mind becomes steady. Whenever a steady condition of the mind is perceived, immediately you stop the breath, no matter in what condition the breath is in. It is called the Kevala Kumbhak or spontaneous Kumbhak.

Spontaneous Kumbhak is a very valuable aid to Dharana. And sometimes, when there is a great deal of Vikshepa, when you are not able to carry on your Dharana properly, when the mind is very, very unsteady and jumping, then also Kumbhak helps. But then, it is Kumbhak done in a deliberate way. Spontaneous Kumbhak, on the other hand, comes about when there is good concentration. When concentration is being successfully carried on, spontaneous Kumbhak becomes invaluable as a secondary aid in that state.

And the benefits of Pranayama are various. Internal health benefits also accrue due to the practice of Pranayama. It imparts a certain strength to the body, and due to the doing of Pranayama, the body is able to ward off fatigue. Even if you sit and do Abhyasa for many hours, fatigue does not approach the body. The body is able to undergo exertion for a long time without fatigue. And successful, sustained practice of Pranayama increases the energy of the body. You become energetic, mentally as well as physically. There is always a freshness in the mind. And Pranayama is a great destroyer of Tamas as well as Rajas. And it is a positive help in increasing Sattva within your nature, within your body and mind. Thus it has a dual effect, namely, one of destroying Tamas and Rajas, and the other of increasing Sattva. And when freshness increases in the mind, the object of meditation becomes very vivid and clear-cut. When there is vagueness of the focal point of concentration or Dhyana Lakshya, proper Dharana does not manifest; but, due to Pranayama, there is a great deal of clarity brought about into the mind and the focal point becomes vivid and clear.

Then, to such a mind, it becomes easy to concentrate. So, Pranayama brings about the unique benefit of clarifying the mind, making the Dhyana Lakshya vivid, and thus precipitating Dharana. This much about Pranayama.

How Asana and Pranayama Help to Combat Rajo-Guna

Now, to recapitulate the rationale behind the third and the fourth Angas—Asana and Pranayama—in Patanjali's system of Raja Yoga. In Raja Yoga, Asana does not mean a posture; it means a seat. You should be seated. And how? Steadily. Patanjali Maharshi adds one interesting further adjective. He says that the Asana should be comfortable. It should give the Sadhaka a feeling of comfort. When you are comfortable, you are happy; when you are uncomfortable, you are unhappy.

So, Patanjali uses the word "Sukha". His definition of Asana is "Sthira Sukham Asanam". You should be seated steadily in a comfortable posture. This is the broad definition of Asana in the Yoga Darshana of Patanjali Maharshi. The body is seated steadily and is in comfort. Why should it be in comfort? Because, if it is not comfortable, you will not be able to maintain the position continuously for a long period. Because, if it is not comfortable, it will give you discomfort and pains and after a little time, you will want to change it. But when it is comfortable, well, then you do not mind keeping it for a long time; and the longer you keep the position the longer your body is steady. The longer you keep the position steady, the longer you are able to curb the Rajo-Guna, the longer you are able to overcome Rajo-Guna. Therefore, the comfortable nature of the Asana is indispensable; it is imperative. The essence of Asana according to Patanjali's Ashtanga Yoga is therefore steadiness combined with comfort, unshaken postural comfort. And Patanjali says that you must go on increasing the time period of your sitting upon one Asana. So, you do your Pranayama sitting on one Asana; you do your Japa sitting on the same Asana; you do your Svadhyaya sitting on the same Asana. What happens then? The mind is diverted and taken out from the body when it is thus absorbed in study, absorbed in Japa, absorbed in Puja... and you are not even aware that you are sitting in one Asana. By thus keeping yourself occupied in various aspects of actual spiritual practice, the Asana becomes prolonged. And as a sort of guide or standard, Patanjali suggests that you should be able to sit steadily in one Asana for a period of at least three hours continuously; during the period you may engage yourself in different spiritual practices and divert your mind away from the body so as to go on sitting in one absolute steady pose for the duration of those three hours. Thus becoming established in Asana, you get into a state of conflict with the Rajo-Guna in the body. And this automatically helps the next Anga of the Ashtanga Yoga, namely, Pranayama.

Now, how does Asana help to proceed with Pranayama? Because, just as Chitta or the mind-stuff and Prana are very closely interconnected, just as mental activity and Prana are interlinked, even so, on the other side, the body and the Prana also are interconnected. This is because Prana pervades the whole body; Prana is almost co-existing with the Annamaya Kosha. And therefore, if the Annamaya Kosha is agitated, then naturally, the Prana also gets into a state of agitation. But, if you have managed to gradually discipline the body and practise sitting steadily for a long period of time, then the Prana also automatically assumes a relative state of steadiness, a comparative state of steadiness. It gets less agitated then before. So, with your success and progress in Asana practice, the Prana also assumes a corresponding state of steadiness. Thus, success in Asana practice becomes very conducive to the practice of Pranayama or the disciplining of the Prana, the regularising of the Prana. And just as steadiness is the very essence of Asana in Ashtanga Yoga, even so, Kumbhaka is the very essence of Pranayama in Ashtanga Yoga. The most important object of the entire Pranayama process in Raja Yoga is to arrest the Prana, is to restrain the breath; because, right at the very beginning of Patanjali's Yoga Darshana, we have a Sutra which gives the definition of Yoga: "Yogas Chitta Vritti Nirodhah". Yoga is curbing the constant thought-activity of the mind-lake, the Vrittis of the mind-lake. And Prana is always in a state of agitation, in a state of Vritti. The mind also is always agitated by Vritti. And if you want to have Nirodha of the activity of the mind, you must make Nirodha of the activity of the Prana. Nirodha of the activity of the Prana means restraint of the breath. It is Kumbhak. So, the various other Pranayama practices that you find in Hatha Yoga—Bhastrika, Suryabedha, Kapalabhati, Ujjayi, Brahmari, Murcha—have no relevance here. In Raja Yoga, Pranayama means inhale-restrain-exhale, inhale-restrain-exhale, inhale-restrain-exhale, inhale-restrain-exhale. It means that and only that. In this way, the crest of the Pranayama, the main essence of the Pranayama, lies in the restraining of the breath. By the restraining of the breath, the activity of your mind, of your mental plane, is restrained. Thus, Asana helps Pranayama, and Pranayama helps ultimately the actual Antaranga Yoga process of slowing down the activity of the mind, the motion of the mind, until it is brought to a state of complete cessation—cessation of all Vrittis. This is the rationale behind the third and the fourth Angas—Asana and Pranayama—in our effort to completely overcome the Raja-Guna mode of the Trigunatmika Prakriti. Prakriti is Trigunatmika, and to overpower the Rajo-Guna mode, Asana helps Pranayama. And Pranayama helps to restrain the mental activity. In this way, it acts as a Sahayogi Prakriya—a helpful process—in the fifth and the sixth Angas of Raja Yoga, namely, Pratyahara and Dharana, withdrawal of the mind and concentration.

15

ALL YOGA IS ONE

The human individual has an apparent outer identity which is seen by, and known to, the rest of the human beings, the rest of the world. It is what they see in a person, what they know about a person. That is the apparent identity of the human being. This apparent identity is limited in time; it has a beginning and an end. This apparent identity is not stable and unchanging; it keeps ever changing. And this apparent identity is subject to inevitable stages of being—birth, growth, old age, decay and death. This is inevitable, this pattern through which every born body has to pass through. This is what Buddha discovered when he first went out of his secluded, carefree, guarded and protected palace environs and it was an eye-opener to him. And this is what set him thinking. Buddha began to ponder: "What is man? What is life? Why do these things happen to men? It may happen to me also". What happened to man seemed to be painful too, because Buddha saw an old man, a sick man, a dead person. All those sights were accompanied by sorrow, grief, distress. They were not joy-giving and happy. So Buddha came to the conclusion that there was a great deal of suffering and distress in individual human life. He set on a quest to find out an answer to human suffering, to find a way out of the predicament of man in Samsara.

So, the apparent outer personality of man, which is the only personality that the world knows, that the world sees, that the rest of the human beings see, is something limited, is something subject to change, subject to ultimate destruction. It has an end and men of wisdom discovered that the outer personality is only a mask that man has taken upon himself and not his true being. The real being is hidden inside. And what is this hidden identity about which those men of wisdom had a faint inkling, but did not know in full? They launched upon an inner quest to try to probe and find out what was this real identity of man. And it is their discoveries about the inner being that form the theme of the Upanishads that are the contents of the great Vedantic scriptures.

The Upanishads deal with the reality of man, with the inner man, with the higher Self in man, with man's true identity. They call it the Nija-Svarupa, one's own real nature. And the Rishis found out that this true identity of man is completely free from all the defects and limitations that characterise his false identity. Man's false identity is subject to change, subject to decay, subject to ultimate extinction. It is limited. It is subject to various types of afflictions and so it is always in a state of turmoil and suffering. But man's true identity, according to the Rishis, is absolutely free from all these characteristics.

The very entity in it is all-full, subject to no change, indestructible, imperishable, of the nature of peace and joy. It was after this discovery that those wise men declared that that inner Self must be known. Knowing the Self, therefore, is the greatest achievement and attainment. Knowledge of the Self is really the supreme goal and purpose of life. And to enable man to attain that supreme experience and once and for all liberate him from all the painful experiences of the embodied existence on earth, to enable him to obtain that state of infinite joy, eternal bliss, peace, perfection and liberation, the ancient seers formulated the different paths.

That also they did not formulate out of their thought by sitting out and trying. They did not try to arrive at a conclusion by deep thinking. No. They themselves tried various methods to attain the Self. They went into a dedicated, whole-souled practice. Then they discovered the Self. God revealed Himself to them. Thus they were able to prove the Self. Thus their practices ultimately led to the tangible experience of the Self, the discovery of the Self. And they put down their experiences, formulating them in the form of a graded series of techniques. These constitute the various Yogas.

Bhakti Yoga, Jnana Yoga and Raja Yoga

If the attempt to discover the Self is done through feeling, through spiritual emotions and divine sentiments, and the love of the heart is directed towards the Divine, then it takes the form of a distinct Yoga. If the attempt to realise the Self is done through pure reasoning, through an analytical exercise of the intellect, through investigation into that which is beyond name and form, that which is beyond appearance, that which is the imperishable in the midst of the perishable, that which is the infinite in the midst of the finite, that which is the eternal in the midst of the non-eternal, then it is another distinct Yoga. In this Yoga, through analysis and sifting, through rejecting certain things and through affirming certain other things, through vigorous and intense exercise of a very sharp intellect and rationality, through inner research, one ultimately begins to get a glimpse of the higher realities. So, this approach is through questioning, through enquiry, through analysis, through deep investigation.

This is the Yoga of the intellect, whereas, Bhakti Yoga is through the heart, through feeling, through love, devotion, prayer, divine sentiments and longing for God. Then there is a third Yoga, the Yoga of mental discipline. The Rishis found out that mind had a power. If the mind is scattered, it is weak; but if it is gathered, it is strong. If intensely brought together, if intensely gathered together, the mind's rays can pierce through the appearance and go beyond to the very substratum or the root, the very ground of appearance. It is just as with the sun's rays.

The sun's rays may be warm or even hot in summer; yet, they do not have the power to do extraordinary things, though they help crops to grow on land. But, if you hold a magnifying glass against the sun, and that convex lens gathers the very same sun's rays which are now falling outside, the rays emerge on the other side in the form of a unified ray. And that unified ray is brilliant; you cannot look at it. It is dazzling light and if any combustible object—be it paper, cotton or wood—is brought against that ray, the object starts smoking and burning. The sun's rays are the same. In a scattered form, their powers are normal; but in an intensely gathered form, their powers are supernormal.

Consider another example. A vast volume of water is collected when you suddenly stop the flow of a river by a dam. You build the dam across the course of the river and then the flow of the waters is halted and water becomes piled up inside the dam. And if this vast volume of water is made to emerge through a small opening, ah, it emerges with such terrible power that it is able to make metal turbines weighing tons spin like tops. What a miracle! Turbines which cannot be moved even by twenty or fifty men whirl at a terrific speed merely through the sheer force of concentrated water. When all the water is concentrated in a small opening and made to gush through, it has terrific impact and power which make the giant generators whirl like toys and generate electricity. So, coming together of any force increases the power of that force tenfold, hundredfold, thousandfold. That is the principle. It is this principle that is invoked by the science of Raja Yoga formulated by Patanjali.

The Power of Concentration—Its Application in Matters Mundane and Spiritual

The essence of Raja Yoga is Dharana or the focussing or bringing together of the entire force of the mind so that it becomes very powerful. That is the key technique of Yoga. The main thing is concentration, bringing the mind together. That is the key technique. That is the very heart of the science of Yoga. And, the uniqueness, the distinguishing special feature, of Raja Yoga is the object to which this concentrated mind is applied, the purpose for which this concentrated mind is utilised. It is utilised to meditate upon your real identity and realise your real identity. It is utilised to enter into a state of unbroken, deep, intense meditation upon your real identity so that you realise your real identity and become liberated. Whereas, the same type of concentration is generated and applied in other fields of activity for other purposes. It is applied by the scientists in doing their research work, by the surgeons in doing very delicate operations, by the Swiss watchmaker in making and assembling very minute and intricate parts of watches. Concentration is there in all these instances. Even a musician concentrates upon his music. But, the Raja Yogic concentration is concentration par excellence. It is concentration taken to its ultimate logical conclusion, so that the mind becomes nothing but one concentrated power. The mind loses all its normal characteristics and becomes one powerful, concentrated ray. And that is directed towards the transcendental Reality, towards that which is beyond phenomena. That is the uniqueness of Yoga, whereas, in all other fields of human endeavour, concentration is there, but only a part of it. And that too is applied only in the phenomenal field of the outer world.

These applications of concentration in the outer field of phenomenal existence produce extraordinary results, no doubt, but of short duration only or of short relevance to man. This is because man, the discoverer of these applications, is himself only a passing traveller. He has no ultimate connection with anything or anybody here on earth. He has no permanent relevance or individuality. So, his discovery too has no permanent significance or relevance to any human individual.

Thus, Nitya-Prayojana is conspicuous by its absence in such applications of concentration in any outer field. And then, man himself is a field for constant conflicts, constant tug of war, constant tension between opposing forces of good and evil, of light and darkness, of that which is sublime and that which is degraded or ignoble. Every moment man is waging an inner battle. So, what happens? More often than not, the power gained by man through intense concentration—the power of the intellect, the power of the disciplined mind—gets misdirected and misapplied. The attainments and achievements that evolve out of this misapplication do not come as blessings to mankind, do not come as results that are conducive to human happiness, human welfare and human progress, but come as curses destroying in one moment what man has painfully built up over centuries in terms of human welfare and human good. Some of the scientists and politicians who have thus developed their power of concentration are giant intellects, no doubt. But then, their intense concentration, their attention, their rationality and their reasoning powers are unfortunately accompanied by egoism, greed, selfishness, hatred, avarice, carnal passion, ambition and a desire to dominate. What happens? Because their nature is qualified by such negative traits and tendencies, the entire motivation for their investigations and research becomes vitiated and the result is human sorrow.

The Danger of Psychic Powers

Power is a very dangerous thing. In the course of Yogic disciplines, the Yogic practitioner may also get various types of powers, lesser and greater. And if he gets them, he becomes elated; he becomes very happy, he becomes fascinated, he becomes curious, he is very very thrilled. Yoga teachers very seriously warn their students to beware, beware, beware. They tell their students: "These powers are terrible dangers on the path. They are obstacles to your progress. Not only are they obstacles, but they are real enemies to your success in this field. They will destroy all prospects of your attaining anything. They will bring about your hopeless downfall. Therefore, beware of them. Shun them ruthlessly, shun them, kick them aside, do not have anything to do with them. Do not pay attention to them". In this way the great Masters and teachers have never hesitated to seriously warn the students of Yoga to beware in the course of their Yogic process and progress about the powers that may come. Because, they are supranormal powers, and when power comes to the hands of man, you know how it corrupts, how it vitiates, how it makes man a beast. It can be seen all around, every day. Even with a little power in his hands, a person will oppress those who are subordinate to him, over whom he has got a sort of hold. That happens everywhere, in gross and subtle ways. So, a clear warning is given by Yogic teachers in this connection.

So, this is the uniqueness of Yoga. Unlike in other fields of human activity, the concentration of mind, which is powerful and effective anywhere, is applied in Yoga, not for phenomenal purposes, but for the attainment of the Eternal Reality, for Self-discovery, for going beyond all limitations and imperfections in order to attain a state of absolute freedom and liberation and total divine perfection. Therein lies the uniqueness of

Yoga. Yoga is an approach through mental discipline. Its key place is concentration. And what follows afterwards is the sublime right application of the power of this concentrated mind. And what precedes concentration, what goes before it, is all a preparation for enabling you to get to a state of concentration. Yama, Niyama, Asana, Pranayama, Pratyahara—all are preparatory processes, preparatory techniques very wisely arranged in order that in case psychic powers come to the Yogi, they may not bring about his downfall. In order that the Yogi may not succumb to the temptation of the supranormal powers, in order that he may not fall a prey to them, our wise Maharshis first of all laid the foundations of absolute selflessness, absolute purity of conduct and character, humility, Tyaga, desirelessness, total renunciation, and aspiration to know one and one thing only.

In this way they anticipated the danger ahead, the danger of the Yogi being tempted by psychic powers, and provided for it at the very beginning of Yoga, at the very threshold of Yoga, at the very point of entry into the portals of Yoga.

The Importance of a Complementary Relationship Between the Outer Life and the Inner Life

It is in the above context that you must understand the invaluable importance of Yama and Niyama and take them with you right up to the very end. Now, very few, if any, will be able to practise Yoga twenty-four hours a day, all the three hundred and sixty-five days of the year. Few are in a position to cut off all connections with the entire world—with family, friends, surroundings, property and so on—and go away into a deep dense interior forest, where no other human being is there. Very few can afford such absolute isolation to lead a hermetical life. By and large, nine hundred and ninety nine out of a thousand have to blend this Yoga somehow or the other with their normal life. Somehow or the other they have to make a sort of blend of both their outer life and their inner life, their secular life and their spiritual life.

There is no other alternative open to them. For them, it has to be in this way only. That being the case, when you have to be in Yoga, and at the same time, carry on your allotted occupations and fulfil your obligations to home and society, there arises an indispensable necessity to carefully ensure that nothing in the outer aspect of your life, in the worldly dimension of your life, either in your domestic set-up or in your professional set-up or in your social activities, assumes a quality or a form that is anti-Yoga, that is unspiritual, that contradicts Divinity and that goes against your entire orientation Godward.

Because, if that comes about, then there will be an altogether undesirable tension between two aspects of your life. It is readily admitted that it is not possible to reject or completely waive the outer aspect of your life—individual, collective, domestic as well as professional and social. At the same time, wisdom dictates that as far as possible you must make all sincere attempts, all earnest attempts, to see that the outer does not contradict the inner, that your earthly life in all its different parts and aspects does not become an obstacle, does not become a serious hindrance to your progress upon your inner path, to your ascent towards Reality, towards light, towards liberation. So, very wisely you have to find out ways and means of how your life of activity, your life of association with other individuals, could be so wisely organised, could be so carefully made, that it does not become a hindrance and an obstacle to your spiritual progress, that it does not range itself in direct opposition to your inner life. Not only that, if you are wise and if it is possible, it is in your interest to see whether you can order your life in such a way that it supplements your inner spiritual life and offers further help in your striving. It is the necessity and importance of this complementary relationship between the outer life and the inner life in your spiritual journey that gave rise to the important science of spiritualising one's entire life, of trying to make even your normal activities into processes of bringing you nearer to God and not taking you further away from God.

This means transforming your normal activities into Yogic activities, because anything that brings you nearer to God is directly or indirectly a part of the Yoga process. Yoga is nothing but moving towards God. Yoga is trying to approach God; Yoga is trying to bring about a connection, a relationship, a link with the Infinite, with the Divine, with the Cosmic Spirit. So, if you so wisely try to organise your life in such a way that it also becomes a process helpful to Yoga, then your life itself becomes a part of Yoga. All your activities are converted into Yogic activities. All your work is transformed into spiritual work. Your whole life becomes spiritualised by this wise way of living and acting and engaging in work. Your work itself becomes a spiritual process; your activity becomes something that takes you nearer to God and ceases to be something that opposes and contradicts your Sadhana or your Yogabhyasa. This technique, this wise process, has assumed the distinct nature of a separate Yoga; it is called the Yoga of spiritualised activity or Karma Yoga, for short.

And this Karma Yoga occupies a unique place in the seeker's life, because it is something that is necessary as a basis for the seeker, no matter what Yoga he is employing as his specific technique of approach to God. This is because the area of outer life is the same in the case of all seekers, no matter what technique they may be adopting—Bhakti Yoga or Vedanta or Raja Yoga—as their individual method of approach to God. All seekers have to deal with the outer life; somehow or the other they have to come to terms with it and wisely make it a complementary process in their Sadhana. Because of this necessity, the importance of Karma Yoga extends to all seekers and is not confined to pure Karma Yogins only. So, Karma Yoga has its importance also for the Vedantin, the Bhakta and the Raja Yogi. Karma Yoga has a distinct place in the life of seekers of all categories. Because, as long as they have to engage themselves in one field of activity or the other, as long as they have to live and move in the outer world, they must know how to make that activity their friend and not their enemy, how to make that activity their asset and not their problem.

Adherence to Virtue—The Common Basis of Every Type of Yoga

The Bhagavad Gita throws a lot of light upon this

important dimension of your life. All the different Yogas, though apparently different in their structure, in their composition, in their outer form, are fundamentally one in the ultimate analysis. How? Because, all these Yogas ultimately raise the Jiva or the individual being who has fallen into a very gross state into the net of desires, selfishness, bondage and ignorance. Basically, all the Yogas have this common motive or intention to take the individual out of his present predicament and gradually help him to ascend higher into a different state of experience and consciousness. They all have this identical objective or motivation or aim. Therefore, in order to achieve this, you have to first shake off the present state of consciousness in order to free yourself, somehow or the other, from the prison-house of your present state of being, where you are completely enslaved by your ego, by selfishness, greed, anger, passion, envy, jealousy, hatred, pettiness and meanness. The normal human individual has so many defects in him that all Yogas lay down the taking up of firm vows to adhere to certain principles of higher life. That takes the life immediately from a lower plane to a higher plane. That helps the person to get established in a higher level of living. It is righteous living, noble living, virtuous living, not unrighteous living, not hating and yelling, not violence and dishonesty, not impurity and evil. So, irrespective of whether you are a student of Vedanta or Bhakti Yoga or Raja Yoga, first of all you have to rise up from your present state. No matter what Yoga you may be practising or you may want to practise, the common basis is Dharma or righteousness of life; the common basis is the adoption of certain noble, ethical principles to live by; the common basis is adherence to virtue. So, character building, Sadachara, right conduct, good conduct, becoming established in a noble pattern of moral and ethical life, righteousness in life—this has to be the firm basis, whether you are a Vedantin or a Bhakta or a Raja Yogi or a Hatha Yogi or a Japa Yogi or a Sankirtan Yogi, whether you are practising Zen or whether you are practising Christian Yoga or Sufi Yoga, no matter what particular background you come from, whether you are Jew, Christian, Muslim or Parsi. Higher life demands that you lay the firm foundation of a blameless, ethical and moral life bidding goodbye once and for all to the ugliness of the ego and its manifestations of selfishness, crookedness, cunningness, falsehood, dishonesty, deceit and all other types of lower impurities. You can have no truck with these undivine factors any longer if you really mean business, if you are really earnest and sincere. That is the plain truth. So, in this matter of an ethical foundation, all Yogas are one, fundamentally one.

Fundamental Unity of the Different Yoga Systems

And then, when you take up serious effort in Yoga Sadhana, no matter what Yoga you may adopt, you must have dedication and intensity. Even if you do a little Sadhana, it should be unbroken, it should be continuous, it should never be given up, it should be daily, daily, daily. It should be daily, daily, daily; it should be unfailingly regular. Regularity is the key to success—unfailing regularity, unbroken continuity. Daily practice is absolutely indispensable. If you are able to do Sadhana for six hours daily, wonderful. If you are able to do it for one hour only, wonderful. If you are able to do it for half an hour only, still wonderful. If you are able to do it for fifteen minutes only, even then, wonderful. But, do not give it up. Even if you are able to do Sadhana for five minutes only daily, it should be as regular as your eating, drinking and sleeping, as regular as your breathing. And if you are really earnest, if you are really sincere, your effort would be where your heart is, where your love and longing is. There the mind must go. That is the truth. And so, if you have real love for the ultimate goal, for the ultimate attainment, you must engage in unbroken continuous effort. Your Sadhana must be a regular, unfailing, daily affair. And while you are engaged in this manner, you should never allow yourself to slide back, you should never allow yourself to slip into the old sensual ruts and grooves, because then all that you might have achieved will become lost. You must hedge yourself against this possibility and you must see that you never go back.

Once you have turned in the spiritual direction, once you have put your hand to the plough, there is no turning back. Be very strict with yourself, be very firm with yourself. Never allow the senses to run riot once again. Never allow the mind to once again fall a prey to desire and craving. That which has been spat out should not be picked up from the earth and put into the mouth once again. No decent person with any sense of respectability will do it. Spat out means spat out. That is the attitude the Sadhaka must take, the Yogi must take. That is called Vairagya. The continuous practice of Vairagya and the keeping up of an unbroken continuity in your Sadhana—what is known as Abhyasa—must be there side by side until you come face to face with your Beloved God or attain Vedantic illumination or

Asamprajnata Raja Yoga Samadhi. Until then, Abhyasa and Vairagya should go hand in hand relentlessly.

In this respect, all Yoga is one. The foundation for all types of Yoga is identical. There is no difference in the basis. The outer form of each Yoga may be different, but the inner anatomy of the progress of the Yogi is the same. It is a fiery determination to keep the effort unbroken and continuous, unfailing and regular and determined. It is a fiery determination never to slip back, never to allow the mind and the senses to fall into old grooves. It is becoming firmly and continuously established in Vairagya. This is the inner form of Yoga Sadhana.

Ultimately, the fruit of Yoga is also identical, whether you come face to face with your beloved Lord through Bhakti or whether you attain Vedantic Aparoksha Anubhuti or Cosmic Consciousness where you feel that everything is the Lord, where you feel, "Vasudeva Sarvam Iti", "Siya Ram Maya Saba Jaga Jani", "Sarvam Vishnu Mayam Jagat". The fruit of Yoga is the same to a Raja Yogi who practises meditation and attain Nirvikalpa Samadhi as to a Karma Yogin who practises Nishkama Karma Yoga with Isvara Drishti or Narayana Bhava in all Nama-Rupa, who sees the manifestation of the Lord in all creatures and serves them and attains cosmic vision, Darshan of Narayan, Darshan of Atma. Once you attain the supreme experience be it through Karma yoga or Bhakti Yoga or Jnana Yoga—there is cessation of all sorrow, pain and suffering. That is the attainment of supreme bliss and blessedness—bliss, bliss, bliss, indescribable infinite bliss, limitless bliss—Paramananda, divine bliss, divine joy. In that state there is no desire, there is no wish, one wants nothing, one has no desire left, all desires are fulfilled and finished. In that condition one is in a state of absolute bliss, one is in a state of total eternal satisfaction. Whatever he has wanted he has got, and therefore, whatever he had to do to get it is all done. There is no more doing, no more striving, no more need for any effort or activity. This outcome is identical, no matter which way you have got on to the roof, whether you took the inside staircase or whether you took the outside staircase, or whether you put the ladder and climbed the ladder, or whether you asked someone to put a rope down and you went up the rope, or whether you asked someone to take you on a helicopter and drop you there. No matter in what way you landed on the roof, you are on the roof all the same. You are in a condition identical with those others who too have reached the roof-top by one means or the other. The attainment is identical. Even so, all the different Yogas ultimately take the seeker to the same supreme summit of blessedness and bliss where there is Sarva Duhkha Nivritti, cessation of all sorrow, where there is Paramananda Prapti, attainment of supreme bliss, where there is Nitya Tripti, eternal satisfaction, where there is that state of fullness, Paripurnata, where man says, "I want nothing" and becomes Apta-Kama, where he becomes Krita-Kritya or one who has done all that there is to be done. That supreme attainment is the fruit of Yoga, call it Jnana Yoga, Bhakti Yoga or Raja Yoga, call it Karma Yoga, Mantra Yoga, Kirtan Yoga, Laya Yoga, Hatha Yoga or whatever.

So, though there is apparent difference of form in the outer structure of the various Yogas differently named, the basis and the attainment are both identical in all cases. Two factors are indispensable and necessary as the very basis to carry you from start to finish, from A to Z, and they are Abhyasa and Vairagya—Akhanda Abhyasa and perfect Vairagya. Without these two, no Yoga can proceed. And the ultimate fruit of attainment is also identical. All forms of Yoga, no matter how completely different they may look on the surface, how clashing and contrary to one another they may seem to be in outer detail, are the same in the ultimate achievement, in the ultimate reckoning. If you take a deeper and inner glimpse, you find that all this clash and conflict is only between the Ganas of Siva and the Vanaras of Rama. The Ganas of Siva and the Vanaras of Rama may clash, but Rama and Siva have no difference. Rama worships Siva and takes His Name and Siva worships Rama and takes His Name. They have no difference. They have got identical Bhava. In the same way, the outer structure and details of the Yogic ascent may be different; the details of practice may be different—they have to be—and they may even look contradictory. And the followers of the different Yogas may even quarrel with one another and say that each one is wrong. But it is all futile and vain. It is all a puerile attitude and approach to Yoga, a limited vision lacking in depth. Those who have inner vision see all Yoga as fundamentally one, as identical from start to finish, based upon Sadachara and self-control and purity of conduct and character and righteous living, and progressing through unremitting, unbroken effort and perfect dispassion, and ultimately culminating in the cessation of all sorrow, in the attainment of supreme bliss—absolute fullness and eternal satisfaction.

16

YOGA STYLES

Although there are many styles of yoga, the differences are usually about emphasis, such as focusing on strict alignment of the body, coordination of breath and movement, holding the postures, or the flow from one posture to another. All of the styles share a common lineage. In fact, the founders of three major styles -- Astanga, Iyengar and Viniyoga -- were all students of Krishnamacharya, a famous teacher at the Yoga Institute at the Mysore Palace in India. Two other styles, Integral and Sivananda, were created by disciples of the famous guru Sivananda. No style is better than another; it's simply a matter of personal preference. More important than any style is the student-teacher relationship.

ANANDA

Ananda Yoga is a classical style of hatha yoga that uses asana and pranayama to awaken, experience, and begin to control the subtle energies within oneself, especially the energies of the chakras. Its object is to use those energies to harmonize body, mind, and emotions, and above all to attune oneself with higher levels of awareness. One unique feature of this system is the use of silent affirmations while in the asanas as a means of working more directly and consciously with the subtle energies to achieve this attunement. Ananda Yoga is a relatively gentle, inward experience, not an athletic or aerobic practice. It was developed by Swami Kriyananda, a direct disciple of Paramhansa Yogananda, author of the spiritual classic, Autobiography of a Yogi.

Note:

Ananda is a worldwide group of individuals who share the search for higher consciousness and the ideal of service to others. We express this service by offering uplifting values and techniques for achieving peace of mind and inner happiness. Ananda, which means "joy" in Sanskrit, was founded in 1968 by J. Donald Walters (Swami Kriyananda) to support others in their quest for spiritual growth.

Ananda is based on the teachings of Paramhansa Yogananda, author of the spiritual classic Autobiography of a Yogi. Yogananda was the first yoga master of India to take up permanent residence in the West. His teachings emphasize direct inner experience of God, which he called 'self-realization.' Yogananda's teachings are nonsectarian, and offer practical solutions to the challenges of modern life.

The Ananda Joy logo, represents the soul's aspiration upward toward God, and outward to embrace all beings in its quest for enlightenment.

ANUSARA

Anusara (a-nu-SAR-a) means, "to step into the

current of Divine Will", "following your heart", "flowing with Grace", "to move with the current of divine will." A new style developed by John Friend, Anusara yoga is described as heart-oriented, spiritually inspiring, yet grounded in a deep knowledge of outer and inner body alignment. Each student's various abilities and limitations are deeply respected and honored.

ASHTANGA

For those who want a serious workout, Ashtanga may be the perfect yoga. Developed by K. Pattabhi Jois, Ashtanga is physically demanding. Participants move through a series of flows, jumping from one posture to another to build strength, flexibility and stamina. It's not for beginners or anyone who's been taking a leisurely approach to fitness. The so-called Power Yoga is based on Ashtanga.

BIKRAM

Bikram Choudhury's yoga is hot, hot, hot, so be prepared to sweat, sweat, sweat. In class, they crank the thermostat up high, then perform a series of 26 asanas designed to "scientifically" warm and stretch muscles, ligaments and tendons. Founder Bikram Choudhury studied yoga with Bishnu Ghosh, brother of Paramahansa Yogananda

INTEGRAL

Developed by Swami Satchidananda, the man who taught the crowds at the original Woodstock to chant "Om," Integral classes put almost as much emphasis on pranayama and meditation as they do on postures. Integral yoga is used by Dr. Dean Ornish in his groundbreaking work on reversing heart disease.

IYENGAR

Ever think standing was just a matter of keeping your body on top of your legs? It's hard to appreciate how involved a simple thing like just standing can be, how much concentration and how many subtle movements and adjustments it takes, until you take an Iyengar yoga class. Of course, the point is that you're not just standing. You're doing Tadasana, Mountain pose, and in yoga in the style of B.K.S. Iyengar, Tadasana is an active pose. B.K.S. Iyengar is one of the best-known yoga teachers and the creator of one of the most popular styles of yoga in the world. His style of yoga is noted for great attention to detail and the precise alignment of postures, as well as the use of props such as blocks and belts. No doubt part of Iyengar's success is due to the quality of teachers, who must complete a rigorous 2-5 year training program for certification.

KALI RAY TRIYOGA

Kali Ray TriYoga, founded by Kali Ray, brings posture, breath and focus together to create dynamic and intuitive flows. The Tri Yoga flows combine flowing and sustained postures that emphasize spinal wavelike movements, economy of motion, and synchronization with breath and mudra. The flows are systematized by level and can be as gentle or as challenging as desired. Students may progress from basics to advanced as they increase their flexibility, strength, endurance and knowledge of the flows.

KRIPALU

Called the yoga of consciousness, Kripalu puts great emphasis on proper breath, alignment, coordinating breath and movement, and "honoring the wisdom of the body" -- you work according to the limits of your individual flexibility and strength. Alignment follows awareness. Students learn to focus on the physical and psychological reactions caused by various postures to develop their awareness of mind, body, emotion and spirit.

There are three stages in Kripalu yoga. Stage One focuses on learning the postures and exploring your bodies abilities. Stage Two involves holding the postures for an extended time, developing concentration and inner awareness. Stage Three is like a meditation in motion in which the movement from one posture to another arises unconsciously and spontaneously.

KUNDALINI

Kundalini yoga in the tradition of Yogi Bhajan, who brought the style to the West in 1969, focuses on the controlled release of Kundalini energy. The practice involves classic poses, breath, coordination of breath and movement, meditation.

SIVANANDA

Sivananda is one of the world's largest schools of yoga. Developed by Vishnu-devananda and named for his teacher, Sivananda yoga follows a set structure that includes pranayama, classic asanas, and relaxation. Vishnu-devananda wrote one of the contemporary yoga classics, The Complete Illustrated Book of Yoga. First published in 1960, the book is still one of the best introductions to yoga available.

SVAROOPA YOGA

Developed by Rama Berch, Svaroopa Yoga teaches significantly different ways of doing familiar poses, emphasizing the opening of the spine by beginning at the tailbone and progressing through each spinal area in turn. Every pose integrates the foundational principles of asana, anatomy and yoga philosophy, and emphasizes the development of transcendent inner experience, which is called svaroopa by Patanjali in the Yoga Sutras. This is a consciousness-oriented yoga that also promotes healing and transformation. Svaroopa is not an athletic endeavor, but a development of consciousness using the body as a tool.

VINIYOGA

Viniyoga is not so much a style as it is a methodology for developing practices for individual conditions and purposes. This is the approach developed by Sri. T. Krishnamacharya, teacher of well-known contemporary masters B.K.S. Iyengar, K. Pattabhi Jois and Indra Devi, and continued by his son, T.K.V. Desikachar. Key characteristic of the asana practice are the careful integration of the flow of breath with movement of the spine, with sequencing, adaptations and intensity dependent upon the overall context and goals. Function is stressed over form. Practices may also include pranayama, meditation, reflection, study and other classic elements. Personal practices are taught privately. Given the scope of practice, the inherent therapeutic applications and the heritage of the lineage, the training requirements for teacher certification are extensive.

17

YOGA FOR CONCENTRATION AND MEDITATION

Concentration is the basis of every human activity. All human beings and animals possess the spark of concentration but everyone does not make proper use of this innate power. For every creative or productive work concentration is a must. Man's story from stone age to the present jet and space age is the story of concentrated thought and concentrated mind. Concentrated thought implies focusing the mind on one subject, one point or one idea. Concentration or Dharana is the sixth limb of the eight-fold path of yoga, once a pandit asked kabir, "O Kabir what are you doing now?" Kabir replied, "O pandit, I am detaching the mind from wordly objects, and attaching it to the lotus feet of the Lord"- This is concentration. A definite aim, interest and attention are the basis of concentration according to patanjali Dharana or concentration is fixing the mind on an external object or an internal point. Concentration is the art of reducing the interruptions of the mind and ultimately eliminating them completely so that the knower and the known become one. Our mind is never free from desires and emotions disturb our peace and harmony. Concentrated mind is very powerful. If we want to develop mental power we must have concentrated mind. If the thought is scattered like the rays of light. It can be brought to one point with the help of concentration. Concentrated mind can influence the health and character, and bring peace and harmony. History is replete with men and women who touched the pinnacles of glory by the power of their concentration. Without concentration our efforts and endeavours will go wastage, and without interest and concentration, meditation is not possible. The fields of concentration is vast and the objects of concentration diversified. It is not easy to develop concentrated mind. Diversified objects, symbols persons, places things. Images natural scenes, sacred and profane things, and sentient things and insentient things, different colours and sounds can come to our imagination in the process of concentration. When wrong things, sexual or pornographic come to our mind, distraction and confrontation appear in our mind. But distraction and confrontation is to be avoided. Mind is one, consciousness is one but for the sake of diversity there are various vrittis or modifications of the mind. When the confrontation between our own vrittis become over whelming then we may have a schizophrenic attack. Most mental patients are victims of this type of attack. The selection of object in concentration is important. The object or symbol selected should be sublime pure or sacred so that our mind is easily drawn to it and integrated with it. Again in the selection of symbol our mind will deviate and wander but practice will integrate the mind with the symbol. The word concentration implies "One-pointedness", just as we need a sharp pencil to write with or a sharp knife to cut with the mind also must be sharpened through the constant practice of concentration.

We have shown rapid strides of progress and development in every sphere. We have conquered the unconquerable, we have made impossible look possible we are mastered science technology but we have not controlled the mind. We are slaves to our desires. We lack disciplined mind. So we cannot lead one-pointed and concentrated lives. It is only though the power of concentration that we can try to make our mind disciplined. Concentration implies diving deep into the recesses of mind and consciousness. In the process of concentration our mind undergoes the process of selection and rejection. What is subtle is to be selected and what is profane is to be rejected. Concentration and meditation are the basic means of dealing with stress and depression. Most of us do not know the proper art of relaxation. Drugs and drinks may provide temporary relaxation but they do not provide the growth of consciousness. Concentration is impaired when so many things cross our mind. In the "Yoga sutra", patanjali says, "astha yoga anushasanam" which means that yoga is a form of control over the subtle faculties experiences of the mind. In our sub-conscious mind many desires appear but we are not aware of those desires. Consciously or unconsciously we are doing so many things—but we are not aware of many things. It is the function of concentration to bring all the desires and objects to one point or objects. We have the potential to fully develop all the faculties to but this is possible only with the help of concentration, when this is achieved, the mind becomes relaxed and receptive and the negative thoughts vanish from our mind. In the system of yoga the faculties of body and mind are subject to the influences of prana and chitta prana shakti is the most important vital energy controlling the physical sensory body.

Our minds and consciousness are engrossed in matter. The senses express their faculties at this level. Even mind expresses it self at this level. There is "Stagnation" at this level. We are all examples of this stagnation of the faculties at this level. In order to evolve ourselves from the level of matter into the higher level of perception we must do mental training of concentration and meditation. Even little acts demand attention and concentration. No work can be done successfully without interest, attention, and concentration. When we sit for concentration and meditation we should nothing of business or office work or domestic problems. Once Lodhi king asked Guru nanak to join him in his muslim prayer (Namaz). After the prayers, Guru Nanak told the king and his kazi that their prayers had not been approved as their minds were wandering thinking about the care of a foal or buying horses. Stunned at Guru Nanak's power of divination they sought his guidance. He advised them that prayers without concentration are not of much value. The reasons for a wandering mind during concentration are three fold. First the mind is neither conscious of its origin of being a spark of divine light nor of its goal of life. Second is the minds negative condition of resulting from past and present immoral actions. Third the mind being of a vagrant and volatile nature is oriented towards wordly passions, attachments and sensual pleasures. The first step towards clarity in concentration and meditation is to purify the mind and cultivate godly qualities like truthfulness contentment and compassion through the yogic principles of yama and Niyama. All of us know the story in the Mahabharata" which illustrates the power of concentration. When acahrya Drona was teaching archery to the kaurva and pandva princes, he asked his pupils to come forward one at a time in order to see a small clay bird that he had placed on a branch at the top of a tree and to shoot an arrow through the eye of the bird. As each prince came forward the Guru asked them the same question, "What do you see"?. I see the forest, the sky the tree the leaves the branches and the bird". The Guru said, "Don't shoot, put your bow down". Then he called the next prince and asked "What do you see"? The second prince replied. "I see the bird". The Guru told him also to put the bow down. All the pupils who come forward failed to understand the teaching that the Guru was trying to impart, because he expected a very specific answers finally Arjuna's turn came and the Guru asked him, what do you see"? Arjuna replied, "I see the bird's eye"?. The Guru asked, "Do you not see the leaves of the tress"? "No" said Arjuna, "I see only the eye and nothing else"? So the Guru was satisfied and said to Arjuna "You have learned well". The intensity of Arjuna's concentration was so powerful that all his faculties of perception were fixed on one single point— the bird's eye, concentration is a state in which there is total one-pointedness.

Thought is very powerful;. Everybody is experiencing the influence of thoughts unconsciously to a greater or lesser degree. If an individual has a clear understanding of the working of the thought vibrations. If one knows the technique of controlling the thought, one can use the thought power move effectively for the benefit of others.

A wrong thought binds but a right thought liberates". Concentration also implies wholeness, unity, equilibrium and balance. All our faculties must beunified. They must work in harmony and balance. Balance is needed in every Balance is needed in every activity. Lord Krishna advises Arjuna in the Gita, "The practice of yoga is not for him who sleeps too much or who keeps awake in excess. He who is moderate in eating and recreation, moderate in his efforts in work, moderate in sleep and wakefulness his practice of yoga destroys all misery". One who goes to extreme is a slave of impulse. He lacks balance. Lack of balance means lack of strength and without strength no great work can be done. It is difficult to keep a balanced mind in all situations. But one shall have to do it. If one wants to have complete concentration. Keeping the balance of mind in pleasure and pain, in success and in failure in praise and in censure in respect and in disrespect is real wisdom. We lose our temper. Concentration can give one balance of mind. It is not easy task but patience and practice for a long time can give the required results. By introspection and self-analysis we can find our own flaws and eradicate them through concentrated through and concentrated mind.

Serenity of mind is another important requisite in concentration. If your mind is restless we cannot make any progress in concentration. Serenity of mind can be achieved by controlling desires and by yogic diet. We must keep our mind free from worries, anxieties, fears and phobias, negative feelings, wild fancies sexual thoughts, and confused ides. Only a calm and serene mind can achieve success in concentration and meditation. There is an old age, "He who has controlled his mind has controlled the world". Through the control of mind we can eradicate all desires, passions impulses and carvings. Our mind is full of vritis--waves caused by thought forms. These vritis or eaves are to be stilled or stopped----Then only we can make progress in concentration. In the beginning the process of concentration may appear difficult but practice, patience, perserversance and regularity will give success in concentration. Concentration has been defined variously by various writers from time to time. In the words of swami Shivananda, "Put your heart, mind, Intellect and soul even in your smallest acts. Some people have wrong notion that whatever they desire they can obtain it by concentration. Merely gaining that upon which we have focused our heart does not mean sure success. A robber concentrates upon robbing a person. He may succeed in it but his concentration does not reflect the righteous means applied to have righteous end. The desire of the robber is not pure.

Concentration means a great self control. One who has no control over himself. He is greedy, cunning, and selfish lacks true concentration. True concentration means strength of mind and strength of character, and cannot be used for negative purposes and negative emotions. The strength of concentration depends on strength of mind, strong determination and positive emotions. Even positive emotions and mental standards are not enough. Mind can create any situation good or bad, ugly or beautiful. Therefore mind itself must be its own subject of concentration. In the Gita Lord Krishan says, "As a lamp placed in a windless spot does not flicker, the same simile is used to define a yogi of subdued mind practising union with the self he is satisfied in he self alone". The average person has multiple outside interests and multiple desires. He is least interested in inward development or the idea of self-realization. Concentration is a faculty of both mind and soul. There is both physical and mental concentration. Physical concentration implies gathering together bodily strength and directing it towards one point. But mental concentration is far more difficult but it gives great power to mind. The true from of concentration requires positive attitude. Often when our mind is full of painful experiences, disappointments, frustrations, anxieties worries and depression, we try to escape from such situations by negative attitudes, by taking drugs and drinks and we get temporary relief and peace. But real peace is not temporary. It is permanent. Real peace and relaxation can come through inner growth and mental control. Regarding concentrated mind swami Ram krishan paramhans has given a beautiful illustration, "Every man should make a legislative effort to keep his mind in a good clean concentrated condition, otherwise it grows unsightly--unlike a metal vessel which becomes tarnished. It is not polished every day.

A golden vessel however does not have to be polished so frequently. So with our mind. Once it touches the supreme, it becomes like the vessel of gold--It retains its shine like splendour, its shining quality even when it is not given any special care. When mind makes its point of contact with the central source of life, and power all our troubles end". So instead of letting the mind revolve round and round our aches ailments, sicknesses, we must fasten our mind to the supreme--- This will give us wholeness and healing.

The mind shows us to so many faces and moods. Sometimes Rajas, some times tamas. These moods are innate in every mind under the influence of Rajas the mind is enveloped in excessive ambition, egotism arrogance and discontent. When this quality becomes dominant a man is consumed by the desire to multiply his possessions and to be more and more interested in external things. His energies are wasted in satisfying materialistic desires. The cycle of his desires is every increasing. He will never find real peace and harmony under the influence of Tamas. Man's mind is entangled in darkness, inertia, and heaviness. This state of mind is dull, slothful and bruthish. A Tamasic mind cannot distinguish between virtue and vice, right and wrong and is led away by animal instincts. The third face of mind is sattwa. The sattvic mind is sereve and illumined. This is the concentrated state through which we become one with the object of our worship.

Practice of Concentration

People often raise the question how to concentrate. Concentration is of no use without following important rules of ethics namely yama and Niyama. It is only though the practice of yama and Niyama and with control of breath that mind can be purified. Concentration will become intense if we remove all the negative thoughts and desires form our mind. Ethical perfection is of great importance in concentration. Interest and attention are the basic requisites in concentration. In the initial stage of practice of concentration one should focus ones mind and thought on some concentrate object on the flame of a candle. The mind can be fixed on any pleasant object. Concentration on the candle flame has been discussed separately under tratak. The power of concentration can also give psychic power and will power. Retire in a quiet room free from flies, mosquitoes, noise, and nay disturbance. Sit in sukhasana and concentrate on rose flower. Think of its colour, shape petals and why it is called the queen of Garden. Through law of association the ideas of some other flowers will come to your mind, and the mind will deviate from the rose flower. Then bring the mind back to rose flower and think of the flower alone. Then with rose the idea of thorns will come to your mind and again the mind will deviate from the rose flower. Bring back the mind to rose flower. Some emotions may disturb you in the process of concentration but these emotions will pass like the pieces of cloud. But you should keep your mind free from any stress, strain, tension or depression, or worry or anxiety. Then train the mind in concentration on different kinds of roses. White rose red rose, pink rose, black rose, and wild rose. In course of time with daily practice you will develop the power of concentration which is the basis of meditation.

Meditation is that state of the mind where is there are no "Vishayas" or sensual thoughts—"Dhyanam nirvishyam manah". A continuous flow of perception or thought is meditation. According to Swami Shivananda,

"Meditation is the keeping up of an increasing flow of continuous thought of one thing or God. All wordly thoughts are shut out from the mind. The mind is filled or saturated with divine thoughts, divine glory, or divine presence". Meditation forms most important aspect among the sight limbs of yoga. Yama (self restraint). Niyama (moral observances), pranayama (Regulation of breath), pratyahara (With drawal of the senses), Dharana (Concentration), Dhyana (meditation) and Samadhi (super conscious state), Meditation is the only way for attaining immortality. Everyone wants to be happy but the paths leading to happiness are not the same. The search for happiness is not focused in the right direction. We waste our time and energy in seeking happiness in the mirage of objects, places and people. In relationship and ideologies in possessions and wanting indulgences. In fact happiness is a function of the subjective. But to seek happiness in the subjective domain is impossible, because subjective can never become an object of seeking. That means to seek happiness in either direction is to miss happiness. That realisation makes the seeker, spontaneously detached, silent, and contemplative. Meditation means all that, "So meditation is the only door to happiness". According to Narayana Guru "To act with awareness is freedom and to act without awareness is bondage". The difference between freedom and bondage is awareness. Self awareness is true awareness with reference to which the thought projected world is seen as a myth.

There appear many obstacles in the process of concentration. This main obstacles are personal which cannot make the process of meditation easy and meaningful. The main impediments in the path of meditation are ailments, and disease, greed, anger, hatred, lust, jealously, inotelerance, arrogance, hypocrisy, and desire for name and fame. The practitioner of meditation should over come these obstacles. Of course it is difficult to have control on these flaws and defects. But by constant practice of pranayama and by will power one can overcome these obstacles. We are living in a materialistic age. In this age most of the people try to have external comforts and external progress. The eternal valves like truth, beauty, goodness affection, love and sympathy are fading sway, corruption and lust for money have hardeved our hearts, silenced our scruples, and corrupted our moral sense. Our cultural is honey combed with dishonest pretences and disco influence. It is rightly said "If you wish to change society first change yourself".

Our main vrittis are kama (Lust), krodha (anger), Lobha and Moha, Anger and lust are bound up with each other when kama is controlled anger will die. Anger can give birth to so many vices. The eight vices which are attached with anger are injustice, rashness, persecution, jealously, captiousness, cheating, taking possession of others property, harsh words and cruelty. These evils upset the balance of mind. Narada says in his "Bhakti sutras". "These propensities though they at first are like ripples, acquire the proportions of a sea on account of bad company". Anger is akin to madness. Some people feel irritation and lose temper on petty things. Their bodies tremble, blood pressure rises and nervous system is disturbed when they are angry. It is anger that sometimes destroys even the good actions of man. Under the influence of anger man can do crimes, murders and most nefarious acts. Anger clouds the vision of man, clouds his judgement and he does not know what he is doing. Anger makes him norms of decency and becomes barbaric. Tolerance and forgiveness are great virtues. It is said that "Forgiveness is the noblest form of revenge. It is true with every human beings that one shows anger towards inferior or weak person, one will hesitate to show anger towards one's superiors or towards strong persons. Anger can be controlled by vichar. If one realise the fact that ones energy, esteem and respect is lost under the influence of anger. If one releases that the self is angry with his servant or with his juniors of inferiors. Anger destroys all that one acquires by tyaga, Dana (cherity) and austerity. According to David Hume Gried and disappointment give rise to anger, anger to envy, envy to malice and malice to grief, again, till the whole circle is completed". Therefore we should overcome anger with the aid of deep breathing or pranayama. Anger that is coupled with hatred is most harmful. Both anger and hatred poison our minds and damage our personality." We can develop the opposite divine virtues such as patience and love. All the barriers must melt away before the powers of love. Anger, jealousy narrow mindedness and selfishness will get themselves eclipsed before the powers of love. Love is the pancea of all evils and ailments. Love cements the negative thoughts and feelings. We know the story of three old men. This didactic story, from "Purity" gives a great lesson once a woman came out of her house and saw three old men with long white beards sitting in her front yard. She did not recognise them. She said, "I don't think I know you but you must be hungry please come in and have something to eat," Is the man of the house home"?. They asked "No", she replied. "He is out". Then we cannot come, they replied. In the evening when her husband came home, she told him what had happened, "Go tell-them I am home and invite them in". The woman went out and invited the men in "we do not go into a house together". They replied "Why is that" she asked. One of the old men explained "His name is wealth", he said pointing to one of his friends, and said pointing to another one "He is success and I am love then he added, "Now go in and discuss with your husband which one of us you want in your home"?

The woman went in and told her husband what was said. Her husband was overjoyed, "How nice"!, He said, "Since that is the case let us invite wealth, let him come and full our home with wealth", His wife disagreed. "My dear why do we invite success?. Their daughter in law was listening from the other corner of the house. She jumped in with her own suggestion, "would it not be better to invite live? Our home will then filled with love!" Let us need our daughter-in-law advice, said the husband to his wife, "Go out and invite love to be our guest". The woman went out and asked the three old men "which one of your is love?. Please come in and be our guest". Love got up and started walking toward the house.

The other two also got up and followed him. Surprised the lady asked wealth and success, "I invited only love why are you coming in?, "The old men replied together". If you had invited wealth or success the other two of us would have stayed out but since you invited love wherever he goes we go with him. The story proves the fact that wherever there is love there is also wealth and success. Where there is love there is patience and forgiveness. True love can overcome lust anger and hatred selfishness, jealousy, greed ego are negative our personality. A person's health or ill health depends on his attitude to life. Healthy attitude is positive attitude and unhealthy attitude is negative attitude. Two people with different attitudes can react differently to a particular situation. Our attitudes and actions are the two sides of a coin. A negative attitude is followed by negative action and negative action gives negative results. William James of Harvad university said, "The greatest discovery of any generation is that human beings can alter their lives by altering our attitude from negative to positive we can achieve health and harmony. Another negative feeling is the feeling of fear. The element fear appears in the life of an individual from womb to tomb. Fear is mans greatest enemy if courage is positive fear is negative, "Vritti" of mind. Sometimes we are compelled to do things against our conscience simply because of fear. Anxiety and fear are bound up with each other.

Everyone experiences anxiety, a diffuse, unpleasant vague sense of apprehension, often accompanied by automatic symptoms, such as headache, perspiration, palpitations, tightness in the chest mild stomach discomfort and restlessness. Anxiety is an alarming signal. It warns of impending danger, fear is a similar alerting signal but should be differentiated from anxiety. Fear is a response to a know, external definite threat anxiety is a response to a threat that is unknown internal and vague. Charles Darwin gave the following psychological description of acute fear merging into terror. "Fear is often preceded by astonishment and in so far akin to it, that both lead to the senses of sight and learning being instantly aroused. In both cases the eyes and mouth are widely opened and the eye brows raised. The frightened man at the first stands like a statue motionless and breathless or crouches down as if instinctively to escape observation. The heart beats violently and quickly, so that it palpitates or knocks against the ribs but it is very doubtful whether it then works more efficiently than usual, so as to send a greater supply of blood to all parts of the body for the skin instantly becomes pale as during incipient faintness. This paleness of the surface, however is probably in large part or exclusively due to the vascomotor centre being affected in such a manner as to cause the contraction of the small arteries of the skin. That the skin is much affected under the sense of great fear. We see in the marvellous and in explicable manner in which perspiration immediately exudes from it. This exudation is all the more remarkable as the surface is then cold and hence the term a cold sweat. The hairs also on the skin stand erect and the superficial muscles shiver. In connection with the disturbed action of the heart the breathing is hurried. The salivary glands act imperfectly the mouth becomes dry and is often opened and shut under slight fear, there is a tendency to yawn. As fear increases into an agency and terror the heart beats wildly or may fail to act and faintness ensues, there is deathlike pallor and the wings of the nostrils and widely dilated. There is a gasping and convulsive motion on the lips.

With anxiety is associated stress and conflict. Whether an event is perceived as stressful depends on the nature of the event and on the person's resources, psychological defense and coping mechanism. All involve the ego a collective abstraction for the process by which a person perceives, thinks, and acts on external events or internal drives. A person whose ego is functioning normally long enough, the person experiences chronic anxiety. Whether the imbalance is external between the pressures of the outside world and the person's ego or internal between the persons impulses (aggressiveness, sexual) and conscience the imbalance produces a conflict. Externally caused conflicts are usually interpersonal. Whereas those that are internally caused are intrapsychic or inter personal. A combination of the two is possible as in the case of employees whose excessively demanding and oritical boss provokes impulses that they must control for fear of losing their jobs. Interpersonal and intrapsychic conflicts are usually intertwined. Because human beings are social their man conflicts are usually with other people.

We often come across people who have nothing else to talk about except the fear of their diseases, pains, aches, sufferings, sorrows, and hardships. They always harbour of ill health and fatigue. They are called hypochondriacs who are always feeling panky about symptoms. Some people fear retirement and old age. Old age may be a handicap for some but for those who utilize it properly old age is not a handicap. Some great thinkers artists, and educationists have given their best to the world in their old age. Winston churchill, Henry Ford,

Thomas Eduson, Rockfetter, Gorge, Bernard Sham, Bertrand Russel, Hellen keller Pablo casals, Isaac Newton, Michael angelo produced best creative things and inventions after the age of 80. Some of us are suffering from the fear of death. But a person who leads a righteous and meaningful life need not bother about death. We should act, act in the present and trust no future however pleasant. Fear is the most common negative emotion.

Fear sacks our physical and mental energy. The intensity of fear varies from person to person. Fear and anxiety play havoc with our physical and mental health. Fear give birth of mental weakness which results in constant stress and strain. It is said, "Cowards die many times before death". According to vedanta philosophy "Fear is the root cause of all misery in the world which devours our strength. We do all sorts of silly things because we have accepted to be weak and pliable." When Alexander the Great invaded India, he saw a saint sitting serenly on a stone near the river Indus. He tried temtping him with material things to come to his country. The saint declined. This infuriated the king who took out his sword, threatened to kill him. The sage replied, "You can kill this body but not the spirit within, for it is unborn undecaying and infinite". The saint was very strong the fearless. Fearlessness is the crux of vedanta philosophy.

Pride is the most dangerous flew of man. The famous adage, "Pride hath a fall" is applicable to all. People boast of riches, beauty, power, strength, intelligence, and learning. Pride clouds the power of reason and logic. Pride is an obstruction to the harmonious development of mind and body. Svetaketu (son of uddala) was suffering from the pride of book learning. He behaved rudely with his father. Uddalka pulled svetaketu down by putting him a question. "Have you learnt, O svetaketu, that science of sciences by knowing which you will know everything"? He replied in the negative. Eventually uddalaka taught him the supreme science of the self. According to Swami Shivananda, it is easy to teach a man who does not know. It is still more easy to teach a man is humble but it is extremely difficult to teach a man who is suffering from the pride of his little learning".

When our mind is free from desire, selfishness, egoism and pride we can enjoy real peace and harmony and our process of meditation will become meaningful. Hatred and jealousy are also negative emotions. We often feel jealous of our friends, relatives, acquaintances and neighbours. When they are in a better position. Jealousy kills a man as canker kills a rose. Jealousy destroys our peace of mind. It is very difficult to remove the stink of jealousy from the mind. Jealousy can be eradicated by destroying the concept of duality. Whenever this wave of jealousy arises in our mind, we should think or feel that the man of whom we are jealous is our own self and he is not separate from us. According to a psychological, law the mind becomes that which it thinks upon. If we think about the flaws or defects of a man, our mind dwells on the bad qualities of the man, we must discard the habit of finding fault with others or ill will towards others. We must look to the good qualities of others. Nobody is perfect, perfection is an attribution to God. We are all mixture of good and bad. We become revengeful or vindictive because of hatred. Besides worry, depression unholy thoughts, hatred and jealousy produce a kind of dark, layer on the surface of the mind. This layer or dust prevents the noble thoughts to get entry inside. Our energy is wasted by worry and jealousy.

We will meditate half-heatedly or with distributed attitude when we are under some grief or sorrow. Grief is the pattern of associated physical and mental responses to a major loss—usually to the loss by death or separation of a loved person. To some the loss of money, status or reputation may be a cause of grief than the loss of close relative or spouse. The psychological elements are complex and include feelings of guilt, anger, hostility, resentment, sense of pain. Everyday we are experiencing internal or external stress that has adverse effect on the correct functioning of the body. These influences include physical factors such as disease or injury or mental factors particularly anxiety symptoms such as fatigue, Nausea, Indigestion palpitations, Insomnia irritation, Headaches and chest pain may develop as stress changes the hormonal balance in the body and lower the effectiveness of the immune system leading to a higher risk of infection.

According to psychological law, "As you think so you become", our thoughts shape our life. When we cultivate sublime or positive thoughts our path of meditation will become easier. If we wish to develop spiritual mind or spiritual behaviours, we shall have to control our anger, ittitability, sex impulses and negative emotions and thoughts our negative in meditation. We should not brood over our past mistakes and failure. This will fill our mind with grief and depression, we should not repeat our follies and mistakes in the future. We must strengthen ourselves with new vigour and virtues. We should rather learn from our past mistakes. Now we are physically and mentally ready for meditation. Select a corner or a place for meditation. The place should be calm and quiet free from mosquitoes, flies, ants and bugs. The place should also be airy. Sit in padamasan or sukhasan, close your eyes spinal column head, should be in easy and erect position. Breath is life and longer breaths have longer life. Breathe is the medium through which the life current (Prana) flows into us. We all breathe but we do not know the correct technique of breathing. Then our next step would be to make our mind introspective. We cannot do it suddenly because our mind is wavering and oscillating. To make our mine one pointed demands steady effort. Lord Krishan says to Arjua in the Gita, "Do not permit yourself to be depressed. This mind which seems difficult to subdue can be subdued through constant practice of dispassion and through discrimination", having relaxed and body. Nerves and mind the practitioner assumes a meditative posture that is steady and comfortable.

The practitioner will then try to make his mind one pointed through concentration. He becomes aware of his breath and synchronizes it with mantra such as SOHAM "I am that". It is only through concentration and uttering mantra that mind can be made one pointed. In meditation deliberate attempt is made to still the activity of the conscious mind. Through withdrawal of the senses one pointedness of mind is achieved. Then concentration flows into meditation, in his "Yog sutra" one such method is mantra yoga. We live in a universe and the universe lives within us. The art of looking within is the mantra of wise living Mantras help draw energy from both external and internal universe. The nature of our thoughts is largely compulsive. We are conscious beings but we live like machines. By chanting mantras with understanding compulsive thoughts are transformed. The mind becomes calm and our perception will be wise with respect to both the external and internal universes. Great are the powers of silence. We must listen to our inner silence. Lotus was one of the Gurus of sage Dattatreya. The lotus grows from muddy waters yet it gives out fragrance. Despite the many bad things happening around us we should strive to be as fragment as the lotus. Silence is created by understanding by chanting a powerful mantra, by having a commitment to grow with worrying thoughts the mind loses its clarity to see what is and starts seeing what is and starts seeing powerful mantra like the mantra of "Om Nama Shivaye" is chanted the higher centres in us open up.

The higher impure the mind is unable to receive the fine vibrations of silence, when our ignorance is destroyed, a great awakening happens within us. Mantra yoga facilitates the awakening of our hidden energies unless there is commitment to grow no growth is possible. Creativity is not doing something new and different it is about bringing a new energy of love and joy. Mantras are like a ladder we must climb it with purity of heart and purity of mind. God is the source of love, happiness and peace. Japa or mantra must become an important part of the practitioner life. The mere repetition of mantra is not of any use. The meaning of mantra must be understood and then the realization of the truth the mantra contains. The mantra yoga also works on the levels of the practitioner sub-conscious mind, influencing his mood and controlling his negative emotions and states such as nager, greed, lust, hatred etc. The ultimate aim of meditation is to experience the self or atman. The self is pure consicousness. The experience of self is beyond time and space when the mind is completely free from desires thoughts and vrittis. It becomes aware of the essence of being. Compared with that of other ritual practices the effect of mantra yoga is ten times as great. If done in secret without outword sound, "the effect is one hundred times as great if done purely mentally a thousand times as great".

There are ten steps of mantra yoga. Like all forms of yoga, the method of mantra yoga has several steps, some of these steps are common to the other forms and some have different implications:-

(1) Devotion (Bhakti) is the first step, the most pertinent and the easiest form of spiritual achievement for the present age of darkness.

(2) Purty (Shuddi) is of two kinds. Outward an inward. Inward purity is the most important in mantra yoga.

(3) The conduct (achara) there are three ways of conduct according to the fundamental qualities of nature. Angelic conduct (Divya-achara) is for the seeker in whom the ascending tendency premoninates the right hand way (dakshina--achara) or way of good actions is for the seeker in whom the expanding tendency predominates, while the left hand way (vama--achara) or the way which makes use of the senses as the means of transgressing them, is the way for those in whom

the descending tendency predominates. (5), Concentration (dharana) is of two kinds outward and inward. Outward concentration is on an external object a picture, image symbol etc, inward concentration is on the inner world within one's mind.

(4) Contemplation (dhyana) consists in witnessing within ones mind the shape of the chosen deity.

(5) Ritual worship (Yojna) is of two kinds--outward and inward. In ritual worship of a deity, whether inward or outward, five ingredients (scents, flowers, incense, lamp and food) are used.

(6) Identification (Samadhi) when the meaning of the mantra has been realised the mind dissolves into the deity the mantra represents, there remains no notion of a separate seeker, search and sought. With identification the seeker has fulfilled his aim.

Mantra yoga like Bhakti yoga emphasises complete surrender before Almighty. When we destroy the walls of falsehood and dishonesty, Ego and greed lust and hatred everything becomes one. When we seek ultimate freedom and bliss, we have to surrender our illusions, when we surrender illusions truth appears. We have built a world of our own but this world is not real. We cannot exists for even a moment without interaction and contact with existence. So freedom and liberation means to drop that which we have identified with the false hood that we have created. For a person who is seeking liberation the only way to truth is the destruction of all walls which means the dissolution of our individuality--That is meditation.

It is said, "A bad workman quarrels with his tools". We have to modify our mind and change our selves. In whatever situations we may be we have to raise ourselves from the low level. Situations will appear to us pleasant when our mind is pure and when our karmas are righteous. The didactic stories of Mullah Nazaruddin are well known to all. Once Mullah Nazaruddin while walking in the desert saw a group of people riding horses. He thought they were robbers and started running. They turned out to be travellers. Seeing the Mullah running the travellers thought he was in trouble---so they started going towards him. Now the Mullah was convinced they were after him and he ran into a graveyard--the travellers followed him there. The tired Mullah lay down on one of the coffins. Then he realised they were not robbers but travellers. They asked him, "Why are you here?" I am here because of you and you are here because of me". Answered the Mullah. This is the law of karma. In other words we attract situations in life. According to Swami Sukhbodana, "we often find ourselves in such situations aligned to our state of being. If our consciousness is not committed to transformation, then we will not grow wiser from situations but complain and grumble expecting the situation to be different. According to yoga philosophy there are two types of growth, horizontal and vertical growth. Horizontal growth means more money name and fame.

People judge others by horizontal growth which means five years back his back balance was 2 lakhs now his back balance is 20 lakhs. The second type of growth i.e. vertical growth means that five years back he was irritative unbalanced person. Now he is calm, poised and balanced person. The more one grows in love, kindness and compassion the more one is truly growing. Growth happening in the vertical dimension changes one state of being. "In ancient India a king sought to resolve a dispute between two of his ministers who wanted to marry the same woman. He told both of them to walk on a rope and whoever did so successfully would win the hand of the woman. One Minister spent a sleepless night to walk the tight rope. The other Minister was very relaxed he felt there was no point in getting agitated when death was imminent anyway. The minister who kept his cool emerged the winner, walking effortlessly on the rope. In order to grow vertically one has to cultivate the art of relaxation and balance.

Harmony, happiness, peace, and joy flower forth in this state of consciousness. One must practise meditation early in the morning at 5 Am. This time is called Braham----Muhurta. In the early morning hours there is calm and quiet atmospheres. All saints and yogis practise meditation at this time. Meditation is the key that can unlock many secrets of life. In concrete meditation the practitioner meditates on the forms of the Lord. In abstract meditation he concentrates the mind on one Idea of god or Atma. A particular kind of meditation is best suited to a particular mind. The kind of meditation varies according to taste temperament capacity of the individual. A devotee meditates on his deity or ishta devata. A Raj yogi meditates on the special purusha or ishwar who is not touched by the afflications, desires and karmas. A Hatha yogi meditates on chakras and their presiding deities. A Gyan yogi meditates on his own self or Atma. A karam yogi meditates on God with pure love. I have discussed only one kind of meditation i.e. mantra yoga meditation different meditation techniques have evolved from time to time by Great masters. Zen masters, Maharishi mahesh yogi, Johnmain Fibetan meditation masters, breathing meditation masters. Anthony De Mello Hara meditation masters joe silva, Therapentic meditation masters, vilayat inayat khan, Taoiost meditation masters, osho Rajnesh, and Douglas harding. One thing common in all kinds of meditation is the control of mind and purity of Heart.